MEDIA LAW
A GUIDE TO UNDERSTANDING
MASS COMMUNICATION LAW
SECOND EDITION

MARK HANEBUTT

Kendall Hunt
publishing company

Cover image © Shutterstock, Inc.

Kendall Hunt
publishing company

www.kendallhunt.com
Send all inquiries to:
4050 Westmark Drive
Dubuque, IA 52004-1840

Copyright © 2016, 2018 by Mark Hanebutt

ISBN: 978-1-5249-4824-5

Published in the United States of America

For Meredith and Eric

CONTENTS

ACKNOWLEDGMENTS

I appreciate the help of fellow lawyers Dick Pryor, General Manager of KGOU Radio, University of Oklahoma, Norman, Oklahoma; Bill Hickman, University of Central Oklahoma professor of journalism, Edmond, Oklahoma; and Jerry Magill (ret.), of Magill & Magill, P.L.L.C., Attorneys and Counselors at Law, Oklahoma City, in reviewing and editing this text.

I also wish to acknowledge University of Central Oklahoma photography professors Mark Zimmerman and Jesse Miller for their photos as well as bibliographer Jordan Piel and Kendall Hunt Publishing senior production editor Beth Trowbridge, project coordinator Bev Kraus and account manager Amelia Pohlmann for their assistance.

Thank you.

INTRODUCTION

This text is meant to give print journalists, broadcasters, photographers, public relations practitioners, advertisers, and those in government and the general public a basic understanding of mass communication law.

It is not meant to be a substitute for the legal training or the comprehensive legal advice that only can come from a skilled lawyer.

Its purpose is to offer students, in laymen's terms, a concise, yet complete overview of the law that affects the mass media profession. Toward this end, and faced with the fact that many students don't understand basic civics, it will start with a review of the purpose and origin of law, the foundation and basic tenets of American democracy, and an overview of the American legal system. Afterward, it will focus on the First Amendment and the boundaries of free expression as defined by the U.S. Courts before examining the various specific areas of media law. The U.S. Declaration of Independence and U.S. Constitution are included in the Appendix.

It is expected that students should understand enough of the law after studying the text to help them know when they are facing possible legal trouble, or more importantly, to help them avoid such trouble in the first place. Beyond that, for specific legal problems, they, as always, should seek advice from a lawyer.

Mark Hanebutt
November 12, 2017
Oklahoma City

CHAPTER 1

The Purpose, Origin, and Types of Law

The Need for Order

It is, as the ancient philosopher Aristotle noted, our purpose in life to flourish. Our focus as humans has always been to discover our individual talents and to develop them. And just as a plant is better able to grow when surrounded by good soil, water, and sunshine, we also have discovered that we are better able to succeed when living in an orderly environment. In short, we have never been able to flourish in the midst of chaos.

Aristotle

MidoSemsem/Shutterstock.com

Therefore, it is in our nature to seek order. Order helps us make sense of our lives and our world. In fact, we spend much of our existence seeking or maintaining order. We struggle to discover the patterns of science, the rules of effective government, and the design principles that allow us to create beautiful art.

Even our philosophies begin there. Ancient man began with the concept of order when first trying to understand his existence. In the Old Testament book of Genesis, we see the writer explain creation as an event that brings order out of chaos. And order, we have discovered, is all around us, whether in the intricacies of the microscopic cell or the movement of the planets.

Little wonder then we feel out of sorts when we can't find order or maintain it. Think of the last time you were sick and your body wasn't working properly, or when you went to work and found your papers in disarray, or when you found yourself surrounded by the chaos of hundreds of screaming holiday shoppers. Think of the last time your well-laid plans didn't work. Chances are you felt more than a little anxious.

It is in this quest for order that we find the law. For the purpose of law is order.

For this reason, law is said to be first among professions, for without law, civilization—our ability to live together in relative harmony—cannot exist, nor any of the institutions or endeavors of man, nor man himself. For although we may be self-centered and self-absorbed in our individual pursuit to flourish, we also have learned that without regard for others' attempts to succeed, such an attitude is often ultimately self-destructive.

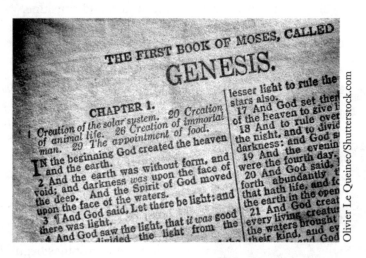

Law, then, is an important thing, a necessary thing. It can guide us and protect us and comfort us. It can give our lives certainty, predictability, and stability. It enables us to live our lives in a state of harmony with ourselves and with others.

It enables us to flourish.

While some law exists to be discovered, as in the laws or principles of science, the law of man comes from the ever-changing experience of trying to find order while living in a world with others. Its value and effectiveness, therefore, will depend ultimately upon the wisdom of those who make it. It should not be too loose or too restrictive. The law, it is said, should fit a man like a good suit of clothes. He should feel comfortable in it.

Law, Ethics, and Morality

Often, we get law confused with morality and ethics. All of them are means by which we attempt to control human behavior. But they are different. Law, as we have noted, is about order. But order—and law—can be "good" or "bad." For example, the Nazis prior to World War II passed laws for the orderly incarceration and ultimate extermination of six million Jews. Never confuse law with good and bad. We may hope the law is good, and most of us may work to ensure that it is, but its ultimate purpose is order.

Morality, on the other hand, is about "right" and "wrong," "good" and "bad." It comes from a culture's determination of what it considers to be humanity's ultimate values. These may come from the collective experience of humans in a society or culture or from the accumulated wisdom of mankind throughout his existence, or it may come from the realm of religion and man's belief of what God has determined to be the essential values or rules of human behavior. This latter view would suggest morality transcends any particular culture or human determination of what is ultimately good and bad. Morality, therefore, would dictate that although the Nazis may have thought Jews were evil, the belief of most, or of God in particular, that human life should be protected would trump a particular society's view that some people are more valuable than others.

Law, of course, often borrows from morality. For example, the Ten Commandments from the Bible lists ultimate values or rules from God, including not killing others, or stealing or lying. These and other values are not just considered moral precepts but legal ones as well since they provide rules of order in any society.

Many laws are neither moral nor immoral. Most, perhaps, are amoral, that is, without morality. For example, the laws regarding where you can

Lena Grottling/Shutterstock.com

park your car or when you can place your trash at the curb have no higher or lower purpose than to direct the orderly flow of traffic and trash.

Ethics, the third category, is about the rational choices we must make between competing values. Morality notes our ultimate values, but it doesn't tell us what to do if those values are in conflict with one another. For example, the Bible's Ten Commandments notes that we are not to lie or to harm others, but what are we to do if we find ourselves in a situation where we must choose between those competing rules?

To illustrate this point, let's say you come home to find your mother upset and discover that she got into a violent argument with a man at the supermarket. She tells you she has a headache and is going to lie down. So as not to disturb her, you go outside and sit on the porch swing. In a little while, you see a man coming down the street. He looks angry, and he appears to be carrying a gun. To your dismay, he turns up your sidewalk and demands to know if your mother is at home. He says he got into an argument with her and is now going to shoot her. Assuming you are a moral person and don't believe in lying or hurting others, you are now facing an ethical dilemma. Do you lie and tell him your mother isn't home, or do you tell the truth and watch as the man enters and kills your mother? (Technically, of course, you could probably argue that you are not hurting anyone, since you are not shooting your mother, and you are only indirectly causing her harm by providing him with the information that she is home, but practically, your mother will be just as dead.)

Although the answer for most of us would be a simple one: we'd lie through our teeth to save mom, it nevertheless requires us to make a decision between two competing values. And that decision should be a rational one. It should not be made on some emotional or gut level because our emotions are not consistent. And consistency with our decision-making helps ensure that we come up with reliable, predictable answers in similar situations. This gives us credibility. It also helps us make better decisions.

Rational thought instead would require us to use some logical approach to solve the problem. We would probably base our decision on some overriding principle—such as trying to make decisions that do the least amount of harm. We might rationally conclude, therefore, that lying, though reprehensible, would result in less harm than telling the truth in this situation, since telling the truth would probably result in our mother's death.

The problem, of course, is that you can't always know in advance the effects of your decision. Nevertheless, we make ethical decisions every day. The question is are we making them rationally and for the right reasons. Ethicists wrestle with different theories of how to make effective ethical decisions.

Law, morality, and ethics all play an important role in defining and maintaining civilization. And although they often overlap, they are different, complex, and deserving of individual study.

We will focus on the law.

Systems of Law

So how then do we come by the law? Before we answer that, we should probably understand what it is.

Law is a system of rules and principles adopted from custom or created by society or its leaders and enforced by some authority to maintain civilized behavior and order.

The history of law is varied and extensive and, as one might expect, covers thousands of years. In modern society, a few countries, particularly those in the Middle East, adhere to religious law while most countries generally have adopted secular systems of civil law or common law or a combination of the two.

Religious law systems follow the code of a particular religion, such as Islamic law, to govern society.

Civil law systems, which trace their origin back to Roman law, follow rules laid down by some authoritative body, such as a legislature, that often include a set of general principles that are used as a basis of deciding each case without reference to how similar cases were decided in the past. As a result, there are no binding precedents. Lawyers consult the law to determine how a judge might rule, though judges are under no obligation to follow a previous decision. Also, judges in civil law systems can take on the role of prosecutors and investigate cases on their own. Civil law systems are the most widely used legal systems in the world. France, for example, follows a civil law system.

Other countries, such as the United States, follow a *common law* system, the second most prevalent system in the world. Adopted from Great Britain, which colonized America, the common law is developed by judges deciding individual cases and then using those decisions as precedents to decide similar cases in the future. Under this system, legal disputes are framed in the form of lawsuits and presented to a trial court. The judge, if it's a bench trial, or a jury, if it's a jury trial, then decides the case after listening impartially to the evidence presented by the attorneys. Following the trial court's ruling, an appellate court may be asked to review the decision. The appellate court may sustain the ruling, modify it, or overrule it. If the ruling is sustained, the court may order the appellate opinion published as precedent so other courts can follow the decision in similar cases.

All states follow the common law system except Louisiana, which was settled by the French and is largely a civil law state.

Although the common law is the basis of the U.S. legal system, in reality our system is more complex, drawing on a combination of types of law, which represent a combination of both the civil and common law systems. The types of law in the United States include common law, the law of equity, statutory law, constitutional law, and executive orders and administrative law.

Common Law

Common law originated during the Middle Ages in England. Earliest common law developed from local custom. In the 12th century,

English King Henry II created a unified system of law when he began sending judges from the king's central court in London to hear cases and resolve disputes throughout the country by applying these local customs. Judges would return to London and discuss their various cases with other judges. Soon these experiences were recorded, and judges began using decisions from prior cases to solve similar conflicts they faced. This legal theory is known as *stare decisis*, or precedent. Judges were bound to follow these earlier decisions when the facts and the cases were similar to their own case. Over time, this practice of adhering to precedent made the law "common" throughout the realm.

The benefit of common law is that citizens can know in advance how they will be treated if the facts in their cases are like those in a previous case. This gives stability, consistency, and predictability to the law, and it promotes confidence in the law. People follow the law largely because they believe in it and trust it.

For example, let's say two peasants live next to each other. One peasant has a radish garden; the other has a pig. They live in harmony with one another. However, one day the radish farmer awakens to find the pig in his garden eating his radishes. He is upset; he needs to grow the radishes to feed his family. He complains to the pig farmer, who is indifferent to his plight. After all, his pig is getting fat eating the radishes.

The harmony that existed between the two men is now gone. They are in a state of chaos. To flourish they must return to a state of harmony; the status quo must be restored. The radish farmer and the pig farmer, realizing the dispute must be settled, bring their case to a judge, who listens to the facts impartially. He asks if there have been any similar cases like this to guide his resolution. He is told there was once a case in the county that involved a horse that ate apples from a neighbor's apple tree. The owner of the horse was ordered to pay for the apples since his horse benefitted unfairly at the apple tree owner's expense.

Although the cases are not exactly alike, they are close enough to result in a fair settlement. The judge orders the pig farmer to pay for the radishes since he, too, benefited unfairly at the radish farmer's expense. The radish farmer is compensated for his loss, the status quo is restored and harmony is reestablished.

The common law is often referred to as "judge-made law." If the facts are similar to a previous case, the judge generally must accept precedent, but if the new case is *distinguishable*, that if the facts are different and the cases are not alike, then no precedent exists. If that happens, the judge must reason through the facts of the new case without benefit of precedent and decide how it should be resolved. The judge's new decision then is the basis of another new law. Since people can get into all manner of different disputes, each new case could theoretically result in a new law unless there is a precedent to follow.

In addition to accepting the precedent, if the facts are the same, or distinguishing the case if the facts are different, a judge may *overrule* the precedent if the law no longer makes sense because of changing times, sensibilities, or circumstances. For example, if a court ruled a hundred years ago that all cars had to pull over to allow a horse to pass, a court today would likely rule that the law no longer makes sense since times have changed and the world is now filled with cars instead of horses. It would therefore likely overrule the law should it come before the court as precedent for a case involving a car and a horse passing one another. Thus, the old decision, once overruled, would no longer be valid precedent to be followed by lower courts.

In other cases, the court may *modify* or change the precedent. For example, if a law noted that a homeowner must maintain his hedge separating his property from a neighbor's, the court may modify that ruling to include any other type of barrier, such as a wooden fence, since not everyone uses a hedge to separate property.

Under American law, decisions of one court are only binding on another court's case if 1. the cases are factually similar, 2. the courts are in the same jurisdiction (the area over which the court has authority to hear and decide cases), and, 3. the decision of the precedent case has been reviewed and published by a higher appellate court. Decisions made by lower courts or courts in another jurisdiction are only *persuasive*, that is, the court may use the earlier decision as a guide but it is not required to follow it.

The thousands of decisions from both federal and state courts are recorded in books known as *case reporters*. Different courts publish their cases in different reporters. Federal courts publish their decisions in various federal reporters, and state courts publish their decisions in reporters covering different areas of the country.

Lawyers research these reporters, depending upon which court they are in, to find law that will support their client's position in a case. If they can find no law *on point*—that is, a previous case that is just like their case—they look for law that is similar. If they cannot find that, then they look to distinguish the case and show the court why a precedent should not be followed because the facts are somehow different. These previously published cases, along with the facts of their own particular case, become the basis for their legal arguments on behalf of their clients.

The lawyers are able to research and find cases through a system of citation that identifies each case. For example, in an important media law case, *New York Times Co. v. Sullivan*, the citation would be *376 U.S. 254 (1964)*. The case name obviously is *New York Times Co. v. Sullivan*. The volume number of the case is *376*. The case reporter in which the lawyer researching the case would look is *U.S.* or United States, which means the U.S. Supreme Court decided the case. The page number is *254*. And the year it was decided was *1964*. Cases can now be found electronically through legal databases such as LexisNexis and Westlaw. Legal encyclopedias, digests, compilations of the common law, journal articles, and other subject-matter texts help lawyers find the cases according to topic.

It should be noted that common law mainly involves state law and not federal law. Federal law is largely a product of federal statute or the *U.S. Constitution*, and so it resembles civil law.

But precedent in the American legal system still plays a crucial part in all court decisions, whether those decisions are by state or federal courts. Cases involving federal law, whether heard by a federal or state court, must adhere to the precedents of the federal courts. Likewise, state courts must follow the precedents of higher courts in their state on matters of state law. Courts in other states need not follow the precedents of other states, though they may find them persuasive in deciding cases.

Equity Law

The common law system may offer some certainty in how a case is likely to turn out, but that doesn't always mean it will turn out fairly. Equity law is used when there is not an adequate remedy under the common law to prevent harm or unfairness. Equity law, therefore, is a different kind of law made by judges. It begins where common law leaves off.

For example, if an industry is going to dump its waste in a river others use for drinking water, it doesn't make sense or seem fair to wait until the water is polluted and people become sick before those harmed are able to go to court and sue for damages. As an alternative, people may seek an equitable remedy, that is, they may ask the court to prevent the harm before it occurs by showing the court evidence that the anticipated harm is about to occur and asking the court to order the industry not to pollute the water.

The law of equity grew out of common law deficiencies in England in the 15th century. Those who felt the common law system had been unfair, would ask the king to intercede and provide a better remedy. As a result, courts of law and equity were formed to offer different types of relief.

Courts of law and equity were later combined in England as well as the United States. Today, courts have the authority to offer both legal and equitable remedies.

To return to the example of the pig farmer and the radish farmer, let's say that after the radish farmer is reimbursed for his loss, he discovers the pig intruding into his garden again. Once again harmony has given way to chaos. The two farmers realize the earlier remedy did not resolve their dispute. So they seek a new remedy from a judge in a court of equity. The new judge realizes the payment of money will not solve this problem since the pig is likely to return repeatedly to the radish garden. If that happens, the two men will be in court every week. He therefore devises another, equitable remedy to solve the problem. He orders the pig owner to build a fence that will keep the pig on his own property.

A legal remedy provides monetary damages, whereas an equitable remedy provides *injunctive relief*, that is, an order by the court that something be done or not be done to prevent harm or solve a problem. These orders often take the form of *temporary restraining orders* or *preliminary injunctions*. The judge has wide latitude in deciding what is fair. These remedies do not follow precedent.

Statutory Law

Legislative bodies—such as state legislatures, Congress, and city councils—create statutory law. The civil law system mentioned earlier is a statutory law system. Thus, even though our legal system is based largely on the common law, the civil law system is incorporated into it.

Whereas common law, created by judges, often deals with small problems between individuals or small groups, and only after a problem occurs, statutory law is created to solve or prevent large societal problems. Criminal laws are examples of statutory laws. Statutory laws are collected in statute books and codified by related topics, unlike the common law, which is kept in books called *reporters*.

Statutory laws begin as bills introduced by a legislative body. For example, once a bill has been voted on and passed by the state legislature and signed by the governor, it becomes the law of the state. Courts then become involved in determining what the law means, particularly, if the meaning of the law is unclear. This judicial interpretation is called *statutory construction* and is a normal and legal function of the court.

For example, if the legislature passes a law that makes it illegal to distribute pornography close to a school, the court must determine what the words "distribute" and "close" mean. Does it include selling, renting, or giving away pornography, or all three? Does it mean within 500 feet or 1,000 feet or some other distance? The court attempts to figure out what the legislature meant. Often courts will look to the reports of legislative debates, minutes of committee hearings of the bill, and other legislative discussions to determine legislative intent. Effective law is written clearly to avoid ambiguity, but even statutes that are well written usually require some judicial interpretation.

Statutory law often finds its way into common law reporters once the court has interpreted the new law in a case. Once this happens, the law is annotated, that is, the law will include a notation at the bottom of the law offering a summary of how the court interpreted the law.

Sometimes, the court will invalidate the law as unconstitutional because it violates the constitution or because it conflicts with another law passed by the legislature or because it conflicts with some well-established common law principles. Statutory law generally trumps the common law since statutory law is made by a legislative body representing the people and is designed to deal with problems that affect all of society not just a few individuals.

However, if the statute is invalidated, the legislature may then decide to revise the law. This interplay between the courts and the legislature refines the law.

Constitutional Law

Constitutions are the basis of government and law in the United States, and represent the supreme law of the United States and of each individual state. The *U.S. Constitution* as well as state constitutions provide a framework or blueprint for government, defining the various powers and limits of the legislative, executive, and judicial branches of government, and note those rights and liberties that government may not take away from the people.

James Steidl/Shutterstock.com

The federal constitution defines the framework and boundaries of federal law, and state constitutions define the framework and boundaries of the laws of each state. City charters, another example of constitutional law, outline various city governments.

Any law or state constitution that conflicts with the *U.S. Constitution* is invalid. And any state law that violates a state's constitution is invalid. State constitutions may give citizens more rights, but they cannot eliminate or reduce those provided for in the *U.S. Constitution*.

Since constitutions are the foundation of government, they are relatively difficult to change or amend. State constitutions can only be changed by a direct vote of the people. The *U.S. Constitution* can be amended either when two thirds of the U.S. House of Representatives and the Senate vote to do so or when two thirds of the state legislatures vote for a Constitutional Convention which then proposes to amend it. In either case, three fourths of all the states must ratify, or accept, the proposed amendment before the Constitution can be amended.

To date, the *U.S. Constitution* contains 27 amendments. The first 10 amendments, known as the *Bill of Rights*, define our fundamental liberties as Americans. This textbook is concerned with the First Amendment, which protects six liberties, including freedom of speech and press, freedom to assemble with others, freedom to petition the government to address citizen complaints, freedom to exercise one's religious beliefs, and freedom from the government endorsing or establishing a particular religion. It says:

> *Congress shall make no law respecting an establishment of religion, or prohibiting the free exercise thereof; or abridging the freedom of speech, or of the press; or the right of the people peaceably to assemble, and to petition the Government for a redress of grievances.*

The *U.S. Constitution* and the U.S. government are a product of the people and the states. It is a constitution of enumerated, or listed, powers designed to accomplish specific tasks agreed upon by the states. We will talk more about this in the next chapter.

Administrative Law

Within both the state and federal governments exists a broad network of agencies created by statutes of the state legislatures or the U.S. Congress to deal with specific tasks. These agencies have the power to create and enforce their own rules and regulations. For example, the Federal Trade Commission and the Federal Communications Commission, both of which will be discussed in this book, regulate the rules regarding advertising and broadcast media respectively in the country.

These agencies also get their power from the state legislatures or Congress that created them and they may not exceed the power given to them. If they do, those same legislative bodies can rescind their power. In short, the state legislatures and Congress get their power from their respective constitutions and the agencies get their power from their respective legislative bodies. Also, agency rulings may be appealed to and voided by appellate courts if they exceed their authority or violate their own rules or the Constitution.

The boards and heads of these agencies are generally appointed by the president or the governors and confirmed by the Congress or state legislatures.

Executive Orders

The president, governors, and mayors may exercise limited powers under their respective constitutions or city charters by issuing executive orders. These orders have the force of law. They can include the classification of some records or even the restriction of citizens to their homes during times of crisis. For example, mayors may issue orders such as curfews to keep people off the streets during periods of civil unrest. Similarly, governors may issue orders declaring martial law and call out the National Guard to quell riots.

If an executive exceeds his authority, the legislature may vote to overturn the decision, or a court may void it, or the next executive may change it.

Areas of Law

The different types of law discussed above can and do deal with a variety of legal problems. For example, cases can be about *torts*—involving wrongs that harm someone, such as personal injuries caused by another (the pig case); *property*—including disputes over ownership or boundaries of real estate; *contracts*—involving the making and breaking of agreements between people; *criminal law*—encompassing both state and federal wrongs against society; and a whole range of other categories.

CHAPTER 2

American Democracy and the Law

Early Events That Shaped American Law

The law in our society, whether it be civil law enacted by legislative body or common law made by judges, comes, as we have seen, from the various branches of our local, state, and federal governments. Government and law, therefore, are intertwined. Both government and law arose out of man's need for order, and both government and the courts work hand-in-hand to make and enforce law. Therefore, before one can get a full understanding of our law and how it works, one must also have a basic understanding of our government.

The roots of American law and government can be traced from several significant documents, developments, and movements in world and English history. Taken together, these had a profound impact and influence on the delegates at the Constitutional Convention in 1787 that determined the shape of our government and, subsequently, our law. These developments include events such as The Renaissance, The Age of Discovery, The Protestant Reformation, and, most important of all, The Enlightenment.

America, of course, was not the first country to experiment with democracy. In ancient Athens, citizens governed themselves in a direct democracy—that is, each citizen voted on issues directly. This system worked for a while because Athens was small and the property-owning males, who were eligible to vote, all had similar interests. But the experiment in Athens failed.

S.Borisov/Shutterstock.com

Countries, subsequently, were mostly ruled by monarchs or other centralized systems of power, such as the Church. However, important events chipped away at this absolute power in the centuries leading up to the American Revolution.

In 1215, King John of England was forced to sign the *Magna Carta*, which placed limits on the king's power over the nobility. The document guaranteed certain protections, such as the right to trial by jury and due process of law. No longer could the king take a person's life, liberty or property at leisure. The *Magna Carta* is often viewed as the forerunner to our Constitution. Nevertheless, the early English kings often ignored the *Magna Carta*.

David Smart/Shutterstock.com

About 1450, perhaps the most significant event in modern world history occurred with the invention of the moveable type printing press by Johannes Gutenberg. The new device spread literacy and education throughout the western world by making information cheap and affordable to the masses. It ushered in the age of shared knowledge and critical thought, which helped signal the beginning of the downfall of centralized governments and their absolute power.

The establishment of the English Parliament, the representative body of the people that passed law, and the growth of its power placed renewed restriction of kings in 1628 with the adoption of the *Petition of Right*. In exchange for the money necessary to fight a war with Spain, King Charles I was forced to sign the document that would limit his right to imprison critics without trial and impose taxes without the consent of Parliament. Most importantly perhaps, it challenged the concept of the divine right of kings. This concept held that monarchs received the right to rule from God and therefore could not be challenged.

In 1644, English poet John Milton continued the onslaught against centralized control when he challenged the right of those in power to censor expression. In his treatise *Areopagitica*, probably history's most eloquent defense of freedom of speech and press, he argued that since God is truth and that since God made man in his own image and wanted man to know him, he gave man the ability to know truth. Truth was not, therefore, revealed through official doctrine by a select line of authority of kings and priests—the view of the day—but to all mankind through inquiry, debate, and reason—characteristics God gave man. Milton's theory grew out of Christian theology as expressed in John 8:32 (. . .*the truth will set you free.*) and was a forerunner to The Enlightenment.

Milton's new philosophy urging individual inquiry in theory made every man intellectually equal to every other man and gave each the right to seek truth on his own. Again, in theory, it gave the common man as much power as the nobleman and priest, and empowered men to govern without benefit of king or spiritual leader to dictate official truth. More, it focused on the concept of personal autonomy, the idea that every man is responsible for himself, an important characteristic of our law. This movement toward independent thought threatened the absolute power of monarchies and theocracies and helped set the foundation for modern democracy.

In 1688, further erosion of the monarchy occurred when Parliament forced William and Mary to sign the English *Bill of Rights* that placed the power of Parliament over the crown. Subsequently, all elections had to be free, trial by jury and the right to petition the government were guaranteed, laws had to be written down and only Parliament could levy taxes.

The Enlightenment—Foundation of American Government

Undoubtedly, the most significant development in regard to the establishment of our government occurred with The Enlightenment. Also known as the Scientific Revolution or the Age of Reason, The Enlightenment brought a different way of looking at the truth. Until then, truth was viewed subjectively, depending upon the whim of tradition or personal interpretation. The Enlightenment looked at truth scientifically, objectively. It was based on fact and evidence, two very important ingredients in our legal system. Truth could be proven.

The Enlightenment in the late 17th century and early 18th century moved us toward a belief in natural law and empiricism—the view that knowledge comes through experience and experimentation. This gave way to what we call the Scientific Method where one starts with a hypothesis and then gathers evidence to prove or disprove it. This rational approach is responsible for all of our scientific discoveries and is the basis of our legal system.

In addition, this rational approach was applied to political philosophy. British Enlightenment philosopher John Locke (1632–1704) in his *Two Treatises of Government*, set forth the idea that people are rational enough to understand what he called the *natural law*, and that this led to a standard of human conduct.

Prior to the development of civil societies or any kind of government,

Georgios Kollidas/Shutterstock.com

John Locke

Locke argued that people lived in a state of nature and that this situation was unworkable because it was unorganized. People could do whatever they wanted and oppress whomever they chose. This led to chaos. To eliminate the problem, rational man understood the need for a civil society to protect life, liberty, and property.

Locke suggested this civil society was formed by a *social contract*, which was an agreement among those in the society to live by its laws and accept its penalties. Although this agreement meant the people would be required to give up some of their liberty to do as they pleased, in return they received an orderly society that protected them.

A second contract was established, Locke said, when a majority of people agreed to use the social contract as the basis of establishing a government. This government, Locke suggested, was to be a limited government to protect life, liberty, and property. Under Locke's view, if the government failed to do that, the people had a right to replace it with a new government. This principle of limited government is tied closely with the concept of *constitutionalism*, which means that the powers of government should be limited and written down.

Locke's view was not universally accepted. Other philosophers argued that law was created by men and not derived from the influence of nature. Political philosophers Thomas Hobbes (1588–1679) and David Hume (1711–1776) thought man's passions and self-interest would trump his ability to reason. They argued the need for a strong government that would curb these impulses. But Locke believed that man had the ability to reason and the duty to reason and that he was rational enough to make decisions that were in his and society's best interest.

Locke's concept of self-government, formed in the years before the American Revolution, had a strong influence on the thinking of the Founding Fathers. His political philosophy found its way directly into the *U.S. Declaration of Independence*. In fact, Thomas Jefferson (1743–1826) used it as the basis for his argument of what government should be but was not under the king's rule. Consequently, Jefferson placed it in the document that announced America's break from Great Britain:

> *To secure these Rights, Governments are instituted among men,*
> *deriving their just Powers from the Consent of the Governed; that,*
> *whenever any Form of Government becomes destructive of these Ends,*
> *it is the Right of the People to alter or abolish it, and institute new*

Government, laying its Foundation on such Principles, and organizing its Powers in such Forms, as to them shall seem most likely to effect their Safety and Happiness.

Moving Toward a Government of, by, and for the People

The British colonists had tried to reconcile with the king prior to the signing of the Declaration of Independence on July 4, 1776, but events leading up to the split made revolution all but certain. The Sugar

Act passed by Parliament in 1764, placing duties on certain imports, gave rise to the exclamation of "taxation without representation." The Quartering Act of 1765, another irritant, required colonists to provide supplies and housing for British troops. And The Stamp Act of 1765, which placed a tax on newspapers and legal documents, increased the Americans' anger further. A fistfight in 1770 between a colonist and a soldier led to the Boston Massacre, killing five colonists. Later, The Tea Act of 1773 left American merchants economically bruised and led to the Boston Tea Party.

Everett Historical/Shutterstock.com

As a result, and to decide on a response to the British, the First Continental Congress was formed and met in 1774 in Philadelphia. The colonists sent a *Declaration of Rights and Grievances* to the British government, but it was largely ignored.

When colonists learned that 700 British soldiers were marching from Boston to Concord, Massachusetts, on the morning of April 19, 1775, to search for hidden arms and arrest rebellious colonists, Paul Revere rode there the night before to warn them. When the soldiers arrived, they found about 60 armed Minutemen had blocked the road. Although it is unclear who fired the first shot, the skirmish that followed gave rise to the phrase "the shot heard round the world," indicating the fight for democracy, which would eventually spread across much of the planet, had begun.

The Second Continental Congress met in Philadelphia in May 1775 in an attempt to raise money for arms and seek alliances from foreign governments. War with Great Britain was not a foregone conclusion; many considered themselves British and did not want to break away. But increasing tensions made reconciliation impossible, and Thomas Paine's *Common Sense* pamphlet, which plainly stated the grievances against the king, turned a majority of the colonists toward separation. By July 1776, Congress had decided to declare America's independence.

Despite the war, the country had no formal central government until 1781 when the Continental Congress ratified *The Articles of Confederation*. This first constitution offered each state one vote, did not provide for a president or court system, and was basically a loose collection of states that would act together only if they wanted to. The states still retained their sovereign powers. And the central government had little power, though it was successful in negotiating foreign treaties, including the Treaty of Paris, which ended the war in 1783.

Following the war, it became apparent that the *Articles of Confederation* was unable to meet the challenges of the new nation. The new government, in debt from the war, could not levy taxes. It had no power to regulate commerce and no system of currency. It relied on the states for money, and they were reluctant to give any.

As a result, another Constitutional Convention was convened on May 29, 1787, to draft a new constitution. Those who attended were considered the best minds of the new country, and Thomas Jefferson referred to them as "an assembly of demigods." Among others, there were George Washington (1732–1799), who had led the country to victory, Benjamin Franklin (1706–1790), noted statesmen, writer, scientist, and leading Enlightenment thinker, and James Madison (1751–1836), who had studied the history of the world's governments. Nevertheless, the task before them was daunting.

Principles of Democracy

The Founders, in determining what the new government would look like, had received clear guidance from Locke, Milton, and other political philosophers as well as from history and their own experience with the king.

Locke's concept of government was based on the theory of majority rule. Though, this too, presented potential problems. A strong majority could impose its own tyranny over the minority as surely as King George III imposed unfair rule on the colonists before the American Revolution. Noting the potential threat, Jefferson, years later warned the public at his first inauguration in 1801 that though the will of the majority should prevail, that will must be reasonable and mindful of the fact that the minority possessed their equal rights that the laws must protect.

The fear of tyranny was and is a constant theme and concern in American government. Determined not to return to a system of centralized power that could impose its authority at will over the masses, the Founders also embraced an idea of the 18th-century French philosopher Montesquieu (1689–1755) who argued that the government's three sources of power—the legislature, the executive, and the judiciary—should not be under one authority, but should be split into three separate branches. If they remained under one authority, he argued that control of any two by a political group could lead to the destruction of liberty. Thus, the Founders divided the government's power accordingly, providing checks and balances against the power of each other.

Since the bedrock principle of any democracy is that the people must be in control of their own fates, free elections were therefore essential to determine the will of the people. It was clear to the Founders that the size of the country both in terms of population and land area would make direct democracy, as in ancient Athens, impractical. (America's founders rejected direct democracy because the new country had almost four million citizens and covered nearly 360,000 square miles at the time of the constitutional convention.) As a result, they determined to create a representative democracy whereby citizens would elect representatives who would then meet to decide government policy and govern in their name. This kind of government is called a *republic*.

Although the original Athenian democracy was small, and no one knew whether this latest, new form of democratic government would work on such a large scale, leaders, such as James Madison, believed that the diverse interest and competing power factions in a large country would

JAMES MADISON

Everett Historical/Shutterstock.com

James Madison

ensure balance and control since no one group could become large and powerful enough to control the others as might be the case in a smaller country.

Furthermore, Madison believed that in a small direct democracy, passions would overrule reason as to common good since each person would look out for himself, but in a representative democracy, those elected to power by the many would have a broader view of what would be necessary for the civic good. He also assumed those who sought election would come from the better-educated class of citizens and offer greater wisdom.

People, of course, who mean to be in charge of their own lives and government, must have access to the information necessary to make wise decisions. They must be able to express ideas, to form opinions, and engage in a dialog with other citizens and their leaders. Thus, the right to share ideas through speech, press, assembly, and petition is an important and necessary ingredient in the democratic process. Consequently, the Founders also made this principle a part of American law in the First Amendment to the Constitution. They expected a Press and public that would be engaged and vociferous and a leadership that would listen to what they had to say.

The Founders also understood that ignorant people could not govern wisely and maintain their freedom; they had to understand the principles of democratic rule. Toward this end, Thomas Jefferson advocated public education. Each generation had to learn anew the philosophies that gave rise to the republic, as well as tolerance and respect for others, the need for compromise, and the government institutions the Founders established. They had to understand political issues and how to participate in the political process. Although not part of the final document, the Founders advocated the need for an educated populace—not for the sake of getting jobs, but for the sake of understanding democracy.

Another important idea involved the concept of equality. Under the British class system, moving up the ladder of social status or wealth, and therefore, power, was extremely difficult. American democracy, in turn, was based on the concept that a man should be able to climb the ladder of success to the extent that talent and hard work would allow.

Thomas Jefferson

Therefore, when Thomas Jefferson wrote in the Declaration of Independence that "all men are created equal," he wasn't saying we all have the same talents, intellect, physical capacity, or social status. He was arguing that each person should have an equal opportunity to rise as far as luck and talent would take him, and that men are equal in their inalienable rights of life, liberty, and the pursuit of happiness, which government should protect.

Toward this end, government was to set up a standard ideal for a free society, an ideal toward which government should work. (The question remained, however, whether the quest for equality would, as the French politician Alexis de Tocqueville (1805–1859) asserted, erode our liberties, for as the quest for equality grows, the rules that promote it are often passed at the expense of individual liberty.)

All of these ideas occupied the Founders time and discussion as fundamental principles of democracy, and all of them found their way into the new government in one way or another.

Drafting the U.S. Constitution

Two plans for the new government were proposed at the Constitutional Convention. *The Virginia Plan* called for a national government with executive, judicial, and legislative branches. It would give the new government the power to tax and pass laws that would directly affect the people. *The New Jersey Plan* more closely resembled the old *Articles of Confederation*, and thus was voted down.

Yet divisions among the delegates remained. *The Virginia Plan* called for a two-house national legislature. The number of representatives from each state was to be determined by the population. Those in the lower house were to be elected by the people, and those in the upper house were to be appointed by the lower house. This arrangement favored states with large populations. Smaller states preferred a single-house legislature in which each state would have an equal number of representatives. To resolve the problem, *The Connecticut Compromise* was adopted. The lower house would be based on population. The upper house would give each state the same number of representatives.

Voting eligibility was another problem. Eventually, it was decided that the standards used by each state would apply to the House of Representatives, which generally meant only adult white males with property could vote. (Amendments would later change this to all citizens 18 or older.) Senators, on the other hand, were to be chosen by the respective state legislatures. (Again, this was later changed to a popular vote of the people.) In this way, the states at the time believed that they could exert some control over the national government.

The convention delegates also didn't think the American people were educated enough or wise enough to choose a president directly. They also feared that a popular election would enable states with large populations to dominate the election and the presidency. Candidates would only need to campaign where population was the densest. And a single national election would be practically difficult at the time given the large area of the country and the limited number of roads on which to travel. To allow the Congress to choose would have given it too much power over the executive branch. The solution was to establish an *Electoral College*, an institution formed from a group of people from each state to decide who would be the president.

These electors, as they were called, were selected by the state legislatures. Each state could choose as many electors as it had representatives and senators in Congress. This gave citizens an indirect power to choose who would be president since the people elected the legislators in each state. Today, the electors are chosen directly by the people. The system, a compromise between the states and the people, has changed somewhat over the centuries, but is still the means by which we choose a president.

(Today, in most states, the presidential candidate who wins a majority of the votes in each state receives that state's electoral votes. The total number of electoral votes coincides with the number of representatives in the U.S. House of Representatives (435) and senators in the U.S. Senate (100) in addition to three votes from the District of Columbia. To win the presidency, therefore, a candidate must garner at least 270 electoral votes. If no candidate wins a majority, the contest is thrown into the U.S. House of Representatives. There, each state gets a single vote. The candidate who wins a majority is elected president. The Electoral College has been criticized as undemocratic, but there are also advantages to the system. To get enough votes, candidates must campaign widely, not just in a few states, and eliminating it would also undermine state interests and power.)

Thirty-nine delegates signed the new *U.S. Constitution* on September 16, 1787, after which it was submitted to the Confederation and to the individual states for ratification. It was not clear, however, that the states would go along with the new proposal. It provided for a much stronger central government, something that the people feared.

The Fight for Ratification

Those who supported the Constitution were *Federalists*, and those who opposed it were *Antifederalists*. The Federalists thought a strong central government was needed to confront the national problems of the day, while the Antifederalists were concerned that the document did not contain a *Bill of Rights* that would protect the people and the states from another new tyranny. This concern was persuasive, and the Federalists promised that a *Bill of Rights* would be added if the document were accepted.

To promote adoption, Federalists James Madison, Alexander Hamilton, and John Jay wrote a series of 85 essays that were published in New York newspapers urging ratification. Known as *The Federalist Papers*, the combined effect of this early editorial campaign was to both show the effectiveness of the Press in promoting discussion of important ideas and provide logical arguments for adoption of the Constitution.

The men argued that small governments were more prone to tyranny than larger ones, that they tended to quarrel among themselves and become easily dominated by stronger, larger nations. Furthermore, they noted that a stronger central government could protect their liberties, and that the new document contained safeguards against tyranny. These included the establishment of majority rule and minority rights, free elections, separation of powers, a free press, and equality under the law—principles they had learned from history and experience.

The writers further noted that the document preserved a federalist system, which divided power between the new federal government and the states, and that the new Constitution limited the powers of the federal government. The United States was the first federalist government. Before that, strong central governments exerted power over the people. Or, at the other end of the scale, a confederation government could only exercise power the states provided; it had no power of its own. But this new system shared power along geographic lines. States exerted power within their boundaries and the federal government had limited power over the nation as a whole. Therefore, the states had control over such things as education, while only the federal government could make treaties.

The separation of powers also meant that *checks and balances* were built into the system to ensure that no one branch of government could undermine or limit the power and authority of another. They needed one another to function. The two houses of Congress had to work together to make law. And although they could pass laws, the president could veto them and the Supreme Court could rule them invalid if they went beyond the boundaries of the Constitution. The president, in turn, had no power to make law, and his veto could be overridden by a two-thirds vote in Congress. If he went beyond his authority, he could be removed from office through a system of impeachment. And the Court had the power of *judicial review*, meaning it could interpret what the law meant, but Congress could determine the size and shape of the federal judicial system. Thus, they were dependent upon one another and limited by one another.

The concept of judicial review was not specifically mentioned in the Constitution, but it had been used in other instances in courts even before the American Revolution and there was evidence that the Founders supported it as a natural duty of the Court. The power was established in 1803 in *Marbury v. Madison*, which established the precedent that the Court could nullify an act of Congress. The Court can also rule invalid any state government action that fails to comport with the U.S. Constitution.

Perhaps, most importantly, the writers of the new document accepted and promoted the idea of popular sovereignty as the basis of government, which meant that the people, not the states or the new federal government, were the source of all legal authority. The people decided their own institutions of government as well as what the law should be. This was a radical departure from the old English monarchy where the king was sovereign.

And although the Founders made it clear in the document that the *Constitution* was the law of the land when it came to the powers noted within it, and that all states had to abide by it and all judges had to enforce it, they also placed within it the power of the people and the states to amend it. The power of the federal government, after all, came from the people and the states. They could change it whenever they thought it necessary. The Founders understood that as times and circumstances changed, the law must change as well. Nevertheless, the Founders made the process difficult to ensure that it was changed for only the most important of reasons.

(Amending the *Constitution* is a two-step process. It includes a proposal to amend and ratification. Amendments can be proposed either by a two-thirds vote of both houses of Congress or by request of two-thirds of the state legislatures demanding a national convention. Ratification occurs either when three-fourths of the state legislatures or three-fourths of specially elected conventions in the states agree to the changes. To date, 27 amendments have been adopted.)

The arguments of the Federalists carried the day. The Constitution was ratified in 1788. The Bill of Rights was adopted during the first Congress in 1789 and was ratified quickly in 1791 as a concession to the Anti-Federalists' concern for protection of individual rights.

What's in the Constitution: Types and Limitations of Power

Under the Constitution, the national government has two different types of powers. *Delegated powers* are expressed in the words of the document itself. They are listed and include such things as the power to tax and spend and regulate interstate commerce.

The document also gives the national government *implied powers*. Implied powers come from the *necessary and proper clause* that is at the end of Article I, Section 8 of the document. The clause gives the government some room to justify using an implied power as a way to carry out a delegated power. The clause states that Congress has the right "to make all laws which shall be necessary and proper for carrying into execution the foregoing (delegated) powers." For example, the Constitution gives Congress the ability to raise an army and navy, but it doesn't say how that is to be accomplished. Consequently, the government has used different methods over the years, including a lottery or a voluntary system of service.

The Constitution also limits the government's powers. It forbids the government from passing *bills of attainder*—laws that would single out people for punishment without due process of law. It also may not pass *ex post facto laws*, laws that would allow the government to punish a person for an act that wasn't a crime when it was done. And it does not have the power to suspend the *writ of habeas corpus*, which prevents the court from arbitrarily holding people in prison without stating the reason for their incarceration. It also may not violate the Bill of Rights.

All powers not given to the federal government are reserved for the states and the people in the 10th Amendment. These are called *reserved powers*. States have the authority to pass laws for the *health, safety, and welfare* of their citizens. This would include the right to establish police and fire departments as well as schools.

Some authority is *concurrent*, that is, both the national government and state government can exercise the same kind of power within their jurisdictions. For example, both may tax and spend, and the *Due Process and Equal Protection Clauses* of the 14th Amendment requires the states as well as the federal government to follow the Bill of Rights.

Other clauses in the Constitution regulate relations of states. The *full faith and credit clause* requires states to honor other states' civil court rulings, such as marriage and divorce decrees. The *privileges and immunities clause* means that all states shall grant to the citizens of other states the fundamental rights guaranteed in the Constitution. And the *interstate rendition clause* allows one state to seek extradition of an accused criminal from another state. Other provisions require states to seek the approval of Congress before entering into agreements with one another. And the Supreme Court has the authority to hear boundary disputes between the states.

The Constitution requires the federal government to protect the states from foreign invasion as well as internal violence. The president has the power to enforce federal court orders and to protect federal property. It also requires the states to maintain a republic-type government, police themselves, hold elections for Congress, consider proposed constitutional amendments, and choose presidential electors.

The Congress

It may be difficult to impossible to make an appointment with the president or the chief justice of the United States Supreme Court, but it is still quite possible to communicate, often in person, with one's

kropic1/Shutterstock.com

representative or senator. Of the three branches of government, the Congress is closest to the people, and therefore arguably the most important.

For democracy to work, the Founding Fathers understood that those leaders closest to the people should exercise the most power. For that reason, the most important functions of government rest with the Congress, whose two main functions are to pass legislation and to represent the people. Only Congress has the power to make law, tax and spend, declare war, make treaties, borrow money, print and coin money, establish bankruptcy laws, regulate commerce, and investigate for the people matters that fall within its jurisdiction. These and other powers delegated to it ensure that the government continues to function on the people's behalf.

As noted earlier, Congress consists of a lower house called the House of Representatives and an upper house called the Senate. The number of House seats each state receives is based on population. The House currently has 435 members. The number was fixed in 1929 with each state having at least one representative. In 1964, the Supreme Court ordered states to apportion their districts to ensure the concept of "one man, one vote" and prevent some districts from controlling others. Each state's share is determined every 10 years after a census is taken.

The Senate is comprised of two senators from each state, or 100 senators altogether. Senators are supposed to look out for the state as a whole, unlike members of the House who are more inclined to look after the interests of their districts and are considered to be closer to the people than the Senate.

Representatives are elected every two years; senators are elected every six years. Each congressional term lasts two years beginning and ending on January 3 after the November elections. Terms of Congress are numbered consecutively. Each term consists of two sessions, one for each year.

The House retains certain exclusive powers. All revenue bills to raise taxes must originate in the House. The lower house also retains the right to impeach officials, approves (by two-thirds vote) Constitutional amendments before state ratification, and elects the president should the Electoral College deadlock in an election. (The right to impeach means the House has the duty to weigh evidence of a possible crime by the president or a member of Congress or the federal courts, and bring charges against them. If that happens, the process moves to the Senate where the Chief Justice of the Supreme Court sits as judge and the full Senate, as jury, listens to the evidence presented in trial by attorneys for both sides and renders a verdict. Thus far, two presidents—Andrew Johnson and Bill Clinton—have been impeached, though neither was convicted. If convicted, officials are removed from office.)

The Constitution determines the qualifications for those running for federal office. Those running for the House of Representatives must be at least 25 years old, have been a U.S. citizen for at least seven years, and live in the state they represent. Elections are held the first Tuesday of November every even-numbered year.

Because our political system has largely evolved into a two-party system of Democrats and Republicans, both the House and Senate are made up of a majority and minority party. One party or the other is always in control. The majority party elects the Speaker of the House. The Speaker's job is to maintain order, assign bills to committees, and to direct floor discussions by determining the order in which members speak. The House does its business through a complex system of committees and caucuses.

Other House leaders include the House Majority Leader and the House Minority Leader who control their respective parties. The Minority Leader is the highest-ranking official of the minority party. Both parties also each elect a "Whip." Whips work with party leaders to keep members in line on issues and gather necessary votes on important legislation. Members usually vote as their leaders wish, because the leaders decide who chairs the House committees where the work of the House is largely done. Although the majority party selects the committee chairs, the ratio of those who are headed by Democrats or Republicans generally corresponds to the ratio of Democrats to Republicans in the House. Committees are organized around particular issues or areas of governmental concern. Thus, those who are on particular committees exert substantial power in those areas.

The major committees in the House include the standing or permanent committees. The most powerful of these include the Rules Committee, which sets rules for debate and can eliminate a bill by not allowing it to proceed; the Ways and Means Committee, which oversees federal revenue matters including borrowing; Social Security, and trade and tariffs; and the Appropriations Committee, which oversees the raising of revenue.

In addition, the House can establish Select Committees for a limited purpose that can last as long as needed. It can also form Joint Committees combining members from both houses of Congress to work on a problem. And it can establish Conference Committees, joining members from both houses to work out difference between House and Senate versions of a bill.

The Senate, or upper house, has a history of being the more elite. One third of the Senate's seats are up for election every two years, unlike the entire House, which is up for election every two years. The vice president of the United States is the president of the Senate, a largely ceremonial role. The vice president can vote on Senate matters only when there is a tie. When the vice president is absent, the President Pro Tempore, a ceremonial title given to the senior member of the majority party, presides in the vice president's absence. The majority and minority leaders and whips positions are similar to those in the House.

The Founders intended the Senate to be less subject to special interests and more formal and above the political fray found in the House. Higher qualifications are required for membership. Senators must be at least 30 years old by the time they are sworn in, must be a resident of the state they represent, and have been a U.S. citizen for at least nine years.

The Senate, just as the House, has specific responsibilities. It has the duty of "advice and consent." It must be consulted on and consent to the ratification of treaties, and it must approve presidential appointments to cabinet positions and executive leadership positions. It also must approve nominations of federal judges and Supreme Court justices.

In many ways, the Senate is simpler than the House, though both do business through a series of committees and subcommittees. Senate rules are short. Unlike the House where members are limited in their time to speak, Senators have few time constraints. Any senator wishing to block a vote can *filibuster* by continuing to speak and refusing to give up the floor during debate, thus stopping all Senate work. (A three-fifths vote of the entire Senate is needed to close the issue and bring it to a vote. This is called *cloture*.)

Although each house of Congress has specific responsibilities, both houses are equally involved in the law-making process. The majority party in each house elects its leader (Speaker in the House of Representatives and President Pro Tempore in the Senate). The majority party in both houses controls committee assignments and the important committees. Key leadership positions in the Senate are elected by the full party membership. Both houses must approve a bill before it can be sent to the president for his signature to become law.

Like the House, the Senate has its own standing or permanent committees, which are similar to those in the House. The most important is the Appropriations Committee, which controls the dispersal of funds. Select committees, joint committees, and conference committees also exist.

While the Speaker of the House is the power in the House of Representatives, the Majority Leader of the Senate retains most power there. Members of the majority party elect the Majority Leader. Duties include meeting with the Speaker and the president on important issues.

The Majority Leader of the Senate consults with the Minority Leader to establish the agenda of the Senate. No legislation in the Senate will come up for a vote without the support of the Majority Leader. Majority party control is important in both houses in deciding who serves on committees and which legislation proceeds.

How a Bill Becomes a Law

With the exceptions noted above, all bills (written proposals for a law) can begin in the House of Representatives or the Senate. Legislation often begins with an awareness of a public problem that needs resolution. Citizens, lobbyists, anyone can suggest a bill be introduced. As a result, members in both the House and the Senate often introduce similar bills at the same time.

Most bills deal with single subjects, but often *riders* will be attached that are unrelated to the subject. Riders are provisions that are unlikely to pass if introduced on their own. They are usually attached to important legislation that their sponsor believes will pass, even if others don't approve of the rider.

A senator introduces a bill by sending it to the Senate desk while a representative deposits a bill in the "hopper" on the House floor. The clerk of the House must assign a number to each bill with the prefix H.R. All Senate bills are given a number with the prefix S. Thus, a bill numbered H.R. 456 would be the 456th bill that was introduced in the House of Representatives that term.

Imilian/Shutterstock.com

If the bill is introduced in both houses, the senator and representative who are introducing the legislation may agree to introduce the same bill. Thousands of bills are introduced each year; only a couple of hundred are actually passed. Not all legislators, as noted earlier, have an equal chance of getting their bills passed. Those in the minority have little chance of getting their proposals through the legislative process. Even those in the majority party may find it difficult since their party leadership may favor some bills over others.

Often bills begin with proposals by the president. Each year the president, by law, must give a *State of the Union* address, noting the overall health of the country from his perspective and offering his vision of where the country should be headed. To this end, the president will suggest Congress pass certain legislation dealing with specific problems. Many of these suggestions are presented as proposed bills by the executive departments and agencies of the executive branch of government. Representatives and senators who agree with the president's policies then introduce these bills in Congress. If the president's party controls Congress, chances are good that the legislation will pass. If, though, the opposition party controls Congress, chances are good that the proposed legislation will fail since the president's opponents do not always share his views.

Once a bill has been introduced, it is assigned to the committee that handles that subject. If the committee doesn't want to pursue it, it is tabled and dies. Most bills do not make it out of committee. (In the House, a *discharge petition*, passed by a majority of the representatives, may be used to remove a bill from the control of a committee and bring it to the House floor for a vote. This is rarely used.)

If the committee decides to review the bill, it is assigned to a subcommittee whose members have knowledge and experience on the subject. They then study it. If the subject is of great importance, public hearings may be held to gather information and discuss the strengths and weaknesses of the proposal. Congress can ask anyone to testify, including experts, government and academic officials, lobbyists, or even ordinary citizens with knowledge of the subject. Such fact-finding hearings can last weeks or months.

Once the subcommittee has done its work, the bill is sent back to the full committee for consideration. The committee then looks at the subcommittee's work and suggestions and goes over it carefully, making what it considers to be necessary changes or revisions. If there are conflicting views, accommodations may be made to secure the necessary votes to move the bill forward. If the bill receives majority approval from the committee, it is "voted out" of committee. If the majority does not approve it, the bill dies.

If the standing committee approves the bill, it is to be forwarded to the full House or Senate where the committee chair will manage the debate. If there are differences between the House and Senate versions of the bill, the committee chair will suggest to the leader of his respective house where committee members should be included in a conference committee to work out a compromise bill.

Once the standing committee approves the bill, and prior to the debate, it is placed on a calendar in the house in which it originated. The Senate has one calendar, and routine bills are considered in the order in which they are placed on the calendar. If a bill generates controversy, the Majority Leader will consult with the Minority Leader and the chair of the committee handling the legislation and any others who have an interest in the bill to schedule debate.

A bill in the House is placed on one of three major calendars—the Union Calendar for appropriations and tax matters, the House Calendar for other public bills, or the Private Calendar for bills dealing with specific individuals or corporations.

Once the bill comes up for debate on the floor of the House of Representatives, the body usually turns itself into a Committee of the Whole, which allows for more flexible procedure and requires only 100 members to be present to debate and propose amendments. If the members present adopt amendments to the bill, the full House must vote to approve them.

In the Senate, where there are fewer members, the process is simpler. Except as noted above, senators debate the bills in the order they appear on the calendar. And while debate in the House is usually limited to an hour, debate in the Senate is unlimited.

If the bill originates in one house, after debate is finished and the bill is passed, it is sent to the other house for debate. If the second legislative body changes the bill, it must again be sent back to the house that introduced it for approval of the new changes. If the house is unable to agree on the changes, a conference committee is formed to work out the differences. Both houses of Congress must pass the bill in identical form.

If the bill passes both houses of Congress, it is signed by the Speaker of the House and the President of the Senate and then sent to the president for his signature. If the president signs the bill, it becomes law. If he disagrees with the law, he can *veto* it, returning it to the house in which it originated, noting his objections. Congress may then try to override the veto by a two-thirds vote in each house. Vetoes are difficult to override, but if the move is successful, the bill becomes law.

The process of passing a bill into law is complicated and depends upon the art of compromise. The acquisition and use of power to accomplish this is called *politics*.

The Presidency

Article II, Section I of the U.S. Constitution notes simply that "[t]he executive Power shall be vested in a President of the United States," a matter-of-fact clause that has come to establish what most consider to be the most powerful position on the planet, power that is checked only by the other branches of the U.S. government.

Created during a time of monarchs, no real precedent existed for the position, and it was left to George Washington to largely establish what the presidency would look like apart from the constitutional mandates charged to it. Since then each president has added to its evolution. And while early presidents exercised modest power, later presidents stood up to Congress, exercising veto powers and providing strong leadership during times of crises. The ebb and flow of power between the Congress and the presidency continues as history changes. (In many ways, intense media focus during the modern era has turned the position into what many describe as an imperial presidency, giving it more power than the Founders intended or the Constitution perhaps permits, and deceiving the public into thinking the executive branch is supreme among others.)

Forty-five men have been elected president since the country was founded. As noted earlier, the people choose the president indirectly through the Electoral College. To be elected, those running for the office of president must be at least 35 years old, have been born in the United States or to parents who are American citizens, and have been a resident of the United States for at least 14 years.

The Founders, not wanting to create an imperial leader like the king they just defeated, established a four-year term for the president, although they did not originally set a limit on the number of terms a

Joseph Sohm/Shutterstock.com

president could serve. George Washington set the standard when he refused to seek a third term. After Franklin D. Roosevelt won third and fourth terms, the 22nd Amendment was passed to limit presidents to two terms.

The president, who lives and works in the White House, is inaugurated on the steps of the Capitol at noon on January 20 following election each fourth November. The oath requires the president to " . . .preserve, protect, and defend the Constitution of the United States." Thus, the president is in charge of maintaining and enforcing the law of the land.

The Constitution gives tremendous authority to the president. The president is the chief of state, thus serving as spokesman for nearly 350 million Americans. As such, the president is the ceremonial head of the nation and a symbol of the government. The president is the only nationally elected official and is in many ways expected to unify the nation, especially during times of crises. During the 1930s, President Franklin Roosevelt tried to bolster the American people during The Great Depression with his radio "fireside chats."

Although the president does not have the power to make law, he can issue executive orders, implementing, and interpreting laws already passed. And he can propose law and veto bills with which he disagrees. (Although state governors have the right of *line item vetoes*—vetoing part of the bill presented to them, but not other parts—presidents have no such authority and must either accept or reject the entire law as proposed by Congress.) A president also may *pocket veto* a bill (ostensibly by putting the bill in his pocket and forgetting it) by not acting on it within 10 days of when Congress adjourns. Threats to veto a bill often persuade Congress to modify the law they passed. The conflict created by the separation of powers forces both branches to work together to get anything done. To get their way, presidents often will go on television and radio to speak directly to the American people in an effort to put pressure on Congress. Congress, meanwhile, can threaten to hold up legislation the president wants.

The president is the nation's chief diplomat, responsible for appointing all U.S. ambassadors and diplomats with the advice and consent of the Senate. The president and his representatives are responsible for negotiating treaties, which are then submitted to the Senate for the necessary two-thirds approval to become law. Executive agreements between the president and another leader do not require senate approval. Both treaties and executive agreements have the same legal force. The president decides which he wishes to pursue. Treaties involve more important matters. (Many in Congress have complained presidents often try to use executive agreements to get around the constitutional requirement of getting the advice and consent of the Senate on important matters.)

The president is also in charge of making foreign policy. Using other agencies such as the Departments of Defense and State, the Central Intelligence Agency, National Security Council, and others, the president is in a position to know the facts concerning foreign affairs probably better than any other official. In many respects, because of the status of the United States as a major power, the president also assumes the mantle of world leader and often takes on the role of negotiator in attempting to resolve disputes between other countries.

The president is the commander in chief of the armed forces of the United States, and although the day-to-day operation of the military is left to the Department of Defense, the president carefully oversees the operation. Placing authority for the armed forces in the hands of the president ensures civilian control of the military and makes a takeover of the country by the military less likely. Only Congress has the authority to declare war, but once declared, the president is in charge of military decisions. Not all military actions in American history have come with official congressional approval, including the Korean and Vietnam Wars, which were considered police actions. Congressional criticism of these actions led to it passing the War Powers Resolution in 1973, requiring the president to seek congressional approval for any military action within 60 days of deployment of troops.

The president also is the chief administrator of the executive branch of government. As such, he oversees a vast bureaucracy of more than two million civilian employees. Although he must receive the advice and consent of the Senate when nominating some positions, he can remove executive officers of the federal government who are unwilling to carry out the president's policies.

He oversees the staff and offices of the president and the White House, including the chief of staff, the press secretary, White House legal counsel, and about 500 others, in addition to eight other permanent agencies, including the Office of Management and Budget, the National

Security Council, the Council of Economic Advisers, the Office of Policy Development, the Office of the U.S. Trade Representative, the Council of Environmental Quality, the Office of Science and Technology, and the Office of Administration.

The president also is in charge of the Cabinet, major federal departments whose leaders are appointed by the president with the advice and consent of the Senate. The Cabinet includes the vice president and the departments of Agriculture, Commerce, Defense, Education, Energy, Health and Human Services, Homeland Security, Housing and Urban Development, Interior, Justice and the Attorney General, Labor, State, Transportation, Treasury, and Veteran's Affairs.

The president nominates all federal judges and justices of the Supreme Court with the advice and consent of the Senate. The president grants pardons and reprieves in federal cases, not including matters of impeachment.

As party leader, the president serves as its main spokesperson and national leader. This role is not mentioned in the Constitution, but it has evolved with the country's party system. As such, the president is expected to attend meetings and rallies, and generate support for the party's candidates for office.

The president is expected to manage the economy, though business leaders in the private sector, not politicians, make most of the decisions that affect the economy. Nevertheless, with the passage of the Employment Act of 1946, the president is responsible for the economic health of the nation.

Although the office of the presidency has gained influence over the years, especially since efforts of President Roosevelt during the 1930s to pull the nation out of The Great Depression, the office is not without its limits. The Supreme Court can and does exercise judicial review over presidential orders just as it does with congressional legislation and can declare actions of the two other branches unconstitutional and invalid. (In 1974, when President Richard Nixon claimed tape recordings of conversations during the Watergate scandal to be privileged executive records, the Court disagreed and ordered Nixon to turn them over.) The Congress can override presidential vetoes and pass laws in spite of his objections. The mass media can hold the office up to intense scrutiny, exposing the presidency to public criticism. And the bureaucracy of government itself is so large as to limit a president's power to affect change.

These safeguards did not evolve by accident. The Founders were not particularly concerned with government efficiency. Their focus was on preventing tyranny. And a government with checks and balances, they figured, would ensure the people's protection.

CHAPTER 3

The American
Legal System

Seeking Truth and Interpreting the Law

We have reviewed two of the three branches of government—the legislative and the executive. The third branch, the judiciary, is the most passive of the three in that it can't act unless cases are brought to it, but

it nevertheless wields tremendous power in government by defining what the law means. Thus, its decisions affect the lives of all Americans. For students of media law, it is essential to understand its basic structure and function.

The philosophies of Milton and Locke are just as critically important to the judicial branch of government as to the legislative and the executive branches. For the Founders understood that effective government must pursue and build on truth, and the pursuit of truth is at the heart of any system of justice.

Copyright © of Mark Zimmerman.
Reprinted by permission.

The American court system is based on the adversarial process—meaning both sides, usually through their lawyers, appear before the court to argue their cases, allowing the judge or jury to discover the truth as it emerges from their competing arguments. This process of finding the truth is a bedrock principle of American democracy as expressed by John Milton in his treatise *Areopagitica*. And it is at the heart of how we determine verdicts in trials. In part, Milton wrote:

> *[T]hough all the winds of doctrine were let loose to play on the earth, so Truth be in the field, we do injuriously, by licensing and prohibiting, to misdoubt her strength. Let her and Falsehood grapple; who ever knew Truth put to the worse, in a free and open encounter?*

Milton's theory is at work everywhere in our government, but especially in our judicial system. Each lawyer gets up in open court before the public and argues to the jury that his client's story is the correct version of the truth. The jury watches the fight—the grappling—and decides where the truth lies by its verdict.

Our Congress makes law using the same technique. It debates bills in the open chambers of the Senate and House of Representatives and before the Press and public in the gallery and then votes on where it thinks the truth lies in the matter.

And we, the people, use it when choosing leaders. We listen to the debates of candidates for office and then cast our votes, deciding who has the better version of the truth.

Our legal system also uses the scientific precepts of the Enlightenment, the other bedrock principle of our democracy. The Enlightenment discovered truth through fact and evidence. In other words, truth could be proven. We reach verdicts in court only after the grappling attorneys have presented facts or evidence supporting their positions. These facts, which can be challenged by the other side, enable the jury to reach a dispassionate, objective opinion on the guilt or innocence of the accused based on evidence instead of personal bias or suspicion.

Although the lawyers are the principal players in any trial, responsible for presenting their cases through evidence, testimony of witnesses, and argument, the judge plays a crucial role in maintaining order and ensuring that the rules of judicial procedure are followed. The judge makes rulings on what the law means, listens to and rules on objections and motions of the lawyers, instructs the jury on how the law should be applied, and in the case of a *bench trial* (heard by the judge instead of a jury), makes a decision on the basis of his own analysis of the facts and the law.

For example, when the individual contacts a lawyer to seek help, the lawyer researches the law and tries to find the particular law that will apply to the client's case and to the client's benefit. In this way, the lawyer attempts to use the law to resolve the dispute in favor of the client. Competing lawyers will argue which laws should apply to any given situation. Since not all cases are alike, judges must decide which law applies. In so doing, the judge interprets the meaning of the law. All judges do this and at every level of the court system. Judges don't just match laws to cases. It would be impossible to write laws to solve each specific problem people fall into. Nevertheless, judges must be mindful that their legal interpretations may be used to establish precedent to decide future cases. They, therefore, want to make wise decisions that provide stability, predictability, and respect for the law.

To illustrate this point, consider the following scenario. Let's say some young people wear black armbands to school protesting the war in Vietnam. The school suspends them because officials fear that it will cause a disruption of classes. The students sue the public school, run by the government, for violating their free speech rights because the First Amendment to the U.S. Constitution states that government can't make laws infringing on freedom of speech.

School officials argue that the court must rule in their favor because the state has a law that gives them the right to maintain order in school. The students argue that the court must follow the First Amendment because they were expressing themselves. But is an armband speech? The judge must weigh the evidence and the laws and decide which law applies.

Let's say at trial, the school can't show classes were disrupted and the lawyers for the students can show that the intent of the First Amendment was to protect expression, and an armband communicates an idea. The judge, therefore, rules that the First Amendment applies. In so doing, the Court has established a precedent of how to rule in future cases where students are using symbolic speech but not disrupting classes.

In this way, too, courts make public policy when judges interpret laws and regulations passed by state legislatures and Congress as they apply those laws to cases brought before them.

A Dual Court System

The nation has a dual court system. This matches the federalist system established by the Founding Fathers. Thus, there is one federal system and 50 state systems, since each state has its own judicial system. Although there are some differences, the systems are basically the same. All of them have a trial court where evidence is presented and decisions are made and the law is applied to solve the problem (otherwise known as fact-finding courts), an appellate court where the decisions of the trial court may be appealed and reviewed to make sure decisions were made properly and according to the law, and a supreme court, or court of last resort, to render a final appellate decision, usually to sort out conflicting decisions on the same matter from different lower courts or to interpret the ultimate meaning of the law.

Although we have discussed six different sources of law, cases that come before the Court generally fall into one of two areas—criminal or civil. Criminal law is usually statutory law in that it is the law passed by a legislative body to protect the public from harm. The state's attorney (if it's a state crime) or a U.S. attorney (if it's a federal crime) brings cases against those defendants accused of crimes. Crimes are either classified as misdemeanors (lesser crimes such as disturbing the peace and punishable by fine and/or less than a year in jail) or felonies (more serious crimes such as murder punishable by fine and/or a year or more in prison, or perhaps death for crimes that carry the death penalty).

States pass criminal laws under their general reserve powers while those passed by Congress are done so under the Constitution's enumerated and implied powers. An example of a state crime would be murder; a federal crime would include failure to file federal income tax returns since the Constitution gives Congress the power to tax and spend and therefore the right also to enforce that power.

The state district attorneys who prosecute state crimes are elected. The president with the advice and consent of the Senate appoints U.S. attorneys. A U.S. attorney is located in each district of the federal court system.

Civil law (not to be confused with civil law systems discussed earlier) involves disputes between private individuals or organizations. The pig example noted above would be an example of a civil case between two individuals. Divorce and personal injury cases would be other examples.

This does not mean that the government cannot be a party to a civil action. For example, the government may be sued for monetary damages when a police officer wrongfully shoots someone. Often, both criminal prosecution as well as a civil action will result from the same case. The 1995 O.J. Simpson murder trial is one example. After he was acquitted of murder, his late wife's family filed a civil suit against him for her wrongful death, which he lost.

Whether a court has a right to hear a case is determined by whether it has *jurisdiction*, a legal term that means the court has the authority to hear a particular matter. The right is determined by either the state or federal constitution or state or federal statute. State courts handle laws related to their state. Federal courts hear cases concerning the U.S. Constitution, federal laws and treaties, and admiralty and maritime law. This is called *subject matter jurisdiction*. In some instances, the state and federal courts share jurisdiction, and the case can be brought in either system.

Courts also determine whether laws passed by a legislative body are constitutionally permissible. State constitutions are the supreme law of states, and the federal constitution is the supreme law of the nation. No state law may contradict the law of its state constitution, and no state or federal law may contradict the U.S. Constitution.

The courts can also hear cases based on who the parties are, or *personal jurisdiction*. State courts generally handle matters related to people living or working within their states. The federal courts hear cases involving ambassadors or other public ministers, cases in which the United States is a party, disputes between citizens of different states involving more than $75,000, and disputes between two or more states.

Jurisdiction also refers to whether a court has *original* or *appellate jurisdiction*. In other words, at what part of the judicial process can a court hear a case? Can it hear the original trial, or can it hear only appeals? Courts that hear trials have *original jurisdiction*. They hear the presentation of facts and law by the lawyers and apply the law. Courts that have *appellate jurisdiction* review the lower courts' decisions to determine if the court followed proper procedure and applied the law correctly. The U.S. Supreme Court has both original and appellate jurisdiction, though most of the time it hears only appellate cases. Its original jurisdiction is limited to certain matters such as disputes between states.

Decisions by state appellate courts, which deal with state law, are binding on the state courts in a particular state, unless overturned or modified by the supreme court of that state. State courts in other states need not follow the precedents of other states, though they may find them persuasive.

Decisions regarding federal law by a U.S. Circuit Court of Appeals are binding only on lower federal or state courts in the region covered by that particular court of appeals. Meanwhile, U.S. Supreme Court decisions regarding the interpretation of all federal law—federal statutes and the U.S. Constitution and cases arising under them—are binding on all federal and state courts.

The legal process generally follows the path, both in state and federal court, of starting at the trial level, then proceeding to the appellate court, and finally moving to the Supreme Court. In some cases, however, appeals can be made directly to the U.S. Supreme Court—those involving the U.S. Constitution, treaties or federal laws from state supreme courts.

As noted, state courts have the final say on what the laws of a particular state mean; the U.S. Supreme Court has the final authority to determine what federal law says. If, however, a decision involving a federal question of law arises at the state level, the U.S. Supreme Court has the final say on the matter. For example, murder is a state crime, and so state law determines what the punishment will be for someone convicted of that crime. But the Eighth Amendment to the U.S. Constitution prohibits cruel and unusual punishment. Therefore, if a state's punishment may be cruel and unusual, a federal question of law arises—whether the state law violates the U.S. Constitution—which can be determined by the U.S. Supreme Court.

Most cases are brought in state court. Although the federal government is large and the laws that come under it are numerous, it is still a government of enumerated or limited powers. Most law, and especially the common law, falls under state jurisdiction. And most of the day-to-day disputes between people occur under state law and at the state level. The state court system, therefore, can be varied and extensive, comprising all manner of courts to handle different problems. Courts can include justices of the peace, municipal courts to handle traffic and city problems, divorce courts to handle family matters, probate courts to handle wills and estates, and a variety of others in addition to the state courts at the county or district level to handle other matters.

Unlike federal judges who are appointed by the president with the advice and consent of the U.S. Senate and serve for life, judges at the city and state level are often elected or appointed by the governor and serve definite terms.

The Federal Courts

At the federal level, two types of courts—the constitutional and the legislative—exist. Constitutional courts are established under provisions of the Constitution. Article III, Section I of the document declares that "the jurisdictional power of the United States shall be vested in one supreme Court and in such inferior Courts as the Congress may from time to time ordain and establish." Thus, Congress could theoretically abolish all federal courts except the U.S. Supreme Court. This likely will not happen since it would effectively shut down the entire federal legal system. It takes a lot of courts to handle all the disputes in the country.

UNITED STATES COURTHOUSE

Most federal courts are constitutional courts. They include the U.S. District Courts, the U.S. Courts of Appeals, and the U.S. Supreme Court. A few others, such as the Court of International Trade, hear cases under the nation's tariff laws and also are part of the system.

Congress creates legislative courts under its legislative powers from Article I of the Constitution. Examples of these courts include The U.S. Court of Military Appeals and the U.S. Tax Court. Although the judges are chosen in the same way all federal judges are selected, legislative judges serve lengths of terms decided by Congress. All cases arising under either constitutional or legislative courts can nevertheless be appealed to the U.S. Supreme Court.

Most federal cases, as noted, arise in one of the 94 federal district courts. At least one federal district court exists in each state, the District of Columbia, Puerto Rico, and various U.S. territories. District courts have only original jurisdiction but hear both criminal and civil cases involving federal matters. Some states have more than one district court. For example, Oklahoma has three—the western district, the northern district, and the eastern district. Districts do not cross state lines. The district courts, in turn, are organized into circuits—areas over which a particular appellate court has jurisdiction. The United States has 13 U.S. Circuit Courts of Appeals that can review cases from U.S. District Courts within their circuits. U.S. Circuit Courts of Appeals have only appellate jurisdiction.

Each court of appeals normally has three judges, unlike the trial court, which has one. The U.S. Supreme Court, as most state supreme courts, has nine. Lawyers who appeal or defend cases at the U.S. Circuit Court of Appeals level file a copy of the trial transcript—that is what was said and done at the trial level—and also their written arguments and the law that they believe supports those arguments. These written arguments are called *briefs*. They give the judges a chance to read the arguments of the lawyers. The lawyers are often allotted time to present oral arguments to the court later. Once the arguments have been made, the judges adjourn the court and gather to discuss the case before announcing their decision.

The U.S. Circuit Court of Appeals must hear all cases appealed to it, usually by the losing party. The government, however, is prohibited from appealing criminal convictions because of the Fifth Amendment to the U.S. Constitution, which prohibits the government from trying the same person twice for the same crime. This is known as *double jeopardy*.

Unlike the other appellate courts, the U.S. Supreme Court is not required to hear every case appealed to it. In fact, in any given term from October until usually June, the high court hears only about 80 cases. It generally chooses to hear only those cases where lower appellate courts have issued conflicting rulings on similar cases, requiring the

U.S. Supreme Court to decide what the law should be. Or it also looks at cases in which it must decide if a law passed by Congress or an action done by the president is within their authority under the Constitution. This is called the court's *power of judicial review*, the ultimate power of the court to be the final word on what is or what is not permitted under the U.S. Constitution. State Supreme Courts have the same power at the state level. Although this power is not found in the U.S. Constitution, the U.S. Supreme Court decided in *Marbury v. Madison* in 1803 that it was the court's logical role in the new government, and the other branches of government assented.

The U.S. Supreme Court generally hears oral arguments from Monday through Thursday two weeks out of each month. The justices spend Fridays in conferences discussing and voting on cases in secret. No record of the meetings is kept. The other two weeks of the month are spent writing opinions.

As at the U.S. Circuit Court of Appeals level, attorneys who argue before the U.S. Supreme Court first submit briefs outlining their arguments. This is followed by oral arguments. The justices frequently interrupt the lawyers to ask questions during their appeal presentations. Each attorney usually gets a half hour to make his presentation.

Justices can issue different opinions on the cases. A *majority opinion* which decides the outcome of the case is usually written by the chief justice if he sides with the majority, or it may be assigned to another justice who has expertise in the area or has a clear philosophical view on the subject. Or it may be assigned to another justice to even the workload among the members of the Court. The chief justice, like the other justices, only gets one vote, but his role is important because he presides over the Court, handles certain administrative duties, and often occupies a persuasive position among the justices.

If a justice agrees with the majority but for different reasons, he may write a *concurring opinion* noting his different reasons for reaching the same conclusion. *Dissenting opinions* are written by one of the members of the Court who voted against the majority. Dissenting opinions are important because they offer reasons why the writer thinks the majority decision is flawed. These decisions sometimes become the basis of a Court's later decision to reverse itself. Decisions of the Court are printed and handed out to the press and the public once the Court has decided a case.

As noted, not all cases reach the U.S. Supreme Court on appeal. The high court decides which cases it will hear. The losing party in the U.S. Circuit Court of Appeals or the highest state court petitions the U.S. Supreme Court for a *writ of certiorari*, which is an order by the high court directing the lower court or state court to send a record of the case up for review. At least four of the justices, known at "the rule of four," must believe there are important enough reasons for the Court to hear the case before the Court will issue the writ. Relatively few writs are issued each year.

The Anatomy of a Lawsuit

No lawsuit is the same, but all follow the same general pattern, with some distinct differences between civil and criminal cases.

• Civil Suits

A civil lawsuit, usually involving a dispute between two private people or organizations, typically begins when a person or organization known as the *plaintiff* contacts a lawyer with a complaint about someone else, the *defendant*. The lawyer listens to his client, writes down the facts of the case as presented by the client and analyzes the case to see if he thinks the case has merit (that is, whether the case concerns something the court could address and resolve). He also must determine the area of law involved and the proper court with the correct jurisdiction in which to file the complaint. And he must decide if the case is likely to succeed in his client's favor. The plaintiff must show that he has suffered some harm or loss to have *standing*, a legal reason for getting involved in a lawsuit. Just being upset that something happened is not enough to get involved.

If the lawyer decides to proceed, he writes up a *complaint* detailing briefly what the problem is. The complaint includes the names of the plaintiff and defendant (John Jones [the plaintiff] v. [for versus] Bill Davis [the defendant]), which identify the case throughout trial and possible appeal. The complaint also includes the legal theory or cause of action for the case (libel, invasion of privacy, etc.), what the basic facts are, and what kind of relief is being sought. The lawyer then files the complaint with the court clerk of the proper court that has juris-diction over the case. The court clerk assigns the case a number and a judge. (Lawyers are not permitted to *forum shop* to match the case to a specific judge.)

A *process server* then delivers a copy of the complaint to the defendant. After this has been done, the defendant has a certain number of days to file a reply. This is called an *answer.* If the defendant fails to answer, the defendant *defaults*, and the court can award the plaintiff whatever he is seeking. Most of the time, however, the defendant—usually through his lawyer, will file the answer, denying responsibility for the alleged wrong. He may even file a *counter claim* against the plaintiff for damages the defendant believes he has suffered at the hands of the plaintiff.

After the case has been filed, the judge then calls the attorneys to a hearing to set deadlines for pretrial proceedings. These schedules help organize the case and enable it to move smoothly through the process of litigation. The lawyers will also present written *briefs* to the court, outlining their case and the arguments and law that support their positions.

Initially, early proceedings may include such things as a *motion to dismiss*, or *demurrer*, which contends there is no legal basis for the lawsuit even if all the facts the plaintiff alleges are true. For example, a defendant may admit that he published the story that angered the plaintiff, but that there is no libel or legally actionable claim for pursuing the case. If the judge agrees and dismisses the claim, the plaintiff may appeal the decision to try to have it overturned so he can proceed with the case.

A motion for *summary judgment* also may be made when the defendant alleges that there is no factual basis for the claim even if the facts cited by the plaintiff are true. In other words, both sides agree that there is no disagreement on the facts and the judge is asked to decide the matter as a matter of law without further proceedings. Motions for summary judgment can occur also during the trial. They must be made with supporting evidence from the party seeking to end the case. A summary judgment means that the judge summarily stops the case and issues a decision because there are no more facts in dispute or the plaintiff during trial has not been able to prove his case.

Pretrial dismissals may be a quick way to end a case before it really starts, saving the cost of trial, but it also has a tendency to deny someone their day in court. Therefore, judges are required to view the case from the perspective that is most favorable to the party opposing the motion before agreeing to dismiss the case.

Any number of other motions or court business may be made before trial, including questions about the meaning of the law, the admission or exclusion of evidence, the identification of which witnesses will testify, and other matters.

Another pretrial proceeding involves a period of information gathering called *discovery* where the lawyers gather facts of the case. This process can take several months. To accomplish this, the lawyers will seek information from the other side by sending each other lists of questions called *interrogatories* or requests for documents called *requests for production of documents*. They may also schedule a time to ask questions of potential witnesses at *depositions*. The witnesses are issued *subpoenas* (orders to attend a proceeding and give testimony or other information), placed under oath, and asked questions that can then be used as evidence in court at trial.

The discovery process gives each side the chance to size up the other's case as well as to gather important information. Discovery also promotes out-of-court settlements before trial. Either side may be more willing to settle the case if they learn that their opponent's case is strong. This, in turn, eliminates a lot of disputes from a court system already clogged with cases.

If, however, no settlement is reached, the case is scheduled for trial. The location of court where the trial is heard is called the *venue*. Trials may be *bench trials* where the judge listens to the facts and the legal arguments and then decides the *verdict*, or outcome. (Where there is no dispute as to the facts, judges listen to the arguments to determine the case as a matter of law.) However, cases also may involve *jury trials* where citizens are asked to come and listen to the facts and render a decision.

Requiring citizens to participate in the legal process further enables the people to participate in their government by directly deciding what is just. Jury decisions also help determine what the law should be in future, similar cases by establishing precedent. In our system, the jury determines the facts—did the defendant do it or not—while the judge decides questions of law such as what law applies in the given situation. Civil suits are decided generally by a "preponderance of the evidence," which is a lower standard than the standard used in criminal cases. Those are decided "beyond a reasonable doubt." A defendant's life or liberty is considered more serious and so the burden of proof required for conviction is greater.

The right to a jury trial is somewhat different in criminal cases than civil cases. A criminal defendant's right to a jury trial is a bedrock principle of our democracy. It further prevents those in power from abusing their authority by putting people in prison without justification. By giving that authority to the people, it further insulates the public from government tyranny. The U.S. Constitution guarantees jury trials for those involved in serious crimes. Nevertheless, most states also allow plaintiffs and defendants in civil disputes to have their case heard by a jury if facts are in dispute and the matter is serious. Either side in a civil suit may request a jury trial.

Jury trials and bench trials both have their benefits. Lawyers may feel they may more easily sway a jury emotionally in some cases and win sympathy for a big money settlement, whereas in other cases it may be to their advantage to have the judge decide the facts as well as the law objectively. Juries must have at least six members but no more than 12. Their verdict must be unanimous unless stipulated otherwise by the parties in the lawsuit.

Jury members are selected from citizens in the community. The area from where the court draws its jurors is called the *venire*. Names usually are taken from the voters' rolls. Citizens receive summons in the mail from the court to appear at the courthouse at a certain time and day to become part of a pool from which the various individual juries will be selected. A bailiff from each courtroom hearing a case usually comes into the room and calls out a list of names. Those called follow the bailiff to a courtroom to be considered for selection for jury duty.

Lawyers and judges determine who is qualified to sit on a jury through a process known as *voir dire*, Latin words meaning "to speak the truth." The process involves randomly calling the potential jurors to the jury box, swearing them to tell the truth, instructing them on the process of jury selection, and asking them questions in an effort to determine who can listen to the facts of a case and render an impartial verdict. Lawyers, of course, in an adversarial setting hope to find jurors that will be at least somewhat sympathetic to their client's case. In some courts, the judge will ask the questions. In others, the lawyers take turns asking the questions. The questions are crafted to determine if the potential jurors may be biased in favor of one side or the other.

Either lawyer may challenge the seating of a potential juror *for cause*, asking the judge to excuse the person from duty. For example, if the potential juror is related to the defendant, the potential for bias is high. The judge then rules on the motion.

Lawyers may also make *preemptory challenges*, in which case they need not offer a reason why someone should be dismissed. Each side gets a limited number of preemptory challenges. In a criminal case in U.S. District Court, for example, the prosecution gets six preemptory challenges and the defense gets 10. The lawyers take turns in making their challenges.

If a person is excused from the jury box, another potential juror is called from those brought to the courtroom to take his place and be examined. Once the questioning is concluded and the jury seated, the judge will ask the attorneys if the jury is acceptable, and if it is, the jury is sworn in.

At this point the trial begins. The plaintiff's lawyer goes first. The plaintiff, after all, is the person with the complaint. It makes sense for the jury to know first what the complaint is so they know what the case is about.

The case usually begins with the lawyer giving an *opening statement*, outlining the problem generally and providing the jury with a roadmap of the case, telling them what they will hear and why it is important to provide their client with relief. The defense follows, asserting why they believe the case is flawed and why relief should not be granted. Both sides usually commend the jury for their service and ask only that they listen carefully to the facts about to be presented.

Once the opening statements have been made, the plaintiff presents his *case in chief.* He has complained that the defendant harmed him in some way that the law prohibits, and so now he must show how the defendant did that. If he is unable to prove his case against the defendant, he will lose. The primary burden then is on the plaintiff.

For example, if someone falsely accuses another person of being a murderer, that person has committed a libel, which is a false statement that harms another's reputation. This is a tort, a legal harm. People have a property interest in their reputation, and if someone harms that property interest, they can be held liable for damages, just as someone could be held liable for running into your car and damaging it.

To prove libel against an individual, the law requires that the plaintiff prove certain things before he can win. In such a case, the plaintiff must prove four things, including that he was defamed (the defendant's words were damaging), that the defamation was about him, that it was published (such as in a letter to others), and that he suffered some harm (such as people no longer want to do business with him). If he is unable to prove even one of these things, he will lose the case. Therefore, the plaintiff's lawyer is keen to make sure he is able to prove all four elements.

To prove his case, the lawyer will call witnesses to the witness stand, wait for them to be sworn in to tell the truth, and ask them questions to elicit facts that prove his point. He may present them with documents or other tangible evidence that needs to be explained to the jury. This process is called *direct examination*. The lawyer is not giving his opinion during the questioning; he is just getting out the factual information that will support his client's contention.

Once the plaintiff's lawyer is finished with his questioning of the witness, the defense's lawyer gets to ask the witness questions. This is called *cross-examination*.

At this point, the defense attorney will attempt to call into question the accuracy or reliability of the witness's testimony.

Once the defense attorney is done with his cross-examination, the plaintiff's lawyer can again ask the witness questions in an effort to rehabilitate or validate what the witness said. This is called *re-direct examination*. Again, when he has finished, the defense gets another chance to question the witness. This is called *re-cross examination*. This back-and-forth process continues until both sides are finished and the witness is excused and can step down from the witness stand.

At any time during the questioning of the witnesses or presentation of evidence, the attorneys can object to the judge if they believe that the other side is doing something wrong according to the law or the procedural rules of the court. At that point, the judge rules on the objection, either *sustaining* it (agreeing with it) or *overruling* it (disagreeing with it). If the judge sustains the objection, the lawyer he ruled against must change his questioning or presentation of evidence in some way. Lawyers can object for numerous reasons since the court rules for the presentation of a case are complex and complicated.

Once the plaintiff has called all of his witnesses and presented all of his evidence to prove the things he needs to prove under the law, he *rests* his case. At this point, the defense lawyer will routinely assert that the plaintiff has not proven his case and ask the judge to declare summary judgment in favor of the defense. Almost as routinely, the judge, believing the plaintiff has proven all of the things he needs to prove, will deny the motion.

Immediately thereafter, the defense will put on its case in chief, calling witnesses and presenting evidence as well as various defenses to show that the defendant is not liable for the harm committed. The same process of direct and cross-examination will continue. When the defense is finished with its case, the defense rests.

To conclude the proceeding, both sides will again address the jury with *closing arguments*. This gives each side the chance to emphasize the basic points of their cases and attempt to persuade the jury to find in their favor. After their concluding remarks, the judge will instruct the jury as to their next task, which is to deliberate as a group and determine if the plaintiff or defendant wins.

The judge will also instruct the jury as to the law and the way it must be applied to the facts of the case. The jury then leaves the courtroom and goes into a separate room to deliberate and determine their verdict and decide what, if any, damages should be awarded. When they are finished, they return to the courtroom and announce their verdict. If the jury is unable to reach a decision, and a *hung jury* is declared, the case ends in a mistrial. If this happens, the case may need to be tried again. This does not often occur.

The judge usually accepts the jury's decision, but the judge does have the authority to overturn the decision if it is contrary to the law or against the weight of the evidence. This also rarely happens.

• Appeals

After the judgment has been made, either the plaintiff or the defendant—usually the losing party—may appeal. Whoever appeals is called the *petitioner or appellant*. The other side is the *respondent or appellee*. The petition for review must include the reasons a review is proper. The facts determined at trial are not in question. Rather, the petitioner is challenging the trial process or the application of the law.

Such reasons may include a contention that the judge erred in some way, that she went beyond her authority, that she permitted or excluded evidence improperly, that she applied the law incorrectly, or that she instructed the jury incorrectly. The reasons may be numerous.

Both sides file written briefs arguing the legal issues and citing various laws to prove their positions along with transcripts of the trial. The appeals court, usually consisting of at least three judges, reads the briefs and sometimes schedules oral arguments before the court. New evidence or testimony of witnesses is not offered. The lawyers stand before the court and argue their positions, often getting only a few words out before the judges begin challenging them with questions. Often, court observers can tell which way a judge is leaning on an issue simply by noting what questions are asked.

Afterward, the judges meet, discuss the case, and vote. As noted earlier, judges can affirm the lower court, affirm in part and overrule in part, overrule it altogether, or send it back down to the trial court for further action. Or they may order a new trial.

If the court's opinion covers a new area of law or modifies an existing law, the judges will order the opinion to be published so it can be placed in law books and serve as precedent for future cases.

The next step in the appellate process is the Supreme Court. If it's a federal case, it will go to the U.S. Supreme Court. Matters of state law are appealed to the state supreme court in the state where the trial was held.

• Criminal Trials

A criminal trial is similar to a civil trial with some notable exceptions. Procedures at criminal trials are generally more formal and involve the state or federal governments, which bring charges of a crime against a defendant in the name of the people. State or federal prosecutors file the charges, depending upon whether a state or federal crime is involved. The defendant can be arrested before or after charges are filed.

A *grand jury* must *indict* defendants charged with serious federal crimes. Grand juries consist of a panel of 16–23 citizens who listen to evidence presented by the prosecutor behind closed doors and then decide if a person should be charged. At the state level, grand juries are not always required to bring charges. The state prosecutor can file an *information*, a formal accusation.

Many state systems hold a *preliminary hearing* at which time the state must present enough evidence to a judge to show *probable cause* that a crime has been committed and that the defendant is responsible.

Following the preliminary hearing, the defendant is *arraigned*. At this time the charge is read to him and he pleads guilty or not guilty. If he pleads guilty, the judge may pass sentence, though the judge will usually order a *presentencing report* so he has a better understanding of the person and the appropriate sentence to give him. If the person pleads not guilty, trial is scheduled. In many cases, the defendant will seek bail before trial. Bail is money given to the court to ensure that the defendant will return for trial. Those charged with serious crimes are generally not granted bail, and the person must remain in jail until trial.

The burden of proof to convict the defendant is on the government, for it is the government that is trying to take away the defendant's life, liberty, or property. The government must show *beyond a reasonable doubt* that the defendant is guilty of the crime or the defendant is *acquitted*.

Finding the Law

The relatively brief time lawyers spend in court on a case doesn't reflect the amount of work that goes into preparing for trial. Lawyers typically spend weeks or months, and in some cases perhaps a year or more, in preparation. They gather facts, witnesses, evidence, and they research the law.

Lawyers know the general areas of law and a great deal of the law itself, but they can't possibly know all of the law. New law is decided every day in the courts and by the various federal, state, and local legislative bodies. It would be an impossible task to know it all. Rather, lawyers are trained to think analytically. They spend years in law school learning important cases, theories, rules, and principles, and how to apply them to their arguments, and they learn how to find the law that applies to any given case they may face.

Legal research is the process of finding the law that applies to a case. Although courthouses and law schools have extensive law libraries that are available to the public, finding the law today is only a click away

on the computer. Databases such as *Lexis-Nexis* or *Westlaw* can make primary legal research relatively easy. Lawyers subscribe to these services and can therefore do research from their offices. Most university libraries also subscribe to the same services so college students can also research the law. In addition, various government websites are available to help locate rules and regulations regarding a particular agency, such as the Federal Trade Commission (www.ftc.gov) and the Federal Communications Commission (www.fcc.gov). Legal encyclopedias such as *Corpus Juris Secundum* and *American Jurisprudence 2d* are useful secondary sources and help with analysis and interpretation. *Black's Law Dictionary* is useful in helping students understand the legal definition of words.

Case law, as noted in Chapter 1, is located in reporters. Different reporters contain federal cases decided at the U.S. Supreme Court or the various U.S. Circuit Courts of Appeals. State cases from state appellate courts are contained in reporters for the various states. State and federal statutes passed by legislative bodies are available in other code and statute books.

Since laws change all the time as old cases are overturned and new cases establish new precedent, lawyers must also research the law they use to make sure it is still good law. This process is called "Shepardizing." All law libraries have a cross-reference index called *Shepard's Citator* that lawyers use to check both state and federal appellate court decisions to make sure the law they cite in cases has not been overturned. Online databases now enable lawyers to perform this function on the computer.

Briefing a Case

Briefing a case is just that, reducing the entire court decision down to its component parts so that it can be easily summarized and understood. A *case brief* differs from a *persuasive brief* where a lawyer presents his arguments on behalf of his client to the court.

Case briefs include:

- the case name which identifies the parties as plaintiffs and defendants;
- the legal citation that identifies where the case can be found in the law books;
- the name of the court that heard the case;
- the date of the court's decision;
- the material (important) facts of the case;
- the nature of the case, including the cause of action or legal reason the plaintiff sued in the first place and the relief sought;
- the legal history of the case (the decision of the trial court where the case was first filed and the subsequent courts that heard and ruled on it as well as who appealed and why);
- the legal issue or point of law in question before the court (what does the appellant claim the lower court did wrong?);
- the summarized arguments of both the plaintiff and the defense;
- the judgment (the court's decision);
- the holding (the statement of law that the court uses to answer the issue);
- the court's reasoning or analysis of the case; and
- the concurring and dissenting opinions from other members of the court

Journalists, like law students, should learn to brief cases to help them understand court decisions.

Bench-Bar-Press Guidelines

Bar Associations in many states publish *bench-bar-press guidelines* to help journalists and citizens understand the legal system and its terminology. Journalists should take advantage of this service early in their careers.

By now, it should be clear that the law is vast, complex, and ever changing. Judges, politicians, and citizens themselves all contribute to its formation. It would take years of study and a library of books and cases to understand it all. Our purpose is to review only one area: the law of mass communication. Therefore, the remainder of this book will focus on the First Amendment to the U.S. Constitution and the various laws and boundaries of free expression in the United States.

CHAPTER 4

The First Amendment: A Look at Speech and Press

Congress shall make no law respecting an establishment of religion, or prohibiting the free exercise thereof; or abridging the freedom of speech, or of the press; or the right of the people peaceably to assemble, and to petition the Government for a redress of grievances.

—First Amendment to the U.S. Constitution

Protecting the Pursuit of Truth

Those 45 words in many ways reflect best what it means to be an American. For no independent people in a democracy can hope to be in charge of their own government without the free flow of ideas and information.

Law may provide the order we need to flourish, but order alone will not ensure our success. Ultimately, our ability to flourish depends on our ability to pursue truth within that order—truth about ourselves and our world, and success there depends on how well we can reflect, question, communicate, debate, and reason—in other words—learn and know.

Truth is the understanding needed to have power over one's life. And the pursuit of truth is the attempt to give ourselves and others that power. And that power, in turn, enables us to flourish and be the best we can be.

When the Founders adopted the principles of John Milton and John Locke as the basis for the new country, they were, in fact, adopting philosophies that were methods of finding truth. America, therefore, more than anything else, is a nation in pursuit of truth. And to be an American is to find the truth so we can make the most of our lives individually and collectively.

Since our ability to flourish is directly tied to our ability to find truth, it makes sense that the law protects our pursuit of it. Thus, the First Amendment is in many ways paramount. It goes to the heart of who we are and what we are about. The six freedoms outlined in the First Amendment—freedom of religion or conscience, freedom from a government-imposed religion, freedom of speech, freedom of press, freedom to assemble, and freedom to petition or demand action of the government—are all in one way or another about our ability to find truth, share it, and act on it without government interference.

Understanding the importance of being able to find and share the truth is vital to understanding what media law is all about. Every law of mass communication in the United States is ultimately about the protections and limitations of our expression of what we consider to be true.

Historians, philosophers, sociologists, anthropologists, and psychologists have always known the value and necessity of this quest for truth. It is more than just a function of the political process; it is a part of being human, of self-awareness, of self-autonomy. It helps us define ourselves. Ultimately any political, social, or religious system that does not take into consideration this basic characteristic of man is doomed to fail. Unfortunately, such is the history of the world.

Even today, less than half of the world's population lives in countries that protect freedom of speech, press, and religion. And leaders in countries that do offer such protection often justify censorship on the basis of national security—whether or not national security is really threatened. Others see the Press as a state tool for propaganda. The Internet, the latest technological development promoting the spread of information, has made such government control more difficult. But it has not eliminated it.

A History of Censorship

The First Amendment, which emerged from such a struggle, did not come to us cleanly or easily. It was born out of censorship and oppression—barriers to truth. When Johannes Gutenberg invented the printing press about 1450 in Germany, he was not inhibited by a strong central government that viewed his tinkering as a threat. And even after setting up the first printing press in England in 1476, William Caxton enjoyed unlimited freedom to print what he wished. But England was not a weak country; it had a strong king and the press quickly came to be seen as a threat to the power of the crown.

Arogant/Shutterstock.com

Leaders then and now understand that information is power and those in control of the flow of information hold considerable sway over what people know and think. The printing press made information cheap and accessible to the masses. Therefore, the early English printers' unrestricted ability to print and publish information that was contrary to the official truth disseminated by the English king and the Church—the other strong power at the time—was seen as a threat, both potential and real, that had to be controlled.

By the early 1500s, the king and the Church controlled all the presses in England by requiring printers to be licensed and by requiring all texts to be reviewed by the authorities before they could be published—an act called *prior restraint*. Books and other writings deemed offensive were banned or censored. Those who defied the power structure were fined, imprisoned, tortured, or even executed. On the other hand, publishers who were favored were awarded lucrative book contracts to print acceptable ideas and information, such as the Bible. These favored printers also worked as informants, exposing those publishers who defied the authorities.

The country, indeed Europe itself, was caught up in a religious and political power struggle at the time, and the press was seen as a potent tool in that battle. The fight was also an economic battle between the aristocracy and the emerging middle class. Both the monarchy and the Church feared uncontrolled distribution of seditious and heretical writings could undermine their efforts to control the populace. Despite the censorship and other attempts to curb the flow of information, the Press ultimately proved too strong for either the king or the Church to control. Free and independent thought eventually won out, undermining the power of the monarchy and the Church and also ushering in democracy. But it was not an easy struggle.

Advocates of Free Expression

By the early 1600s, a few champions of free expression began to emerge. In 1644, John Milton wrote his unapproved treatise *Areopagitica* against government censorship.

> *[T]hough all the winds of doctrine were let loose to play on the earth, so Truth be in the field, we do injuriously, by licensing and prohibiting, to misdoubt her strength. Let her and Falsehood grapple; who ever knew Truth put to the worse, in a free and open encounter?*

Milton was angered that the Church and state had attempted to destroy a pamphlet he had written earlier justifying divorce. He argued that an open *marketplace of ideas* furthered the cause of truth, and therefore society and mankind. Milton argued that if all ideas could be heard, even those contrary to popular notion, debate and reason would sort through them to find the truth. It was not a universally held opinion, and even Milton did not support the distribution of subversive ideas. He did not, for example, support the Catholic Church, superstition or ideas he considered evil.

MidoSemsem/Shutterstock.com

John Milton

Ironically, Milton later accepted a government appointment as a government censor. By 1651, he was censoring ideas himself, promoting a strict Puritan government that allowed for little tolerance of those who did not share his convictions. Nevertheless, he was among those who first pushed back against the concept of "official" truth.

Others went even further to promote the free expression of ideas. During the same year Milton wrote his treatise, a Puritan minister named Roger Williams, who had been exiled for his religious beliefs, argued that Catholics and other religions should be permitted free expression of their ideas. About the same time, a radical Puritan group called the Levellers distributed tracts that condemned censorship and licensing, also arguing that free expression is essential to religious freedom.

Despite these and other pleas, licensing and censorship in England continued. Although power was shifted from the king to the British Parliament, the suppression of ideas did not stop. In 1662, Parliament even went so far as to limit the number of printing presses. It also prohibited writings contrary to Christianity or the government.

English political philosopher John Locke entered the fray in the late 1600s, arguing again that censorship should not be within the power of the government. Locke had asserted in his *social contract theory* that it wasn't the people who should serve the government, but the government that should serve the people. He said that man had certain natural rights, including life, liberty, and the right to own property and that the people's ability to communicate with one another was central to maintaining those rights.

Furthermore, Locke argued that people had the authority to make a contract with the government in which they would give government the right to govern if the government would, in exchange, protect their liberties. The government itself had no rights beyond what the people gave it. Therefore, it had no right to censor, license, or prohibit people from expressing themselves.

Locke listed reasons why the English licensing act should be eliminated when it came up for review in 1694. Parliament allowed the law to expire more because of its negative effect on trade and the difficulties of administering it than on the eloquence of opponents' arguments. Other factors also contributed to its demise, including Parliament's enactment of a Bill of Rights and the emergence of the two-party political system, which encouraged robust debate among those seeking a seat in Parliament. The two parties—the Whigs and the Tories—needed the Press to argue their positions to the people.

Yet for the next 100 years, Parliament continued to pass laws to stop expression it considered illegal, dangerous, or immoral. Laws against *seditious libel* (writings that criticized the government or its leaders) were one example. The concept of seditious libel held that if people said bad things about their government, the government would lose public support and not be able to govern.

And if the government criticism was warranted and accurate, officials believed it actually created more harm since the people would have even less reason to support the government. The maxim was "the greater the truth, the greater the libel."

In the early 18th century, the prevailing attitude still was that the people were subject to the crown. It wasn't important that the truth prevailed; it was important that the government could lead effectively. Today, some still adhere to this view even though truth is the ultimate, effective defense against any charge of defamation or libel.

Early Suppression in America

The view of Parliament and government officials on press control was the same in the English colonies across the Atlantic. Licensing, taxation, and other restraints on the Press, official and otherwise, were present in America as well. Censors reviewed publications for offensive expression until the 1720s. And religious leaders, who were seeking freedom to promote their ideas, nevertheless established close relationships with the government and succeeded in inhibiting the speech of those who had differing religious or political beliefs.

Laws in America restricting expression existed almost 30 years before the introduction of the first newspaper. In 1662, Massachusetts's statutes required printers to get government approval before publication. *Publick Occurrences, Both Foreign and Domestick* was published without a license by Benjamin Harris in Boston on September 25, 1690, but the authorities forced it to cease publication after only one issue.

Even after licensing laws were abolished in England, officials in America continued to insist that they had the power to license publications. Benjamin Franklin's older brother James did not get permission to publish his newspaper, the *New England Courant*, and ended up in jail in 1722. So successful was the colonial government in its efforts that years after the end of licensing, newspapers still often carried the phrase "published by authority" on their newspapers' mastheads.

Seditious libel prosecutions and special taxes on newspapers continued to burden publishers, but government efforts were becoming less effective as the colonists became more independent and publishers began to resist.

In 1735, the trial of John Peter Zenger, publisher of the *New York Weekly Journal*, became a turning point in the struggle. Zenger had printed attacks on unpopular New York governor William Cosby, charging corruption. Cosby ruled by royal appointment and was therefore legally immune from criticism under the law of sedition. Cosby had Zenger jailed, thinking this would silence him and other critics.

Under the law, Zenger was obviously guilty. He had, in fact, broken the law by criticizing the government. However, his highly respected criminal lawyer Andrew Hamilton convinced the jury that no free man should be convicted for criticizing the government if the allegations were truthful and fair. As a result, the jury ignored the law and Cosby's specially appointed judge and acquitted Zenger.

(Such an act is called *jury nullification*, which means the jury simply nullifies a law by ignoring it. Such an action is rare, but legal scholars see it as an important part of the legal and legislative process. If numerous juries ignore the same law, it should be a signal to the legislature to change or repeal it.)

The Zenger verdict was a victory for free expression, but it did not eliminate the English law of sedition. However, news of the verdict spread throughout the colonies and to England, and after 1735, the number of seditious libel cases dropped. Those that were prosecuted by the government weren't successful.

Passage of the Stamp Act in 1765 added to the publishers' growing intolerance of government interference. The Act required publishers to buy special revenue stamps for their newspapers. Many refused to pay the tax and defied the authorities.

As the government's control of expression waned, publishers became more aggressive and their presses more robust. Growing tensions between England and its colonies only added to their determination to print the truth as they saw it.

The problem of censorship, nevertheless, did not go away. The country was not as connected as it is today. Communication was limited, and roads were little more than trails. People lived in communities that were miles apart, and they tended to live among those who shared similar beliefs about religion and government.

Outsiders were not well tolerated, nor were differing opinions. Despite their struggle against government censorship, the people still did not fully understand that freedom of expression was intended for everyone, including those with whom they disagreed. As a result, people often self-censored, afraid that they would be harmed if they spoke their minds.

This chilling effect was apparent in the early 1770s just before the American Revolution. As the propaganda war heated up and more colonists urged separation from England, they insisted freedom of the press and the right to criticize government were essential to liberty. Those who still considered themselves English subjects and did not want to break from England found it difficult to publish pro-English ideas in some American cities. They attempted to distribute ideas at their own peril. They were attacked and their presses destroyed. Over time, the separationists were able to suppress these loyalists' views and move a majority of the country to their side.

The community censorship that existed then is still prevalent today. Those individuals or groups with ideas that are not popular with the public are often pressured to remain silent, not because of government censorship—which would be illegal, but because political activists and public interest groups who disagree with their positions work to drown out contrary views. Since the First Amendment only protects against government censorship, such action is legal.

In some instances, economic pressure is applied to coerce speakers to be silent. In 2007, radio personality Don Imus had his show pulled from the airwaves after he referred to Rutgers' female basketball players as "nappy-headed hos." Civil rights groups complained, and businesses pulled their advertisements from the program. Ironically, it was Imus's popularity and ability to attract listeners—and therefore ad revenue—that enabled him to return to the airwaves eight months later.

The lesson from before the American Revolution as well as today is the same: Milton's marketplace of ideas cannot exist if some can speak but others cannot, no matter how disagreeable the message. Freedom of expression must exist for everyone or it cannot exist at all.

The First Amendment: Discovering the Framers' Intent

Given their experience with the king, there is little doubt the Framers of the Constitution and the Bill of Rights, including the First Amendment, agreed that government censorship of ideas was wrong. Nevertheless, the record of Congressional discussions at the time the Bill of Rights was drafted does not give a clear picture of what the Founders were thinking. It is likely that it meant somewhat different things to different people. Most scholars today doubt that the Founders envisioned a society in which government was prohibited from regulating speech and press in all circumstances—despite the fact the First Amendment notes that "Congress shall make *no* law. . . ."

Harry H Marsh/Shutterstock.com

The general opinion of the day was that punishment of harmful speech after the fact was a legitimate exercise of government. Therefore, punishment for defamation, as in the case of libel, was appropriate. Sir William Blackstone in 1769 noted that under English common law the government could not, nor should it, censor speech before publication, but added that "if he publishes what is improper, mischievous, or illegal, he must take the consequences of his own temerity."

Nevertheless, modern scholars agree the action to punish speech after the fact did not include the right of government or the courts to punish seditious libel. One of the reasons for the American Revolution was to end the British Crown's ability to silence its critics. A hallmark of

American freedom is the right to criticize government and its officials, though this, too, did not come without a struggle, even after the First Amendment was ratified.

Ways to Interpret the First Amendment Today

The term "free speech" was not clearly defined by the Founders, but most scholars and the courts have since interpreted it as "free expression." This could mean any attempt to communicate with another by nearly any means—by writing, speaking, printing, or photographing. But it can also include *conduct*—that is through some form of action.

The courts refer to this as *symbolic speech*—the ability to communicate an idea—actor to audience—through some form of demonstration, such as burning a flag to protest against or show displeasure with the government, or by dancing nude at a strip club, or even by fully disrobing to protest full body security scans at airports.

The U.S. Supreme Court has ruled such communication is legal under the *symbolic speech doctrine* if two elements are satisfied—1. The person's action or conduct must be an attempt to convey a particular message; and 2. Given the situation and location at the time of the act, there is a good chance that at least some people who see it will understand the message.

Likewise, the term "free press" is generally agreed to mean the right to disseminate information and ideas to the public at large through any means or device that makes that possible. In the 1790s, that meant the printing press, which produced newspapers, books, pamphlets, flyers, or posters. Today, it has come to mean TV, radio, motion pictures, telephones, the Internet, and whatever invention might come next.

Scholars and the courts agree that it would make little sense in the 21st century to interpret the First Amendment literally and allow protection for only information that is printed on paper by a printing press. Still, as new media are invented, the courts will no doubt struggle to determine how and when First Amendment protection is applied.

It is important to note that the U.S. Supreme Court has made little distinction between free speech and free press. They are largely treated the same.

The U.S. Supreme Court has the task of defining just what free expression is all about. Given the limited record of what the Framers meant by free speech and press and more than 200 years of technological and social change, it is easy to understand why the Court has struggled to interpret its meaning.

Trying to figure out just what the Founding Fathers had in mind is a slippery slope that leads to speculation. On the other hand, allowing the Court too much flexibility to determine the definition without guidance from the past could enable it to redefine the amendment at will, diluting its protections. The Court largely sidesteps the problem by avoiding broad interpretations and ruling instead on the merits of each individual case, thereby allowing the body of case law to give meaning to the amendment. However, the Court tends to lean toward protecting fundamental liberties such as freedom of speech and press when they come in conflict with other liberties.

The Court will often weigh the need for Constitutional protection on one side against the competing interests on the other. Or the Court may look at the particular circumstances surrounding the case. For example, political speech receives the highest protection because it concerns questions of politics and government and goes to the heart of democracy. Commercial speech, which concerns matters of advertising and commerce receives less protection. Obscenity, blackmail, perjury, fighting words, defamation, and other narrow categories receive no First Amendment protection. (We will look at these in detail later in the book.)

Where the speech occurs can also influence the Court's interpretation. Political speech on the courthouse steps or a similar traditional public forum receives broad protection, while speech that occurs in a nonpublic forum, such as a military base, receives little. (This, too, will be reviewed later.)

This is not to say the Court has not looked to various First Amendment theories or strategies to help guide it. These have taken shape largely during the past 80–90 years after the Court began to take a closer look at First Amendment concerns. These theories are discussed next.

• Absolutist Theory

A few have argued that the Founders were clear in their intent when they said, "Congress shall make *no* law . . ." regarding limitations on the First Amendment. They argue that the government may impose no restrictions whatsoever. It may not censor under any circumstance.

The Court has never embraced this theory as a whole. Even the Founders recognized that some expression could be punished, including defamation. The Court also has ruled consistently that there is no First Amendment protection for obscenity, defamation, and other limited categories.

• Ad Hoc Balancing Theory

When two values, such as freedom of the press and the need for military secrecy conflict, the Court must find a way to balance the two. Perhaps the public's need to know what a new weapons system costs is more important than the military's need to keep it secret, or perhaps the military's need to keep its location of missiles secret is more important than the public's need to know the location of the weapons. This is called *ad hoc balancing*, which means the Court reviews each conflict on a case-by-case basis without regard for how it ruled on other previous similar cases. All sides of the case are viewed equally.

The problem with this strategy is that it can lead to uncertainty. Citizens can never know in advance which speech will be protected. This can have a chilling effect and frighten people into keeping silent on important issues. It also promotes inconsistency, since individual justices will rely more on personal bias than on guidance from previous cases or theories. The law could change quickly as members of the Court come and go. As a result, this strategy is not widely used.

• Preferred Position Balancing Theory

Some values are more important than others in our democracy. They are called *fundamental values* in that they go to the heart of who we are as Americans. They define us. Those values guaranteed by the First Amendment fall into this category. For example, freedom of expression, which is specifically guaranteed in the Constitution, is considered more important than the freedom to receive welfare benefits, which is not.

This does not mean fundamental values trump other rights all the time, but under this theory it means the Court, when deciding a case where a fundamental value is at stake, will weigh the matter leaning in favor of the fundamental liberty. Therefore, if someone sues the government because it is trying to take away their right of expression, the Court will presume that the government action is unconstitutional, forcing the government to defend its action and prove the censorship is warranted and not in violation of the First Amendment. The burden is on the government, which is trying to take away the liberty, not the citizen who presumably has the right to retain it.

Thus, the preferred position balancing theory is like the ad hoc balancing theory but instead of looking at each side equally, the Court weighs the matter from a position that initially supports the fundamental value. This provides more certainty to the law in that when the government is attempting to take away an important liberty, the citizen understands in advance that the government will probably lose unless it can show a very good reason for doing so.

• Marketplace of Ideas Theory

This theory returns to the argument of John Milton—that the best way to find truth is through the exchange of ideas competing in an open marketplace. There people can weigh the merits and demerits of any proposition and through thought, debate, and reason test them as true or false and either accept or reject them.

The limitations of this theory are that not everyone has equal access to the marketplace and that it encourages an unending stream of seemingly unworthy speech that drowns out matters worthy of discussion. Large conglomerate media outlets have more power to control the media, and thus the discussion, than the average citizen. Those media outlets may tend to present content that serves their interests of generating large audiences and selling advertising, even though much of the information they provide may have little significance.

Still, the Court has noted the importance of providing and encouraging an environment of competing ideas and has noted as such in some of its rulings. In addition, the development of the Internet and social media has given more voice to the masses, enabling any citizen with a cell phone or computer to disseminate information and ideas to the world.

• Access Theory

Given that large conglomerate media companies have more access to the marketplace than the average citizen, some First Amendment scholars have noted that the marketplace of ideas is more illusion than reality, social media notwithstanding. As a result, some analysts have suggested that owners of newspapers, magazines, broadcast stations, and other media outlets open their pages and airwaves to the public to give more people a voice. This theory suggests that such action should be mandatory. If the owners refuse, the government should intervene and compel them to do so.

The Supreme Court has rejected this theory, noting the First Amendment does not give the government the right to oversee an editor's decision of what to print or broadcast. Neither does the government have the right under the Constitution to confiscate private property without due process of law. Newspapers and broadcast stations are privately owned.

• Self-Realization Theory

This idea suggests speech should be protected regardless of whether it is beneficial to society simply because it enables citizens to express themselves and thereby define who they are as individuals. Promoting a candidate, political position, or idea on a T-shirt is a form of self-expression and fulfillment whether it convinces someone else to agree with the position. It also helps define the culture and the political direction of the country.

• Meiklejohnian Theory

Philosopher Alexander Meiklejohn argued that the only reason free speech and press should be protected was so the democracy could function. He believed all other speech, including private speech, was less important and should receive less protection or none at all. Therefore, under this theory the only expression that needed protection was expression related to public matters.

Meiklejohn supported his theory using the town hall analogy. He noted that the moderator had the right to limit the speech to the political issue at hand, and that all could speak, but only the topic being discussed. It was not, he argued, a place where anyone could talk about anything they like just for the sake of self-fulfillment.

The problem with this theory is determining just what constitutes political speech. If one complains about the construction of a new Walmart store near a residential neighborhood, is it a matter of public expression that relates to self-government? Or is it just someone complaining about a private concern? Could it become a matter of political speech if not already? At what point does private concern become public issue? And if the expression of a private concern is not protected and cannot be shared, how can the subject ever grow to become a public issue? Public issues often start as private matters.

Nevertheless, some U.S. Supreme Court justices have embraced the theory, noting that free expression is protected ultimately for the sake of ensuring that the democracy functions.

The Future of the First Amendment

As in the past, a number of factors will determine the future health of the First Amendment. It will depend upon those we elect to federal and state office, the men and women appointed to the Supreme Court, technological advances and limitations in the media, and the events that shape our history.

The future of the First Amendment will likely not depend upon just the words written by the Founders in the 18th century, but upon the attitudes of citizens today—and tomorrow. Much of that will depend upon our educational system and whether we continue to pass on the lessons of democracy and a basic understanding of civics.

Unfortunately, opinion polls often show the public has a lack of knowledge when it comes to our basic principles and institutions of government. People often are too willing to curb the free expression of artists, politicians, and activists whom they find offensive.

Respect for the amendment also often increases and decreases with national threats. During times of national strife when people are fearful, they often are willing to give up their freedoms in the name of security. During good times, they are more prone to support their freedoms.

Former Chief Justice William Rehnquist noted in his book *All the Laws but One: Civil Liberties in Wartime* that even the high Court interprets the law differently in wartime than peacetime. Nevertheless, he said that citizens are becoming more protective of their civil liberties and less willing to abandon them over matters of national security. But that was in 1998 before the September 11, 2001, attacks on the World Trade Center in New York City and the Pentagon in Washington, D.C.

Those terrorist attacks changed things. Congress passed the USA Patriot Act, which increased the government's power to monitor citizens' Internet and telephone communications and keep more things secret. In response, the fight over free expression heated up. The website WikiLeaks posted thousands of pages of sensitive government information collected by the federal surveillance program of the National Security Agency. The result was a call to pass new legislation to prevent future leaks. And government contractor Edward Snowden leaked information showing that the government was collecting phone records of millions of citizens. Amid charges of treason, he fled the country, but not without calls from some in Congress demanding a stop to the program.

Fortunately, the Knight Foundation's annual "Students on the Future of the First Amendment" survey has revealed a growing support for freedom of speech—at least for the moment. The private nonprofit foundation that supports journalism and media innovation found in a survey of 12,000 high school students conducted in the spring of 2016 that 91 percent said it was important to be able to express unpopular opinions. That number was up from 83 percent in 2004.

Still, the attitude was not without its limits. The survey also discovered that just 45 percent supported unfettered speech when it offended others, and only 36 percent backed unlimited speech if it's considered to be bullying.

The survey found that those students that frequently consume news and are engaged with news on social media show stronger support for the First Amendment. The survey noted that 71 percent of students discussed news on social media, 62 percent got news from mobile devices and 64 percent got news from online videos.

Support for the First Amendment also seems to hold true for the country as a whole. Every year the First Amendment Center of the Newseum Institute, a non-partisan organization headquartered in Washington, D.C., that promotes, explains and defends the First Amendment, conducts a survey to examine Americans views on the law. In its 2017 survey, the organization found that only 31 percent said the amendment goes too far in protecting speech, press, religion, assembly and petition.

Said Lata Nott, executive director of the First Amendment Center: "We're glad to find that most Americans still support the First

Amendment, although it's troubling that almost one in four think that we have too much freedom."

The reason may be that Americans, generally, don't understand basic Constitutional provisions.

Also in 2017, the Annenberg Public Policy Center's annual Constitution Day Civics survey found 37 percent of Americans could not name any of the rights guaranteed in the First Amendment and only 26 percent could name all three branches of the government. In 2011, 38 percent could name all three branches. In both 2011 and 2017, thirty-three percent could not name any of them. Perhaps most troubling was the fact that 39 percent of Americans say Congress should be able to prevent the news media from reporting on any issue of national security unless the government approves.

"Protecting the rights guaranteed by the Constitution presupposes that we know what they are. The fact that many don't is worrisome," said Kathleen Hall Jamieson, director of the center at the University of Pennsylvania.

To be sure, the Internet has revolutionized free expression and made government censorship more difficult. Social media was in many ways responsible for the successful anti-government uprising that helped bring down Egyptian president Hosni Mubarak in 2011. And as new technology makes communication easier, government officials' efforts to control information likely will become more difficult.

Still, the threat of censorship and oppression has been with us since before the invention of the printing press, and despite our continued technological achievements, the fight of some to keep information secret has not abated. If history is any guide, the struggle for free expression will continue.

TO REORDER YOUR UPS DIRECT THERMAL LABELS:

1. Access our supply ordering web site at **UPS.COM**®
   or contact UPS at 800-877-8652.
2. Please refer to label #0277400801 when ordering.

0277400801   RRDRF

CHAPTER 5

The Boundaries of Free Expression

Few would argue that yelling fire in a crowded movie theater and causing a mass panic, or publishing the movement of troop ships during wartime so that the enemy could locate and sink the ships, or libeling someone with impunity and destroying a person's reputation falsely would be good things.

The dissemination of some kinds of information can cause great unjustifiable harm. But determining just where the line between free expression and prohibited expression should be drawn is not always easy. And the government and the Court have struggled to find that line since the founding of the Republic.

The Alien and Sedition Acts of 1798

In fact, less than 10 years after the drafting of the First Amendment, some of the very men who supported its adoption had all but abandoned it. Fear that the violence of the French Revolution could spread to the United States prompted President John Adams and his Federalist-dominated Congress to pass the *Alien and Sedition Acts of 1798.*

The legislation made it a crime to publish false, seditious, or malicious material against the United States, Congress, or the president. Neither could anyone publish material that would urge people to resist federal law. The law was in reality an attempt to silence newspapers that supported Thomas Jefferson's rival Republican Party, which had been attacking Adams and other Federalists in power.

Although the First Amendment had been passed in large part to end the government's ability to censor its critics, judges appointed by the Federalist administration were now upholding convictions of those editors accused of sedition. Nevertheless, the effort backfired. Upset that Adams was using the law to silence his critics, the public voted him out of office in the election of 1800. Once Thomas Jefferson took office, he pardoned all of those who had been convicted under the law, and the Sedition Act was allowed to expire in 1801.

Two other periods of widespread censorship occurred in the United States during the 19th century and early 20th century, and as was often the case, both occurred during times of national crises. With the growing tension between the North and South over the issue of slavery, some officials attempted to silence abolitionist newspapers. And once the Civil War began, governments in both the North and South censored the Press widely for what both claimed were military reasons.

Toward the end of the century, facing a tide of immigrants, a faltering economy, a loud women's movement, and a growing inequality between rich and poor, the country found itself in the middle of a different kind of revolution—a social and economic one.

The reality was that the American dream was not working for everyone. Squalid living conditions, disease, lack of adequate wages and protection for workers plagued the labor pool while the rich oil and railroad barons got wealthier during the Gilded Age of the 1890s. With little to lose, those with nothing were becoming more attracted to socialism, anarchism, and unionism and pushed for change. Fearing such movements would lead to open revolution, states and cities passed laws attempting to silence such dissent.

In 1914, as World War I broke out across Europe, the threat only increased. As the warring countries squared off and common laborers found themselves in the trenches fighting to prop up crumbling monarchies headed by rich aristocrats, the ideas of economic philosopher Karl Marx and other socialists spread and took root in Russia, resulting in the Communist Revolution in 1917.

As a result, the communists ousted the Russian monarchy, and Russia abandoned the war. Meanwhile, the rich capitalists and industrialists in the United States, which was now in the conflict, saw the spread of socialism and unionism as a direct threat to capitalist countries. Fearing

Everett Historical/Shutterstock.com

it also would undermine the war effort and threaten American security, they urged Congress to pass laws allowing censorship that would prevent the spread of such radicalism. In fact, it was during this period that suppression of speech reached its highest level in American history. Trade unionists, socialists, and anarchists attempting to foment radical change found their newspapers and pamphlets censored or destroyed.

The Espionage and Sedition Acts of 1917 and 1918

The two main laws that Congress passed to silence dissenters opposing the war were the *Espionage Act in 1917 and the Sedition Act in 1918.*

The Espionage Act, in addition to dealing with legitimate problems of spying, made it a crime to interfere with the war effort though dissent, insubordination, disloyalty, mutiny, refusing military duty, or by sending information that violated the law through the mail. The law also prohibited citizens from willfully obstructing military recruiting and enlistment efforts. Those who violated the law could receive a $10,000 fine and prison sentences of up to 20 years.

The Sedition Act, which amended the Espionage Act, went even further and made it a crime to say, write, or publish disloyal or profane messages in contempt or scorn of the government, the Constitution, the flag, or a U.S. military uniform. Again, those who violated the law could receive a $10,000 fine and up to 20 years in prison. Nearly 900 people were convicted.

In addition, the U.S. Post Office used the laws to censor thousands of books, newspapers, and pamphlets.

It was out of the turmoil of the First World War and these two laws that the Court finally attempted to address the problem of what speech is protected and how much free speech is too much free speech under the First Amendment. Based on the old common law doctrine adopted from England known as the *Bad Tendency Test*, which made it possible to convict anyone whose speech tended to create a low opinion of public officials, institutions or laws, the new test did offer more protection for unpopular speech—to a point.

The Clear and Present Danger Test

The case that established the new test was *Schenck v. U.S.*, 249 U.S. 47 (1919). Charles Schenck, the general secretary of the Philadelphia Socialist Party, published 15,000 leaflets that protested U.S. involvement in World War I. The leaflets encouraged young men to resist the military draft. Schenck was arrested and convicted for violating the Espionage Act. He appealed to the U.S. Supreme Court, arguing that his First Amendment rights had been violated.

Justice Oliver Wendell Holmes wrote the majority opinion for the Court, rejecting Schenck's argument:

> *We admit that in many places and in ordinary times the defendants in saying all that was said in the circular would have been within their constitutional rights. But the character of every act depends upon the circumstance in which it is done. The question in every case is whether the words used are used in such circumstances and are of such a nature as to create **a clear and present danger** that they will bring about the substantive evils that Congress has a right to prevent.* (Emphasis added.)

Thus, the Court for the first time ruled that the First Amendment was not absolute. The government, under certain circumstances, could stop speech if the speech created a clear and present danger to a national interest that at the time was deemed more important than free speech.

Although some might find the ruling contradictory given the wording in the First Amendment that Congress shall make *no* law, it must be noted that the U.S. Constitution contains protections for other rights as well and gives Congress power to protect the country. It would be improper to ignore the rest of the document out of hand to protect one part of it. And it especially makes no sense to protect speech if the speech that is being protected would bring about the destruction of the country during wartime. Of what use is a First Amendment if the country that protects the First Amendment is destroyed? This, Congress has a right under the U.S. Constitution to prevent. Thus, Holmes was saying that under certain conditions, speech must take a back seat to more important matters. He said it depended upon the "proximity and degree" of the danger.

Holmes was criticized for the Schenck ruling. That 15,000 leaflets could undermine the country or the war effort seemed farfetched to many. Yet the test, now known as the *Clear and Present Danger Test*, stuck and influenced the Court's decisions on free speech limitations for 50 years.

Nevertheless, the Court was not sanctioning the wholesale rejection of free speech anytime it suited the government. If the government wanted to stop someone from speaking, it had to prove that the danger it faced was greater than the need for free expression.

Even Holmes modified his position only months later in *Abrams v. U.S.*, 250 U.S. 616 (1919). Jacob Abrams and four others were convicted in another case involving the Espionage Act after they had passed out antiwar leaflets. Although the high Court upheld the convictions, Justice Holmes dissented.

> *Congress certainly cannot forbid all effort to change the mind of the country. Now nobody can suppose that the surreptitious publishing of a silly leaflet by an unknown man, without more, would present any immediate danger that its opinions would hinder the success of the government aims or have any appreciable tendency to do so.*

The Doctrine of Incorporation

The federal government was not alone in its efforts to curtail free speech. States, also fearing changes to the American political and social landscape, added to the suppression by passing their own sedition statutes against *criminal syndicalism*, which, among other things, prohibited anyone from displaying a red flag, or other symbols deemed unpatriotic.

The legal question then became whether the states could interfere with First Amendment liberties.

The Court soon answered this question in *Gitlow v. New York*, 268 U.S. 652 (1925). Benjamin Gitlow and three other socialists were convicted of violating a New York criminal anarchy law after they published a document entitled the "Left Wing Manifesto." Gitlow said the law violated his First Amendment rights and argued that the U.S. Supreme Court should overturn an 1833 decision that said the First Amendment only applied to the federal government.

Taken literally, the First Amendment says *Congress* shall make no law abridging freedom of speech, which means the Congress of the United States or the federal government may not interfere with the right of free speech. It doesn't say anything about the states not being able to violate the First Amendment.

When the Founders established the federal government, they weren't particularly concerned that the states could interfere with their rights. The people, they figured, were close enough to state leaders to prevent tyranny there. The Founders, and the people, were more concerned with the new, larger, more powerful federal government. They figured it would be easier for the federal government to abuse their liberties. Thus, the Bill of Rights was adopted to protect the people from the U.S. government, not the state governments. Therefore, the Court had ruled in the 1830s that the First Amendment only applied to the U.S. government.

But that was before the American Civil War and the adoption of the 13th and 14th Amendments to the U.S. Constitution, which came after the war. The 13th Amendment abolished slavery and the 14th Amendment extended citizenship rights to the newly freed slaves. In addition, the 14th Amendment prohibited the *states* from denying citizens their right to life, liberty, or property without due process of law. Otherwise, no doubt some of the southern states would have denied former slaves their rights as citizens after the war. A majority of states had ratified the amendments, so they had become the law of the land and all the states were bound to follow them. (Remember, only the states and the people, not the federal government, can change the U.S. Constitution.)

Gitlow argued in his appeal that the term "liberty" in the 14th Amendment referred to those freedoms in the First Amendment, and therefore, the states as well as the federal government had to uphold them.

The Court agreed. The Court's decision, therefore, incorporated or read into the 14th Amendment the rights of the First Amendment. This has come to be known as the *doctrine of incorporation.*

Since then, most of the liberties noted in the Bill of Rights have been incorporated through the 14th Amendment onto the states. Thus, the protection of American liberties has been greatly expanded.

Nevertheless, Gitlow lost his appeal. The Court ruled that the state had a right, in this case, to prevent his actions.

More Speech, Not Less

The Court took another tack two years later in *Whitney v. California*, 274 U.S. 357 (1927), presenting a different antidote to the problem of radical speech.

Charlotte Anita Whitney had been convicted of violating California's criminal syndicalism law after she attended a meeting of the Communist Labor Party. Despite the fact that she had argued against the Party's militant policies, her conviction was nevertheless upheld because she was a member of the organization and it advocated government change through violent action.

Yet, in a concurring opinion, Justice Louis Brandeis looked at the Clear and Present Danger Test differently. Although he agreed with the test, he suggested the remedy to radical, seditious speech was more speech, not less. He wrote:

> *Those who won our independence by revolution were not cowards. They did not fear political change. They did not exalt order at the cost of liberty. To courageous self-reliant men, with confidence in the power of free and fearless reasoning applied through the processes of popular government, no danger flowing from speech can be deemed clear and present, unless the incidence of the evil apprehended is so imminent that it may befall before there is opportunity for full discussion. If there be time to expose through discussion the falsehood and fallacies, to avert the evil by the processes of education, the remedy to be applied is more speech, not enforced silence.*

Like the Alien and Sedition Acts of 1798, which were not renewed, the Sedition Act of 1918 was also largely allowed to expire. Most of the Act was repealed in 1921. And while the majority of the Espionage Act of 1917 was allowed to stand, it only dealt with wartime threats. Not until 1940 was another law passed to eliminate seditious speech in America. And again, it emerged during a time of crises—World War II.

The Smith Act of 1940

The Smith Act, like those before it, made it a crime to advocate the violent overthrow of the country or join a group that advocated such action. The law did not require proof that such a violent act was planned or about to occur, only that the defendant was urging people to act. The law was primarily aimed at communists.

Government prosecutions were limited, probably because most citizens were in favor of going to war after the attack on Pearl Harbor. Nevertheless, the Act was used more widely during the late 1940s and early 1950s during the Cold War. Given the growing Red Scare after World War II and the emergence of Sen. Joseph McCarthy's campaign to root out communists in American government, the mood of the country grew more receptive to the law. As a result, at least 121 people were convicted under the Act.

As the paranoia waned, however, so did the zeal for prosecution. In 1957, the Court overturned a conviction of some communists because the government could not prove that the defendants posed an actual threat. The Court said that their advocacy was only an abstract suggestion. The Court's new requirement that the government prove the defendant was calling for direct action rather than just advocating an idea, made prosecution of the law more difficult. As a result, the law was almost never used again.

The Brandenburg "Imminent and Likely" Test

The Court had used the Clear and Present Danger Test in one form or another for 50 years by the time it heard *Brandenburg v. Ohio*, 395 U.S. 444, in 1969. Nevertheless, the Court wasn't particularly comfortable with the old test. The wording was too subjective, and political and social events had too much influence on it. Thus, the Court attempted to refine it one more time. The effect was to further loosen the government's grip on seditious speech.

Clarence Brandenburg, a Ku Klux Klan leader, had made nonspecific threats against the government at a rally of KKK members, calling for "revengeance" and urging that "niggers" be sent back to Africa and Jews back to Israel. He was subsequently convicted under Ohio's criminal syndicalism law. He appealed, arguing his First Amendment rights had been denied.

In its ruling, the U.S. Supreme Court went beyond speech protection afforded in earlier decisions and said that even a call for lawless action was protected as long as it wasn't "imminent lawless action." The Court noted:

> [T]he constitutional guarantees of free speech do not permit (state regulation) . . .except where the speech is directed to inciting or producing **imminent** lawless action, and is **likely** to incite or produce such action. (Emphasis added.)

The Court ruled that Brandenburg's speech, though offensive, was not directed toward inciting lawless action that was likely to occur. As a result, his conviction was overturned and the Ohio law invalidated.

The Brandenburg rule remains the test today for determining just how far one can go in advocating lawless action. The test involves four parts. To be illegal, the speech must be:

1. Directed toward inciting or producing—in other words, what was the intent of the speaker? Was the speaker intending to incite action?

2. Imminent—how much time had elapsed between the speech and the likelihood of lawless action? Would it be immediate? The Court must find that the intended lawless action is going to happen right away.
3. Violent or illegal action—a criminal law or statute must exist forbidding the action.
4. Likely to do so—the evidence must show that there is a substantial probability that the action will occur.

All four of the elements must be present before the speech can be ruled outside First Amendment protection.

The Brandenburg Test also has been used in other cases to determine whether a book, film, web posting, video game, or other media artifact incited someone to commit a crime. Because of the stringent requirements of the Brandenburg Test, it has been all but impossible for someone to prove that the media in such cases is responsible for the illegal actions of another.

For such a case to succeed, the Court noted that it would have to find that the material was specifically "directed" to cause violence. In other words, that was its primary purpose. That a movie or book contains violence, and that violence may prompt someone to decide to commit a crime, is not enough. Just because violence appears in movies, video games or even the nightly news does not mean it is designed to prompt lesser minds to act violently. It also would need to be reasonably foreseeable to the manufacturer of such material that it was "likely" to cause such harm.

This is not to say, however, that such a case could not exist.

The Strict Scrutiny, Intermediate Scrutiny, and Rational Basis Tests

It is out of these free speech challenges as well as cases involving other fundamental liberties and constitutional interpretation that the Court developed three tests to help it decide the limitations of government power. And two of these tests help it determine what government action is impermissible under the First Amendment today and when government interests may not supersede individual rights.

These tests are called the strict scrutiny test, the intermediate scrutiny test, and the rational basis test. The tests evolved from the earliest days of the Republic. They are among the most important tools of the Court in ruling on Constitutional matters. We will refer to them repeatedly in this text.

The origins of the tests can be traced back to perhaps the most important case in U.S. constitutional law—*Marbury v. Madison*, 5 U.S. 137 (1803). In that case, as noted earlier, the Court decided for the first time that the role of the U.S. Supreme Court in the new country was to pass judgment on what was permissible under the U.S. Constitution. This power is referred to as *the power of judicial review*. Thus, it is the Court that will decide what actions of the Congress and the president are constitutionally valid.

The concept of strict scrutiny, intermediate scrutiny, and rational basis grew out of this power of judicial review.

In another early case—*McCulloch v. Maryland*, 17 U.S. 316 (1819), we see an early example of the most widely used of the tests—the rational basis test. In that case the issue was whether the Congress had the authority under the U.S. Constitution to create a national bank. In deciding the case, Chief Justice John Marshall interpreted the last clause of Article I, Section 8 of the U.S. Constitution. The clause notes that the Constitution gives Congress the authority to make all laws that are "necessary and proper" to carry out its powers. Although the Constitution did not say specifically that Congress could establish a national bank, it did not say it couldn't. Thus, Marshall deferred to Congress if it could show that the power to charter a bank had some rational relationship to its legitimate constitutional interest or duties.

Almost all government action that comes under constitutional review is evaluated under this test. And unless the government action is irrational or arbitrary, the government action is almost always upheld as constitutionally permissible. Consequently, it is very difficult for the government to fail this test, and the presumption is that, unless someone can prove otherwise, what the government has done is valid if it falls within the scope of its constitutional duties.

But when fundamental liberties, as those found in the Bill of Rights, are infringed or when a question of equal protection under the law is involved, the constitutional stakes are much higher. Few would argue that Congress's power to pass a law to build a road is as important as its power to pass a law to take away someone's free speech rights. When the government seeks to do that, the Court takes a much closer look at the government's actions. It is then that one of the other two tests is used.

If a law, for example, is designed to stop someone from saying something—that is, it is directed at the content of what they are saying—the Court evaluates the law using the <u>strict scrutiny test</u>.

Content-based laws that come before the Court are presumed to be invalid, and the burden is on the government to prove otherwise. In essence, given the above example, the government has passed such a law to censor people, and that undermines the free exchange of information and ideas in a democracy, a fundamental right protected in the U.S. Constitution.

Therefore, the Court views such laws with great suspicion, and it subjects them to a vigorous test. For the government censorship to stand, the government must show that the law is:

1. <u>Necessary—it is needed to achieve the government's goal.</u>
2. <u>Compelling—it has to be something of great importance or interest to the government, such as national security, and</u>
3. <u>Narrowly tailored—the law must fit and advance the government purpose and not impose an unnecessary burden on speech. In other words, the law must not curtail more free speech than is necessary to accomplish its goal.</u>

Roe v Wade, 410 U.S. 113 (1973), involved a case of strict scrutiny review that ultimately invalidated state laws that prohibited abortion.

The Court held that the right to privacy is a fundamental right. As such, it said a woman has the right to decide whether to terminate her pregnancy. The state of Texas had argued that it had a compelling interest to protect an unborn child. Although the Court said the state had a legitimate interest, it ruled that the state's interest did not become more compelling than the woman's interest until the fetus became "viable," that is, it could live outside the mother's womb.

To return to an example involving free speech, the Court might also uphold a law that made it a crime to publish the location of U.S. troop ships during a declared war. Although free speech is important, it would not, in such an instance, be more important than preventing the defeat of the country.

Today, this would also be applied to the *Schenck* case. The government would have to show its attempt to silence him was necessary, that it had a compelling reason, and that the law designed to accomplish that was narrowly tailored. Its compelling interest, of course, would be the clear and present danger that faced the country at the time—World War I.

The strict scrutiny test was first applied in the case of *Korematsu v. United States*, 323 U.S. 214 (1944), in which the Court ruled that Japanese-Americans could be excluded from certain areas during World War II.

On the other hand, if the government is not trying to stop someone from speaking on some subject—that is, the law is not directed at the content of their speech—but is trying to *regulate* their speech only as to *when they can say it, or where they can say it, or how they can say it*, then the Court will use the <u>intermediate scrutiny test</u>.

The Court is more likely to uphold laws that are not aimed at stopping speech on the basis of content. These are called *content-neutral laws.*

The Court established the intermediate scrutiny test in 1968 when it reviewed the case of David O'Brien who had been convicted of burning his draft card in protest against the Vietnam War. Federal law made it a crime to destroy draft cards on the theory that requiring all 18-year-old males to carry their draft cards helped the draft run smoothly and promoted national security. O'Brien argued that it infringed on his First Amendment right to free speech.

In *United States v. O'Brien*, 391 U.S. 367 (1968), the Court disagreed with him. The Court looked at the purpose of the law and the words in the law and found that it was not directed at the content of his speech, that is, it wasn't saying he couldn't express his displeasure with the war. The law allowed him, the Court said, to voice or otherwise express his dissent in any number of other ways. The Court said any infringement on his speech was minimal and the government had an important interest in protecting the military.

Thus, the Court crafted a new intermediate standard between the rational basis test and the strict scrutiny test. Now often referred to as the *O'Brien Test*, it contains three parts. Laws are considered constitutionally permissible if they:

1. Are not related to the suppression of the content of the speech—particularly ideas with which the government disagrees or might want to suppress.
2. Advance an important or substantial government interest—that is the interest is more than just convenient or reasonable, but less important than compelling, as in the strict scrutiny test,
3. Are narrowly tailored—the law must fit and advance the government purpose and not impose an unnecessary burden on speech. In other words, the law must not curtail more free speech than is necessary to accomplish its goal, and
4. Leave open other ways for the message to get out.

Most laws reviewed under this standard are upheld. The standard, therefore, is more stringent than the rational basis test but not nearly as presumptively fatal to the government action as the strict scrutiny test.

Regarding speech, strict scrutiny, therefore, deals with content-based laws while intermediate scrutiny deals with time, place, and manner laws.

Forum Analysis

When it comes to time, place, and manner restrictions, the court takes a close look at the forum or place where speech occurs since it can also affect whether expression is permissible or not. The Court has identified four different kinds of forums, including traditional public forums, designated public forums, public property that is not meant for expressive purposes, and private property.

Traditional public forums include places where people historically have assembled to express themselves, particularly on matters of government and public policy, and often through speeches or protests. These include street corners and sidewalks, the courthouse steps, and public parks among other traditional venues. The Court has ruled the First Amendment gives people speaking in these places the most protection from government interference since such forums have been critical to open debate and dissent in United States' history. The presumption is the public has a right to use such places for expression.

This right, however, does not give individuals license to interfere with the intended purpose of the location. For example, one could not stop traffic any time one wished to hold a parade. Neither would one be able to block the courthouse steps so others could not enter.

The government may establish reasonable rules, hours, and policies regulating the use of public forums, though they cannot block their use indefinitely. Often, the government will require citizens to get permits. These rules are permissible if they are content neutral, in other words, government officials cannot allow some to get permits and others not because of what is being expressed. Government officials, therefore, may not use their unbridled personal discretion in deciding under these rules which person gets a permit. If that happens, the government will face a strict scrutiny test from the Court instead of a time, place and manner test.

Designated public forums are places the government has created specifically for expression, such as school classrooms, community auditoriums, city halls, or public fairgrounds. There is no presumption the public can use them whenever they like. They were created for a specific purpose, though the government may choose to allow them to be used for other expressive purposes. Thus, the government has more discretion in determining how and when they will be used.

The Court must find evidence that the government had intended to establish such a forum before it will be recognized as such. This can be shown through some stated government policy or other official intent or action.

The government is not required to establish such forums and once it does, it does not have to maintain them indefinitely, but as long as the forum exists, the Court will treat it the same as a traditional public forum.

Nonpublic forums include government property that is off limits for public expression. It would include places like military bases, prisons, utility poles, airport terminals, mailboxes, and public places where speech has no history and would interrupt the function of government were it allowed to occur.

The Court usually allows the government to decide what is off limits. However, the Court has said the government may ban the public from such places only if the ban is reasonable, rational, and viewpoint neutral.

Private property includes everything from your front yard to the nearby shopping mall. The First Amendment generally does not give people the authority to use someone's property to express themselves.

However, the Supreme Court has ruled that when an enclosed area of a shopping mall or a parking lot is widely used for public assembly and expression it may take on characteristics of a public forum and the owner may be required to allow such gatherings.

Moreover, the Court ruled in *Pruneyard Shopping Center v. Robins*, 447 U.S. 74 (1980), that a state may expand First Amendment liberties in its own constitution, allowing free speech rights at shopping malls, provided they follow the owner's reasonable time, place, and manner restrictions. The ruling has not been widely expanded, and this area of law is unclear.

Unprotected Speech

Speech that creates a clear and present danger of imminent lawless action that is likely to occur represents only one kind of expression that is unprotected under the First Amendment. Other areas include obscenity, defamation, false or deceptive advertising, a narrow class of speech called "fighting words," and whenever the government can demonstrate a "compelling interest" in limiting First Amendment activity. (These will be discussed individually later.)

Prior Restraint

The Court prefers to deal with problematic or unprotected speech after the fact, that is, to allow the speech to occur and then decide what to do about it later. As with Mr. Schenck, who was punished after circulating the seditious pamphlets that created a clear and present danger, those who defame others or invade their privacy today face legal consequences afterward.

The reason is clear. Such is the essence of democracy—the ability of the people to receive information and decide themselves what to do with it. For the government to interfere beforehand is to censor, and the Founders understood that censorship is the great evil of a free and open society. It threatens freedom because it prevents people from getting the information they need to govern their society and their lives.

Freedom of the Press cannot survive in such an environment. Even William Blackstone, the English legal scholar, understood the danger to the Press as early as the 1760s before the American Revolution, defining freedom of the press as freedom from prior restraint. Thus, whatever else it was intended to mean, the First Amendment was written primarily to protect speech and press from government interference— in advance.

The modern Court seems equally clear on the matter, noting in *Nebraska Press Ass'n. v. Stewart*, 427 U.S. 539, 559 (1976), that if "a threat of criminal or civil sanctions after publication 'chills' speech, prior restraint 'freezes' it."

Nevertheless, the Court under certain limited circumstances permits censorship, or its legal term—*prior restraint*. The action could take the form of a license, a court injunction, or even a prohibition against using the mails. All are permitted when some great harm would otherwise result.

The government's burden to justify such action is heavy. The Court demands that any prior restraint be narrowly tailored, interfering with the least amount of speech necessary and that the government interest be significant. The harm it seeks to prevent must be a *special societal harm*. Such harm today would include matters of national security or preserving someone's right to a fair trial. But it can also include somewhat lesser matters, such as requiring someone to get a city permit before holding a parade.

The Supreme Court has noted that certain procedural safeguards also must be in place protecting those whose speech is being restrained. These include requirements that:

1. The government standards must be narrowly drawn, reasonable and definite so they only restrict the speech in question.
2. The government agency seeking to prevent the information from getting out must promptly seek an injunction allowing it to restrain the speech.

3. <u>The Court must make a prompt and final determination of the validity of the restraint.</u>
4. <u>The government must bear the responsibility of proving that the speech is unprotected.</u>

• *Near v. Minnesota*

It had been more than 10 years since the *Schenck* case when the U.S. Supreme Court ruled in *Near v. Minnesota*, 283 U.S. 697 (1931), that prior restraint or censorship by the government was always to be the exception and not the rule and that it only would be permitted in very limited circumstances. The landmark case involved a Minnesota state law that allowed officials to declare any publication deemed to be "malicious, scandalous, and defamatory" a public nuisance and close it down.

In an attempt to clean up Minneapolis, *The Saturday Press*, a small weekly published by Howard Guilford and J.M. Near, had printed inflammatory attacks on certain public officials, claiming that law enforcement was doing little to stop gambling, bootlegging, and racketeering in the city. Further, the newspaper charged the police chief with gross neglect of duty and said he participated in corruption.

In 1927, city and county officials brought legal action against Near and Guilford under the public nuisance law, and a district court judge ruled in their favor, issuing an injunction against future publication or distribution of the newspaper. A year later, the Minnesota Supreme Court upheld the ruling, declaring that the U.S. Constitution gave the state broad police powers to regulate public health and welfare.

But the U.S. Supreme Court reversed the state decision and declared the law unconstitutional. In a 5–4 ruling, the Court said that the nuisance statute was not directed at punishing but censoring, which was not consistent with freedom of the press and was in violation of the First Amendment.

Nevertheless, Justice Charles Evans Hughes, who wrote the majority opinion, said that in some kinds of circumstances prior restraint might be permissible, such as in cases of obscenity or national security.

• Pentagon Papers

Perhaps the most famous modern case involving prior restraint occurred during the Vietnam War. Known today as the *Pentagon Papers case*, it pitted President Richard Nixon against the editors of *The New York Times* and the *Washington Post.* The case, *New York Times v. U.S.*, 403 U.S. 713 (1971), marked the first time in U.S. history that the federal government tried to prevent major newspapers from publishing information that the administration alleged would harm national security.

The case began when the newspapers started publishing stories that were based on stolen copies of a top-secret 47-volume Defense Department study entitled "History of the United States Decision-Making Process on Vietnam Policy." The study revealed questionable decisions about the war that had been made by the four presidents who had been in office before Nixon—Truman, Eisenhower, Kennedy, and Johnson. The documents had been pilfered by Defense Department whistleblower Daniel Ellsberg and given to the editors.

Frontpage/Shutterstock.com

The Vietnam War was an unpopular war that had split the country into two philosophically. The result was a political stalemate that left a country of "hawks" and "doves." Meanwhile, the war dragged on.

After the newspapers published the first stories on the subject, U.S. Attorney General John Mitchell asked the editors to stop publication of any more of the articles. The editors refused, and the government went to court to seek an injunction against the newspapers. Given the high stakes involving national security and freedom of the press, the case was appealed and taken up quickly to the U.S. Supreme Court.

The government argued that publication of the material would harm national security. The newspapers argued first that the secret classification system was a sham designed to let government officials sway the public, and second, that the injunction violated the First Amendment. The result was a 6–3 ruling in favor of the newspapers that lifted the injunction and allowed publication of the articles to continue. The Court had said that the government failed to show that publication of the articles would further harm the war effort. Therefore, it failed to show the compelling interest that would trump First Amendment concerns. Yet the Court did not say that the prior restraint sought was unconstitutional, only that the government failed to show it was necessary.

The government later unsuccessfully prosecuted Daniel Ellsberg for copying the classified material. In 2011, the government finally released the study that prompted the case—40 years after the newspapers published the information.

* * *

The number of prior restraint cases is vast and includes a whole range of legal issues. The following examples show the extent to which the Court has addressed the problem.

• Hate Speech

In *R.A.V. v. St. Paul*, 505 U.S. 377 (1992), the high Court said **hate speech** cannot be banned on the basis of content when it overturned a St. Paul, Minn., ordinance that punished those who burn crosses or express racial or religious hatred. The Court ruled that a youth who burned a cross in front of a black family's home could not be punished for communicating hateful messages based on race, gender, religion, or the like just because they were offensive.

Said Justice Antonin Scalia, "Let there be no mistake about our belief that burning a cross in someone's yard is reprehensible. However, St. Paul has sufficient means at its disposal to prevent such behavior without adding the First Amendment to the fire." "Sufficient means" might have included charges of arson or trespassing.

Nevertheless, hate speech is not the same as a **hate crime**, which *is* illegal. The court ruled unanimously in *Wisconsin v. Mitchell*, 508 U.S. 476 (1993), that the First Amendment does not protect violence motivated by hatred of religion, race, national origin, sexual orientation, or gender. The case involved a group of black youths who watched the movie *Mississippi Burning* and then seriously beat a white youth. Chief Justice William Rehnquist wrote for the Court: "A physical assault is not by any stretch of the imagination expressive conduct protected by the First Amendment."

Fighting words also are not protected under the First Amendment. In *Chaplinsky v. New Hampshire*, 315 U.S. 568 (1942), the Court upheld the conviction of a man who was convicted of calling another man a "damned fascist" in a face-to-face confrontation at a time when the country was at war with Nazi Germany. The Court said those "words which by their very utterance inflict injury or tend to incite an immediate breach of the peace" are outside the realm of First Amendment protection.

However, just because words are insulting or offensive does not mean they can be defined as "fighting words." There must be evidence that uttering them would tend to cause a breach of the peace. Thus, the court will look not only to the words used, but also to how close the speaker was to the receiver when the words were spoken and what kind of effect they were likely to have.

Threatening speech is also unprotected expression. For speech to be characterized as a threat, it must be directed toward someone with the intent of causing fear of bodily harm or death.

As noted, burning a cross is not, by itself, against the law. But if it is done with the **intent to threaten or intimidate**, the Court has ruled that it is outside First Amendment protection. In *Virginia v. Black*, 538 U.S. 343 (2003), the Court said Virginia's total ban on cross burning was unconstitutional if it involved, for example, burning a cross at a political rally in an open field as a form of symbolic speech. The Court, however, said the law was valid when used to prosecute someone who burned a cross on a neighbor's yard to intimidate them.

Profanity or offensive speech is also protected under the First Amendment. In *Cohen v. California*, 403 U.S. 15 (1971), the Court held that Paul R. Cohen was within his rights when he entered a Los Angeles courthouse wearing a leather jacket with the motto "Fuck the Draft" on it in protest of the Vietnam War. Justice John Marshall Harlan wrote that it was "nevertheless often true that one man's vulgarity is another's lyric."

The Court added that court administrators, like school officials, have the right to maintain order, but so long as the speech doesn't create a disruption of government operation, it is protected speech. Of course, obscenity (a narrow class of expression that will be dealt with later), intimidation or fighting words would be outside the scope of protection.

Neither are **offensive images** outside First Amendment protection. In *Brown v. EMA*, 131 S. Ct. 2729 (2011), the Court refused to establish a new category of unprotected speech when it struck down a California law that prohibited the sale of violent video games to minors, noting that the law failed strict scrutiny review applied to content-based speech.

• Symbolic Speech

On occasion, nonverbal expression, or symbolic speech, may also qualify for First Amendment protection. Marching through the street, wearing armbands, burning the flag, or engaging in some other conduct to express an idea can also be a form of important communication. Nevertheless, the Court has not held that every kind of conduct qualifies. The conduct, the Court said, must be "closely akin to pure speech" to receive protection. And, like any other kind of speech, the government may be able to show a compelling reason to prohibit or regulate it.

For example, when David O'Brien burned his draft card to protest the Vietnam War, the Court upheld his conviction in *United States v. O'Brien*, 391 U.S. 367 (1968), noting that although he was expressing himself, the government had a legitimate interest that overrode his expression (see above).

But when Gregory Lee Johnson burned the American flag at the 1984 Republican National Convention in Dallas in violation of a Texas law that made it a crime to desecrate the flag, the Court used a strict scrutiny test and ruled the law unconstitutional. In *Texas v. Johnson*, 491 U.S. 397 (1989), Justice William Brennan wrote, "[i]f there is a bedrock principle underlying the First Amendment, it is that the government may not prohibit the expression of an idea simply because society finds the idea itself offensive or disagreeable."

• Compelled Speech

Freedom of speech also means freedom *from* speech. In *Wooley v. Maynard*, 430 U.S. 705 (1977), the U.S. Supreme Court held New Hampshire could not require citizens to display the state motto "Live Free or Die" on their license plates if they found it offensive to their moral convictions.

George Maynard and his wife had covered up the motto on their license plates because as Jehovah's Witnesses, they found it offensive. As a result, Maynard was issued a traffic citation for violating a state law that made it a crime to cover up the motto. Maynard was convicted and appealed. Eventually the case found its way to the U.S. Supreme

Court. Writing for the 6–3 majority that overturned the conviction, Chief Justice Warren Burger said the state statute requiring citizens to display the motto effectively required citizens to "use their private property as a 'mobile billboard' for the State's ideological message."

This is not to say a state has no control over messages on its license plates. In *Walker, Chairman, Texas Department of Motor Vehicles Board, et al. v. Texas Division, Sons of Confederate Veterans, Inc., et al.*, 576 U.S. _____., 135 S.Ct. 2239 (2015), the Court held that license plates constitute government speech and citizens cannot require states to display messages on them.

The case stems from a Texas policy that differentiates between general-issue and specialty license plates. In the latter instance, citizens can propose a plate design comprising a slogan, a graphic or both. If the Texas Department of Motor Vehicles approves the design, the state will make it available for display. In the case at bar, the Texas Division of the Sons of Confederate Veterans and its officers proposed a specialty plate with a Confederate battle flag. The state rejected their request and they sued, alleging a violation of the First Amendment's free speech clause.

The Court, in ruling for the state, held that the First Amendment does not bar the government from determining the content of what it says. The Court added that states have long used license plates to convey government speech, promoting tourism, etc. What appears on them, therefore, conveys how they are identified in the public mind, the Court noted. Since each plate is government property, serving a government purpose of vehicle registration and identification, the state has the right to regulate what's on it. The Court said license plates are not traditional public forums, that they are essentially government IDs which they have a right to control.

The Court noted that just as a state cannot compel a private party to express a view with which the private party disagrees, citizens cannot compel a state to promote their personal messages on government property.

• Censoring Government Employees

Although government workers do not give up their First Amendment rights when they become public employees, the government, in certain situations, can have more control over their expression than private citizens. The government can prevent workers from disseminating classified information and prohibit political campaigning, though officials may not fire employees for making political statements.

In fact, the mistaken belief that a police officer had engaged in political activity was at the center of a recent U.S. Supreme Court case. In *Heffernan v. City of Paterson, Jew Jersey, et al.*, 578 U.S. ____., 136 S.Ct. 1412 (2016), the Court held that when an employer demotes an employee out of a desire to prevent the employee from engaging in protected political activity, the employee is entitled to challenge that unlawful action under the First Amendment.

The case involved a police officer, Jeffrey Heffernan, who, as a favor to his bedridden mother, agreed to pick up and deliver to her a political campaign yard sign. Although Heffernan was not involved in the campaign, other officers saw him speaking to the politician's campaign staff while holding the yard sign. The next day his supervisor demoted him from detective to patrol officer as punishment for his "overt involvement" in the campaign. Heffernan filed suit, complaining his First Amendment rights had been violated.

Although Heffernan had not engaged in any political speech, the Court ruled he had been demoted under the mistaken belief that he had engaged in such protected activity. The Court noted that the constitutional harm – discouraging employees from engaging in protected speech or association – is the same whether or not the employer's action rests upon a factual mistake.

The Court, nevertheless, said lower courts should first decide in such cases if the employer had acted under a neutral policy that could prohibit police officers from overt involvement in any political campaign, and whether such a policy complied with constitutional standards.

When an employee signs an employment contract with the government, the Court says that contract is binding. In *Snepp v. U.S.*, 444 U.S. 507 (1980), the Court ruled former CIA agent Frank Snepp violated his contract with the government when he resigned and wrote a book alleging CIA ineptness in Vietnam without getting prior approval from the CIA as required by the agreement.

Outside employment can also be a problem for government employees. In 1989, Congress amended the Ethics in Government Act to make it illegal for almost all federal workers to receive payments for writing articles or giving speeches, even for subjects outside their official duties.

The U.S. Supreme Court ruled on this in *U.S. v. National Treasury Employees Union*, 513 U.S. 454 (1995), holding that the ban was too broad and violated the First Amendment. Justice John Paul Stevens, writing for the Court, said the ban that prevented senior officials from writing about policy matters was permissible, but that lower level employees should have the same First Amendment rights as private citizens.

• False Speech

In 2005, Congress passed the Stolen Valor Act which made it a crime to falsely represent having received or been awarded a medal or decoration from the U.S. Armed Forces. The U.S. Supreme Court overturned the act in *U.S. v. Alvarez*, 567 U.S. 709 (2012), in a 6–3 decision, noting that Xavier Alvarez's lies about receiving awards were "a pathetic attempt to gain respect that eluded him." Justice Anthony Kennedy said that the First Amendment contained no general exception for false statements. He said it was preferable that the American people ferret out and refute false claims rather than criminalize them by an act of Congress.

• Taxation as Censorship

Governments have used taxation to control and intimidate the Press for centuries. The Stamp Act, which taxed colonial newspapers, was one of the major grievances that led up to the American Revolution. Unfortunately, adoption of the First Amendment after the war did not stop government efforts to tax crusading newspapers into silence. Yet the Court has been clear that such government antics are not to be tolerated.

In *Grosjean v. American Press*, 297 U.S. 233 (1936), the Court said that an attempt by Louisiana governor Huey "Kingfish" Long's political machine to pass a special tax against the largest newspapers in the state who were opposed to him amounted to an attempt at censorship. The Court has said that newspapers like any other business are subject to taxation, so long as they are not taxed in a discriminatory manner.

• *Son of Sam* Laws

Both state and federal governments have passed laws that permit authorities to take away book profits from criminals recounting their crimes and give those profits to their victims. Referred to as *Son of Sam laws* after David Berkowitz, the serial killer who called himself Son of Sam, the statutes often pose constitutional problems.

In fact, the Court held that New York's Son of Sam law was unconstitutional in *Simon & Schuster v. New York State Crime Victims Board*, 502 U.S. 105 (1991), noting that it financially burdened speech content. Thus, the state would have to show a strict scrutiny compelling interest to justify the law, which it could not do. Justice Sandra Day O'Connor said that the law, as written, was over-inclusive because it could apply to too many legitimate literary works, including Henry David Thoreau's *Civil Disobedience*.

Since then, several states have attempted to pass narrower laws. Some have passed judicial scrutiny.

• Grand Jury Testimony

In *Butterworth v. Smith*, 494 U.S. 624 (1990), the Court invalided a Florida law that made it a crime for a reporter to write about the things he told the grand jury. The Court said it did not involve information that he secretly learned from the grand jury itself. Chief Justice William Rehnquist said that the reporter was merely recounting information he already possessed. Interfering with that was a violation of the First Amendment.

• Elections

In a highly controversial 5–4 decision, the U.S. Supreme Court invalided a federal law that prohibited corporations and unions from using their money to campaign for or against political candidates. In *Citizens United v. Federal Elections Commission*, 558 U.S. 310 (2010), the Court said that the statute that addressed campaign expenditure reform violated the free speech rights of the organizations. The case centered on efforts by the conservative lobbying group Citizens United and its attempt to present a film critical of Hillary Clinton. Critics charged that the ruling would corrupt the political process further by giving more power to those lobbyists and special interest groups with the most money. But the majority said spending money was essential to disseminating speech.

• Internet

The Court has found that some media enjoy more freedom than others. The printed media—newspapers, magazines and the

like—enjoy the most freedom. They are not constrained by lack of ink or paper. Over-the-air broadcast media—TV and radio—are subject to greater regulation given the limitation on the number of broadcast channels available. Though even here, the Court has sought to prohibit content regulation by the government unless it is narrowly drawn.

With the development of cable broadcast, the Court has held that there is a gray, middle ground that contains slightly more regulation than newspapers enjoy, but less than over-the-air broadcast stations are subjected to. The reasons are both technical and historical. Cable TV is able to carry nearly an unlimited number of messages, yet these electronic media have a history of limited government regulation. *Sable Communications v. FCC*, 492 U.S. 115 (1989).

However, the Court has held that the Internet is more similar to newspapers and thus deserves the widespread protection found in the printed media. The Court made the ruling in *Reno v. American Civil Liberties Union*, 521 U.S. 844 (1997), noting that the provisions of the 1996 Communications Decency Act prohibiting transmission of indecent material was unconstitutional. Justice John Paul Stevens said the Court recognized that each medium of communication had unique problems and limitations, but that it found no unique reason why the Internet should receive more regulation than print. Unlike over-the-air broadcast there was no limit on the number of channels.

Net neutrality, or the idea that messages on the Internet should flow freely and democratically, is still a matter of debate, and it remains to be seen if the Net retains its open status or becomes more regulated like cable.

• Distributing Literature

As noted earlier, the government may adopt content-neutral time, place, and manner restrictions under the First Amendment. Thus, the government may require that people get a permit before holding a parade on a city street or organizing a rally in a public park. But these laws may not discriminate against those who wish to promote controversial views in a public forum. The same is true for those who would wish to distribute controversial literature there.

In *Lovell v. City of Griffin*, 303 US. 444 (1938), the Court held that a law that required the city manger's permission to distribute pamphlets violated the First Amendment rights of Alma Lovell, a Jehovah's Witness, who was fined for circulating religious tracts. The Court said that the First Amendment protects the right to distribute literature as well as to publish it.

In another Jehovah's Witness case—*Schneider v. State of New Jersey*, 308 U.S. 147 (1939)—the Court said an anti-littering ordinance could not be used as a pretense to infringe on First Amendment liberties. The Court said that the government had a right to prevent littering, but to suggest, it was permissible to stop someone from handing out literature on the off chance it might later end up as litter went too far. If the government wanted to stop litter, the Court said, it had to arrest those who littered.

• Signs

The U.S. Supreme Court has also addressed the issue of government regulation of signs. In *Reed et al. v. Town of Gilbert, Arizona, et al.*, 576 U.S. ____., 135 S.Ct. 2218 (2015), the Court ruled a town's regulation of signs was content-based and did not survive strict scrutiny.

The case involved Gilbert's comprehensive sign code that prohibited the display of outdoor signs without a permit, but exempted 23 categories of signs, including ideological signs, political signs, and temporary directional signs, such as those that directed people to a public or church gathering. The Good News Community Church had been cited by the town for exceeding the time limit for displaying temporary directional signs and failing to include an event date on the sign. Clyde Reed, pastor of the church, sued, alleging the code violated the group's First Amendment rights.

The Court agreed, holding that when a law attempts to regulate speech on the basis of content, as it did here because the sign code singled out certain categories on the basis of their messages and then subjected them to different restrictions, the law violates the Constitution. The Court also said the town did not show a compelling governmental reason for requiring different sign restrictions.

The Court added that its decision did not prevent governments from enacting effective sign laws to resolve problems with safety and aesthetics so long as they were content neutral.

• Abortion Protests and Other Picketing

Anti-abortion demonstrations outside medical clinics and doctors' homes have led to concerns about public safety as well as legal questions over time, place, and manner regulations. The U.S. Supreme Court in *Frisby v. Schultz*, 487 U.S. 474 (1988), first addressed the problem when officials in the Milwaukee suburb of Brookfield, Wisconsin, banned demonstrations near homes after anti-abortion activists picketed in front of a doctor's house.

Activist Sandra Schultz sued, charging that her First Amendment rights had been violated. The Court, nevertheless, upheld the city's ban, noting that although residential streets are generally considered public forums, the space in front of a person's house is not. The Court said that the city had to let the protesters walk up and down the street carrying signs, but it could prevent them from lingering too long in front of a particular house.

The Court said a person is entitled to some privacy and freedom from harassment in their own home. Noted Justice Sandra Day O'Connor: "The First Amendment permits the government to prohibit offensive speech as intrusive when the "captive" audience cannot avoid the objectionable speech . . ."

A different kind of protest problem confronted the Court in *Organization for a Better Austin v. Keefe*, 402 U.S. 415 (1971), after Jerome Keefe, a real estate broker, was accused of trying to scare white residents into selling their homes cheaply to avoid the blacks he claimed were moving into the neighborhoods. The Organization for a Better Austin countered his move by circulating fliers that attacked Keefe. Keefe then got a court order preventing their distribution. The Supreme Court set aside the injunction, noting that peacefully passing out pamphlets enjoys First Amendment protection.

Although passing out fliers may be constitutionally protected, soliciting money is not. The Court ruled in *U.S. v. Kokinda*, 497 U.S. 720 (1990), that the U.S. Postal Service could prohibit solicitations at post offices. In a 5–4 decision, the Justices held that representatives of the National Democratic Policy Committee were not permitted to set up a table at a post office to distribute fliers and solicit funds.

The Judges who dissented said that they believed the post office qualified as a traditional public forum, and the ban was not a valid time, place, and manner restriction.

Thus, the government can prevent solicitations, though not literature distributions, at government buildings that are open to the public but not considered traditional public forums. The government may regulate solicitations at traditional public forums under time, place, and manner rules.

Finally, the Court has ruled that picketing at funerals can be a form of protected speech. In *Snyder v. Phelps*, 131 S. Ct. 1207 (2011), the Court ruled 8–1 that the Westboro Baptist Church, which often protests homosexuality by picketing at the funerals of soldiers, had a right to picket the funeral of Marine Lance Cpl. Matthew A. Snyder, who had died in Iraq. Though the church had attracted national wrath as a result of its actions, the Court said the protesters complied with time, place, and manner regulations and that their picketing related to political and moral questions.

Schools The U.S. Supreme Court has viewed public schools and universities as limited-purpose public forums, subject to reasonable content-neutral time, place, and manner restrictions. Therefore, schools may impose limited speech restrictions on students and teachers to advance their educational objectives, but the schools may not dictate speech content except to prevent a disruption of the educational mission. The rule does not apply to private schools where administrators can curtail free speech generally at will.

The standards that apply to public grade schools, high schools, and universities differ depending upon the age and maturity of the students, location of the speech, and the goals of the institution. Public grade schools and high schools may regulate, among other things, dress, hours of use, and content of school-sponsored publications.

The Court views university free speech and press rights more liberally. University policies are supposed to enhance student discussion of issues and ideas as part of the broader educational mission. Thus, the Court does not grant university administrators the same degree of deference when it comes to regulating student or teacher expression.

Case law regarding campus speech is mixed.

Perhaps the most important case supporting student expression reached the Court more than 40 years ago after some junior and senior high school students were expelled from school for wearing black armbands to school to protest the Vietnam War.

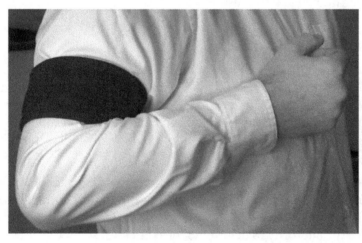

Copyright © of Mark Zimmerman. Reprinted by permission.

John Tinker, his sister Mary Beth Tinker, and a friend sued after the principal expelled them. School officials argued that they had the right to curtail the students' expression to prevent a disruption of school functions, but the Court said that the officials could not show evidence that any disruption was about to occur or likely to occur.

In *Tinker v. Des Moines Independent Community School District*, 393 U.S. 503 (1969), the Court declared the students' actions were symbolic speech protected by the First Amendment. Justice Abe Fortas, in a now-famous opinion, spoke for the Court: "It can hardly be argued that either students or teachers shed their constitutional rights to freedom of speech or expression at the schoolhouse gate."

The law after *Tinker* seemed clear—schools could not interfere with student speech unless the offending expression was inside or next to the school, made during school hours, and the school could show it would disrupt school functions.

But the Court added another standard in *Morse v. Frederick*, 551 U.S. 393 (2007), when it ruled that school officials could prohibit speech that contravened school policy. The case emerged after Joseph Frederick and some other students displayed a banner reading "Bong Hits 4 Jesus." The school's principal tore down the banner after Frederick refused to do so. When she suspended him for 10 days, he sued, alleging a First Amendment violation. The Court held that although the speech was nondisruptive, officials could nevertheless prohibit speech that advocated illegal drug use.

The Court has also dealt with campus speech that is offensive or inappropriate.

In *Bethel School District v. Frasier*, 478 U.S. 675 (1986), the Court ruled that student speech at a school-sponsored event might be curtailed to comply with the school's educational purpose. In that case, Matthew Frasier made a sexually suggestive speech in front of 600 students. He was suspended for violating the school's policy forbidding profanity and obscenity.

And in another, more widely discussed case, the Court distinguished between what is student expression and what is a school's curriculum. In *Hazelwood v. Kuhlmeier*, 484 U.S. 260 (1988), the Court said school officials have the authority to determine the content of a school-sponsored newspaper.

The case involved a high school journalism class that produced a student newspaper under the direction of a faculty adviser who reviewed the content prior to publication. The principal also reviewed the content and removed some stories that dealt with pregnancy, divorce, and other issues deemed too sensitive for young readers. The students sued, charging a constitutional violation.

In ruling for the school, the Court said that when a school sponsors a student forum, it becomes part of the school's curriculum and it has the authority and obligation to exercise control over it. However, the Court added in a footnote that the ruling did not apply to the university student press.

Although schools have control over their curriculum, such control does not extend to flag salutes and pledges of allegiance. In *West Virginia State Board of Education v. Barnette*, 319 U.S. 624 (1943), the Court sided with some students who were Jehovah's Witnesses who argued that a school policy requiring them to participate in such activities violated their religious beliefs. The Court said that the school could not indoctrinate students in particular ideologies.

Finally, speech codes adopted by numerous universities across the country as part of a move toward *political correctness* have been held to be an unconstitutional abridgement of freedom of expression. The codes, which are designed to prevent verbal harassment of minorities and eliminate other offensive campus speech, are in violation of the First Amendment because they target disfavored speech, curb the free flow of information and are overly broad.

CHAPTER 6

Libel

The Value of Reputation

For thousands of years, society has recognized the value of a person's reputation. Even the earliest civilizations viewed it as an individual property interest, a valuable personal asset that needed legal protection. Laws against defamation—or the harming of reputation—can be traced back to the ancient Romans and even the Ten Commandments, which include a charge not to bear false witness against another. As such, these societies understood that insulating people from unfair humiliation was important in promoting and maintaining social order.

The earliest recorded defamation case in Western Civilization may well be the trial of Socrates in 399 BCE. Socrates was convicted of

Socrates

slandering the Greek gods and was sentenced to death. Although in most parts of the world the penalty for defamation is not nearly as severe today, modern societies still take it seriously.

American laws regarding defamation can be traced directly from English common law, and they are considered no less important by the Court today than they were before the American Revolution, as the late Chief Justice William Rehnquist noted:

> *"The right of a man to the protection of his own reputation from unjustified invasion and wrongful hurt reflects no more than our basic concept of the essential dignity and worth of every human being—a concept at the root of any decent system of ordered liberty."*

As noted in Chapter 4, defamation—*a false communication that harms another's reputation by holding him up to contempt, ridicule, causes him to be shunned, damages his business, or otherwise causes him disrepute*—is unprotected speech under the First Amendment and illegal. Under American law, it is considered a *tort*, a civil wrong involving two or more parties that the Court resolves usually through the payment of money.

However, a few states still have criminal libel statutes that make defaming another a crime if it leads to a breach of the peace. In those situations, conviction could result in a fine and/or time in jail. These laws are left over from earlier times when English laws like seditious libel made it a crime to criticize the government. Criminal libel laws are rarely used today.

Of all the areas of mass communication law, defamation is the most troublesome. About two-thirds of all legal complaints lodged against the media each year concern matters of defamation. The problem has grown worse because of the Internet and other electronic media. Writers and editors are spending less time checking facts before they publish and broadcast them. This, in turn, increases the chance that false and defamatory information will be spread.

As bloggers and other individuals—many without journalism training—set up their own websites and begin publishing without the benefit of another pair of eyes to check their work, the number of cases will also, no doubt, increase.

Public relations practitioners and advertising copywriters can find themselves in trouble, too. And those outside the media are equally liable for their communication. Libel and slander can often be found in letters to the editor, Internet chat rooms, and in daily business settings.

To compound the problem, some are suing the media for defamation even when defamation doesn't exist. In an effort to eliminate criticism and prevent the discussion of controversial issues, some individuals and businesses that come under scrutiny for possible wrongdoing are suing the media to shut them up. These anti-speech lawsuits are called *SLAPP suits* (strategic lawsuits against public participation).

The plaintiffs don't expect to win since no defamation exists. Any criticism the media has made of them has been valid and a matter of public concern, but by instigating a lawsuit that will require a costly defense, they are able to harass the media into silence.

Libel suits can be very expensive. And for those who lose, multi-million dollar judgments are not uncommon. Although most of the verdicts are reduced or overturned on appeal, the cost of defending such a suit can run into millions of dollars even if the defendant is innocent.

As a result of this chilling effect on legitimate speech, 28 states and the District of Columbia have passed *anti-SLAPP statutes.* These laws let a judge quickly dismiss such suits if the defendant can show the communication was constitutionally protected speech that was a matter of public concern, and the plaintiff is unable to show there is sufficient evidence to prove he will likely win. In addition, attorney's fees may be awarded to the defendant if the case is found to be without merit.

For legitimate cases of defamation, however, the law's purpose remains clear. Regardless of the state or jurisdiction, American libel laws are designed to accomplish three goals: compensate those harmed for losses they incurred as a result of the defamation, punish the offender, and discourage others from engaging in such behavior.

Elements of Defamation

To prove a *prima facie* case of defamation—that is, on the basis of the facts presented by the plaintiff alone without regard to possible defenses—the plaintiff must prove four elements at common law. If the plaintiff fails to prove all four things, the case fails to move forward and the plaintiff loses. The following sections discuss the elements of defamation.

• Defamation

The plaintiff must show that the defendant used defamatory language. Statements that impugn a person's virtue, sanity, integrity, honesty, and other such matters can all be defamatory. The damage can be conveyed by the words themselves, such as calling someone a "thief," or it can be accomplished by reporting things out of context.

For example, it is harmless by itself to falsely report that a tennis player won a match on a Saturday instead of on a Sunday, unless the tennis player is a devout Jew. By proving that he is true to his beliefs, the plaintiff through this act of *inducement* can prove that the false report harms his reputation through *innuendo* by implying he is really not faithful to his religion if he is willing to play on the Sabbath. Thus, reporting facts accurately and in context is important. Even simple mistakes can lead to a case of defamation.

Words need not be used to defame. Pictures, photographs, cartoons, and any other communication that conveys a false and harmful message can be actionable.

Any living person can be defamed. One can't libel the dead. But a corporation or other business relationship can be defamed by false reports of dishonesty, financial instability, or other matters that would undermine the venture.

• Identification

The plaintiff must prove that he was identified as the subject of the defamation. In other words, he must be able to show that the language was "of or concerning" him and that a reasonable reader, listener, or viewer would understand that.

Although a person certainly can be identified by name, he might also be identified in some other way, as through a description. This is called *colloquium* and means that the plaintiff is able to prove identification by presenting additional evidence that shows the defendant was referring to him by some other means.

Defamation is a personal tort. Only the individual who has been defamed can sue. Thus, the plaintiff must prove that the defamation is about him personally.

As a result, large groups or classes of people cannot sue for defamation since individuals in the group were not singled out for scorn. It is not possible to defame a religion, race, or ethnic group. But if the defamation involves a small group in which the members could individually be identified, then each person may file suit if they can show they were a part of that group.

• **Publication**

The defamatory statement about the plaintiff must have been communicated to a third party. Someone else besides the plaintiff must have received and understood the message.

The plaintiff needs to only prove the defendant intended to publish the information. The plaintiff does not need to prove that the defendant intended to defame him. Thus, a mistake can lead to a charge of libel, as in the example of the Jewish tennis player falsely accused of competing on the Sabbath.

Each time a defamatory message is repeated, it is considered another publication for which the plaintiff may sue. However, this does not apply to multiple printings of the same issue, as in the case of a newspaper publishing several thousand copies of one day's news. This is called the *single publication rule*, which has been adopted by most courts. Thus, all of the copies are considered a single publication.

Whoever has control over the content of the defamatory statement and helps publish it may be held liable for any damage. These individuals are referred to as *primary publishers*. This would include newspaper and magazine publishers, editors, reporters, radio and television station managers, advertising account executives, bloggers, and the like.

Newsvendors who sell or distribute the material are generally not liable for the defamation unless it can be proved they knew of the defamatory information or should have known about it before distributing it. They are called *secondary publishers*.

If someone repeats the defamation, they are known as a *re-publisher*. They, like a primary publisher, can be held liable even if they believe the defamation is false. Reporters and others often mistakenly believe that if they accurately quote someone who is libeling another, it relieves them of any responsibility for the libel they are spreading. This is not true. All they have done is accurately repeated the libel.

• Damage

In many cases, the plaintiff must prove the damage to his reputation. In other words, he must show that as a result of the defamation, people thought less of his integrity, honesty, etc., and so his business suffered and he is therefore entitled to some kind of specific monetary award. In other instances, damages may be presumed. The distinction often turns on the kind of defamation involved.

The law recognizes two forms of defamation—*libel*, or printed or recorded defamation, and *slander*, which is spoken defamation. Of the two, libel is considered the more damaging because it can theoretically do more harm. Once words are spoken, they dissipate into the air and their ability to damage is gone. But libel, or printed defamation, can be seen or read repeatedly and therefore continue to do damage. Libel can include words, pictures, cartoons, and any other communication that is somehow made permanent. A libelous statement repeated orally is still considered libel.

The legal distinction between libel and slander has become less pronounced with the advent of radio and TV. Though both utilize the spoken word, and thus generate problems of slander, the ability of broadcast media to reach large audiences has given them the ability to inflict an equally extensive amount of damage. Too, since broadcast messages are often scripted or recorded on audiotape or videotape, the difference between libel and slander, when it comes to the media, is often indistinguishable. For some cases, however, and for those not involving the mass media, the distinction still can be important.

Most courts consider mass media defamation to be libel. To classify it as such, courts will look to how permanent the defamation is (is it recorded?), how many people did it reach, and how spontaneous was the statement (Did the defamer think about it before he disseminated it?).

When it comes to libel, the Court recognizes two kinds—*libel per se* (libel on its face) and *libel per quod* (when the addition of outside facts make it libelous). To falsely call someone a "heartless thief" is *libel per se*. The words themselves carry the sting. To report inaccurately that someone played tennis on Saturday instead of Sunday and finding out later that he is devoutly Jewish (as in the example above) is libel per quod.

In almost all libel cases, damages may be classified as *general damages* for such intangibles as pain and suffering, or they may be *presumed* damages and need not be proven. Judges and juries award these damages to cover the general loss to a plaintiff's reputation. A few Courts require damages for libel per quod cases to be proven. These are referred to as *special damages*. To prove special damages the plaintiff must show a specific monetary loss, such as the loss of a business deal or inheritance. The humiliation alone will not suffice.

With regard to slander, or spoken defamation, damages are usually not presumed. The plaintiff must prove special damages. This is true unless the slanderous statement harms a business or reflects on someone's ability to conduct his business (such as saying someone is a cheat), or charges that someone has a loathsome disease, or claims someone is immoral (such as suggesting someone is an adulterer), or suggests a woman is unchaste. In those instances, damages may be presumed.

* * *

Defamation, until 1964, was largely a matter of state common law, but First Amendment concerns and cases have added elements of federal law in situations involving public officials, public figures, and private people engaged in matters of public concern. This has been done to protect the mass media. This combination of federal and state law makes this area of law more complex and complicated today when dealing with such matters. As to state defamation law, the principles are similar from state to state, however important variations remain. Journalists and others should familiarize themselves with the media laws in the states where they work.

The above four elements are left over from English common law and involve "simple" libel or libel that does not involve public officials, public figures or private people engaged in "matters of public concern." When such cases do involve those people, however, the plaintiff must prove two more elements—falsity and fault. Since stories that appear in the media are generally about public figures or "matters of public concern," most plaintiffs suing the media must prove these two elements. (Private persons speaking on private matters who are libeled fall under the common law requirements and need not prove the additional two elements.)

* * *

• Falsity

The plaintiff—if he is a public official or public figure, or a private individual speaking on a matter of public concern—must prove that the offending statement made about him was false. (Under traditional common law requirements, the defamatory statement was *presumed* to be false. The burden was on the defendant, if he wished to defeat the claim against him, to prove that the offending statement he made about the plaintiff was true.)

• Fault

The plaintiff must show that the defendant was at fault in making the defamatory statement. Again, the fault requirement varies depending upon whether the plaintiff is a public official or public figure, or a private person involved in a matter of public concern.

For public officials and public figures, the fault requirement is *malice*. Malice is defined by the Court as "knowledge of falsity or reckless disregard for the truth." The plaintiff, therefore, must prove with "clear and convincing evidence" that the defendant knew that the information he was about to publish was false or that the defendant entertained serious doubts about its veracity. In other words, the defendant knew he was lying or entertained serious doubts about the information he was about to publish. (The common dictionary definition of malice being ill will or hatred does not qualify. How the defendant *felt* about the plaintiff doesn't matter.)

A *public official* is someone who has been elected or appointed to office and is responsible for making public policy, spending public money or overseeing public welfare. As such, the public has a rightful interest in the official's performance and can comment on him with regard to matters that affect that person's job performance. This does not mean that just because someone is a public official that the media can write anything about them they want and claim that if they are sued the public official must prove malice. Even public officials have private lives. The matter being discussed must relate to their fitness for office or their performance on the job.

The same can be said for public figures. Just because someone is famous does not give the media carte blanche to write whatever it pleases. The public person must have done something that generates interest in which the public has a rightful concern.

Public figures are divided into two different classifications—all-purpose public figures and limited-purpose public figures.

An *all-purpose public figure* is someone who has achieved *pervasive fame or notoriety* and as such is widely known in the public eye. A movie star or sports celebrity would qualify as an all-purpose public person. Since they have voluntarily put themselves on the public stage, they are open to public commentary and criticism.

A *limited-purpose public figure* is someone who has voluntarily taken on a major role in some public controversy. A community activist advocating for a certain outcome in a public dispute would be such an example. Such individuals are considered public figures only for matters concerning that controversy. Again, the public has a legitimate interest in their involvement. The classification comes from *Gertz v. Welch*, 418 U.S. 323 (1974), and will be discussed later.

If the plaintiff is a *private person speaking on a matter of public concern*, the fault requirement is *negligence*. Negligence is a lesser standard than malice, and is defined as "failure to exercise reasonable care." The Court will determine if negligence exists by asking whether the defendant made a good faith effort to determine the truth of the report before publishing it. Did the defendant fail to read relevant documents or not edit his work properly? Damages are limited to actual injury, which requires evidence of some harm to reputation. Damages are not presumed. The level of fault is less in situations involving private people speaking on matters of public concern because private people don't have the same access to the media that public people do, and they are, therefore, less able to defend themselves. The Court, in essence, is making it easier for them to win their lawsuit.

To determine if something is a "matter of public concern," the Court will look to the *content, form, and context* of the matter that was published.

In short, public people have a harder time winning against the media. They must prove those in the media knew or questioned what they were reporting was false. Whereas, a private person speaking on a matter of public concern needs to only prove that the media did not do its job with the proper care needed.

*   *   *

The U.S. Supreme Court added the previous two elements as a result of what is arguably the most important media law case in U.S.

history—*New York Times Co. v. Sullivan*, 376 U.S. 254 (1964). Other cases later expanded and refined the law regarding media libel. They also are reviewed below.

The New York Times Co. v. Sullivan and Public Officials

The case emerged during the turbulent civil rights era of the 1960s. Blacks, often with white support, participated in nonviolent marches through the streets of mostly southern cities in support of racial equality. Much of the white Press in the South ignored the protests, but larger, northern media outlets often covered them. The press coverage angered many segregationists, especially when the stories detailed violent acts against the protestors, often with the approval or, in some cases, participation of government officials.

littleny/Shutterstock.com

As part of the effort to detail abuses and garner support for their cause, a coalition of civil-rights leaders placed a full-page advertisement/editorial in *The New York Times* under the headline "Heed Their Rising Voices." The "advertorial" charged that police in southern states had used violent and illegal tactics against the protesters.

Although the essential claims of the text were true, it did contain some minor factual errors. (For example, when Alabama State College students protested, the ad claimed police "ringed" the campus. In fact, the police were there, but they did not "ring" the campus.)

As a result, several public officials, including Montgomery, Alabama, police commissioner L.B. Sullivan, sued for libel in Alabama state court, an appropriate venue since the newspaper had been circulated there and libel involving the media was only a matter of state law at the time. Sullivan's case was the first to go to trial. He sought $500,000 in damages from the *Times*. Sullivan had not been identified by name in the article, but he argued that it was nevertheless "of and concerning" him since he was in charge of the police. The jury quickly found in his favor. The case was appealed to the Alabama Supreme Court, which also ruled in his favor.

As a matter of state law, the case was over. However, in an effort to overturn the judgment, *Times'* leaders appealed to the U.S. Supreme Court claiming an issue of federal law was at stake—the First Amendment.

In a 9–0 decision, the Court agreed, reversing the Alabama Supreme Court decision and ruling that the First Amendment required Sullivan to prove a higher standard of fault against the newspaper than simple libel required. The Court said Sullivan would have to prove that the *Times* published the article knowing it was false or that it entertained serious doubts as to its veracity. Simple factual errors would not be enough. The Court called this new standard *actual malice*. Henceforth, the Court said all *public officials* who believed they had been libeled because of allegations about their job fitness or job performance would have to prove malice.

Justice William Brennan explained that the new rule was important to protect the Press and promote unfettered debate of important issues in a free society.

"We consider this case against the background of a profound national commitment to the principle that debate on public issues should be uninhibited, robust, and wide-open," he noted, adding that those in public service should understand that their actions would be scrutinized and criticized by the public. He said because of their status in the public eye that they also had more recourse to defend themselves in the media than ordinary citizens.

The result of the ruling was to embolden the Press, especially in terms of its "watchdog" role of government. Suddenly, those in the media didn't need to worry that simple errors would get them into trouble.

The Impact of *The New York Times Co v. Sullivan* Case

The ramifications of the ruling were enormous. For the first time, the Court drew a distinction between libel involving private people and private matters, and libel involving public officials and matters of public concern that were reported in the media.

When it comes to the former, the Court said First Amendment free press rights are not at issue, and federal law need not apply. In those cases, the law remains what it has always been—a simple state common law tort in which the plaintiff needs to only prove the four elements of defamation, identification, publication, and damage.

But in cases involving public officials and matters of public concern that find their way into the media, the Court said it must look not only to state libel law requirements when deciding matters of defamation but also to the federal First Amendment protections of the Press.

The Court reasoned that the First Amendment was established to eliminate seditious libel. The people, in a democracy, had a right to criticize those government institutions and officials who were established and elected to do their bidding. Further, as a people who would mean to be their own governors, they had a right to know about and discuss matters of public concern. Such is the essential nature of any democracy and of any democratic government. The First Amendment was adopted to protect that interest by protecting the media's efforts to maintain the free flow of information about these things—which included public officials involved in issues that would be of legitimate interest.

The Court further reasoned that without the *Times'* case ruling any simple mistake impugning someone's reputation that found its way into print or onto the airwaves, as part of a matter of public concern, could become a case of libel. The news media deal with thousands of stories a day. The fear of getting just one of them wrong would create a chilling effect and undermine this essential tool of democracy. In short, the media would be too scared to print or broadcast controversial matters that might incur the wrath of public officials.

Thus, to protect that First Amendment interest, the Court said in the *Times'* ruling that the plaintiff in such cases must prove two additional elements—falsity and fault.

The falsity element was important, too, because the Court in essence said the only reason the First Amendment protects a free press is to enable it to disseminate matters of public concern to the people so they can govern themselves. Therefore, it makes no sense to protect the Press when it undermines that mission by lying. The law will not become a party to that which undermines the democracy. Consequently, if the plaintiff can show that the media defendant knew what he was publishing was false or entertained serious doubts as to its truthfulness, First Amendment protection drops and the plaintiff wins.

The ruling has been hailed by those in the media as establishing a bastion of free Press protection, but not all legal scholars and judges agree with it. Some assert the Supreme Court read its own views into the First Amendment. They note that such an interpretation is nowhere to be found in the text as provided by the Founders. Nevertheless, the Court held that without this interpretation, seditious libel laws would again return to curb government criticism as they had before the American Revolution.

In any case, when it comes to free press rights, the decision has been the law of the land for more than 50 years and is not likely to be overturned.

The short of it is that for the first time, as a result of this case, a *public official* suing a mass media defendant over matters of public concern had to prove the elements of falsity and fault.

Public Figures

Subsequent libel cases expanded and refined the Sullivan rule. The *Times* case applied to *public officials*. But the Court held in two other cases it considered simultaneously that the malice requirement would also apply to those who were *public figures*. Although they had no control of government affairs, public figures, too, were of legitimate public interest, had placed themselves in the public spotlight, and had access to the media to correct any damage to their reputation.

The cases were *Curtis Publishing Co. v. Butts*, 388 U.S. 130 (1967), and *Associated Press v. Walker*, 388 U.S. 130 (1967).

In the first case, an article ran in *The Saturday Evening Post* (published by the Curtis Publishing Co.) about an attempt to "fix" a 1962 football game. The article alleged that Wally Butts, athletic director at the University of Georgia, had been on the phone with Alabama head coach Paul "Bear" Bryant giving him game plans before an upcoming contest between the two rivals. The magazine based its false report on notes taken by Atlanta insurance agent George Burnett who said that he accidentally overheard the telephone conversation between the two men. Editors made no effort to check out the story or review and verify the notes. Nor did they check with any other sources.

The Court said there was ample evidence to support a finding of "highly unreasonable conduct constituting an extreme departure from the standards of investigation and reporting ordinarily adhered to by responsible publishers." The Court said the editor's actions amounted to a *reckless disregard for the truth* and voted 5–4 to uphold Butts' half million dollar judgment.

In the second case, Edwin Walker, a retired major general, sued the *Associated Press* for stories that alleged he personally had taken command of violent protesters. The stories reported that he led the protesters in a charge against federal marshals who had been sent to the University of Mississippi to help maintain the peace during attempts to enroll the first black student there in 1962. Walker denied the allegations and said that he counseled the whites to remain peaceful. He denied leading the charge. The false statements about his actions were attributed to other media.

The Court unanimously overruled Walker's half a million dollar judgment against the *Associated Press*. The Court said the cases differed. In the *Butts'* case the magazine had ample time to check the facts of the story, but did not. While in the *Walker* case, time was limited. The wire service was on deadline to get the story out, and the reporter who covered the story had a reputation for accuracy. Furthermore, Walker's conduct was in line with his previous statements critical of desegregation.

The Court held both men to the same fault standard as public officials since they were involved in issues "in which the public has a justified and important interest." Thus, the ruling extended the *Times'* rule to *public figures*.

Limited-Purpose Public Figures

More often, a person can be a public person in a very limited sense. Unlike all-purpose public figures, these people are in the public eye because they have often stepped forward to influence the resolution of a particular controversy. Such people would include local activists.

The Court took up the question of limited-purpose public figures in *Gertz v. Robert Welch, Inc.*, 418 U.S. 323 (1974) and found that in some instances it is possible to step in and out of the limelight. In other words, in some situations a person can be considered a private person while in others he might be considered a public person.

Elmer Gertz was a private lawyer engaged to represent a black family in a civil suit for the wrongful death of their son who had been killed by a Chicago police officer. *American Opinion*, the magazine of the ultraconservative John Birch Society, ran an article calling Gertz a communist who was out to discredit law enforcement. Gertz sued Robert Welch, the publisher. Gertz initially won a $50,000 judgment, but the trial judge overturned the verdict. The Court said Gertz had not proved malice, which he needed to do because he was held to a public figure as a result of his advocacy of civil rights reform. Gertz appealed to the U.S. Supreme Court.

In a 5–4 decision, the Court made a distinction between private people and public figures. The Court said Gertz was a prominent lawyer, but had done nothing to reach public figure status *in this case*. He was simply a lawyer in private practice doing his job. He had made no attempt to put himself on a soapbox and sway public opinion on the matter of civil rights. Had he done so, and had the case concerned his activities in such matters, he would have been considered a public figure and had to prove malice.

The case, therefore, drew a distinction between public persons and limited-purpose public persons.

The question of limited-purpose public people also came up in *Time, Inc. v. Firestone*, 424 U.S. 448 (1976), which involved a divorce action of a Florida socialite named Mary Alice Firestone, who was married to Firestone tire heir Russell Firestone. Because of the prominence of the family, the press coverage was extensive.

Time magazine reported that one of the grounds for divorce was adultery, but since Florida law prohibited alimony in matters of adultery and alimony had been awarded, the allegation was false. Mary Firestone sued. Although she gave two press conferences on the divorce, the Court said that she was not a public figure since she had not thrust herself into a public controversy. She had been drawn into it.

The Court's decision in this and other cases prevents *bootstrapping* or creating a matter of public concern by putting someone's name in the news and then claiming they are a public figure and must prove malice to win a libel suit. Although the Court said that it might be possible for someone to become a public figure without acting, the Court said that the plaintiff in almost all situations must voluntarily enter into a public controversy and seek to affect its outcome before such a distinction could be made. Further, the public controversy must have existed prior to the publication of the material that gave rise to the defamation.

Thus, as a result of this decision and others, the Court has modified its ruling somewhat when it comes to public figures. Just because someone is famous or someone has been dragged into court does not make that individual a public person for purposes of libel law. The general rule today is that unless someone voluntarily thrusts himself into the resolution of a public controversy or in some other way voluntarily enters the limelight, they may not be considered public figures. Under this rule, therefore, even famous people may not qualify. The Court seems to be saying it all depends upon what they are doing as to whether they generate a matter of public concern.

It should be noted again that without proof of malice, private plaintiffs are unable to win presumed or punitive damages against the defendant. Punitive damages are awarded to punish the defendant for defaming the plaintiff. Thus, private persons suing the media who only need to prove negligence can only receive damages for harm actually incurred as a result of general injury to reputation, such as loss of friends, humiliation, etc. These are otherwise known as general damages. Or the plaintiff may be entitled to special damages, which means that the plaintiff must show a pecuniary loss as a result of the defamation, such as the loss of a specific gift or inheritance.

Businesses as Public Figures

Businesses and corporations can be classified as public figures and sue for libel if the business tried to affect the outcome of a public controversy regarding a public issue. In this regard, it would be considered a limited-purpose public figure. In making such a distinction, the Court might look to several factors, including:

1. Whether the business used a highly unusual advertising campaign to draw attention to its cause.
2. Whether the business was well known.
3. Whether the business was regulated in some way by the government.
4. Whether the business comment focused on a matter of public concern.
5. Whether the business generally attracted media scrutiny.

• Product Disparagement

Casting aspersions on a business product instead of a business is often referred to as *trade libel*, or more properly, *product disparagement*. As noted, in certain situations, businesses can be classified as public figures. In product disparagement, the defamation isn't of a person, but a thing, and therefore, cannot be properly defined as libel. Nevertheless, untrue claims about a product can and do harm businesses and are actionable.

To win a case of product disparagement, the plaintiff must prove that

1. The statements about the product are false,
2. A specific monetary loss has occurred as a result of the false criticism, and
3. Actual malice is present.

Many states have passed laws protecting certain products or services, including banks, insurance companies, and even vegetables. The statutes often require the defendant to prove that what he said about the product was true.

Public Persons and the Passage of Time

Generally, someone who is a public person today will be considered a public person later, but only for matters that related to their public status in the first place.

In 2002, the 10th U.S. Court of Appeals ruled in *Revell v. Hoffman*, 309 F.3d 1228, that the former associate deputy director of the Federal Bureau of Investigation retained his public status with regard to a libel suit based on a book about the Oklahoma City bombing. Noted the Court:

> *That the person defamed no longer holds the same position does not by itself strip him of this status as a public official for constitutional purposes. If the defamatory remarks relate to his conduct while he was a public official and the manner in which he performed his responsibilities is still a matter of public interest, he remains a public official within the meaning of New York Times.*

It is important to note that the Court found that public interest in the issue was still present. If public interest is no longer present, retaining public person status is dubious.

Defenses to Libel

The burden of establishing a libel case rests with the plaintiff. But once all the necessary elements of libel have been shown and the prima facie case has been made, the burden shifts to the defendant to prove, nevertheless, why the case against him should fail.

In most cases, the defendant has an easier task. While the plaintiff must prove that each and every element of libel is present before the case can move forward, the defendant only needs to prove that one of the elements is missing.

In other cases, however, the defendant's task can be equally difficult. Often the information that led to the libel claim may be true, but may be inadmissible in court because it was based on hearsay. In the case of an investigative story, the reporter may have used confidential sources and is unable reveal their identities without breaking an oral agreement. Without the means to corroborate his report, the defendant will lose.

In addition to understanding those elements of libel that must be established by the plaintiff, media students must also understand the various defenses that are available to counter a libel claim. The following is a summary of them.

• Truth

The most complete defense to any libel claim is truth because libel is, by definition, a false claim against another that damages their reputation.

If the defendant can prove that what he said about the plaintiff is true, he can show that no defamation exists. To call a *convicted* murderer a murderer is not libelous. It is a true statement.

However, in matters of public concern, the burden, as noted earlier, is on the plaintiff to prove falsity; so only in cases involving matters of private concern does the defendant need to prove truth. (Even in those cases, some states now require all libel plaintiffs to prove that the libelous statements are false.)

• Summary Judgment

Perhaps the best defense in any libel case is not to have to give one at all. As previously discussed, if the case cannot move forward because the plaintiff cannot prove one of the elements of libel, the defendant can move for summary judgment. If the Court grants the motion, the case ends and the plaintiff loses. In a *summary judgment* ruling, the Court decides the case without trial. Nearly three-fourths of all cases end in summary judgment.

However, the U.S. Supreme Court has said that in making such a ruling, the Court must review the motion to dismiss in a way that's most favorable to the party opposing the motion. That means that if there are any facts that need to be settled at trial, and the defense moves for summary judgment, the judge must deny the motion so the dispute can be resolved. Either side can move for summary judgment.

• Statute of Limitations

The time to file a lawsuit is limited. In most civil and criminal matters, *statutes of limitations* determine how long someone has to file a civil suit or the state has to file a criminal action against a defendant. The plaintiff or the prosecutor can't afford to wait too long. If too much time passes, the statute of limitations bars their case and the defendant avoids trial.

The statute of limitations for libel varies from one to three years, depending upon the laws of the state where the trial is to be held. The clock begins ticking the day the libel was published, posted or broadcast and the public had access to it.

Lightspring/Shutterstock.com

• Privilege

The Founders understood that democracy required open and robust debate. Consequently, Article 1, Section 6 of the U.S. Constitution creates an **absolute privilege** for members of Congress to say anything during debates on the floor of the House or Senate and not be sued. Since the founding, this absolute privilege has been expanded to include other national, state, and local legislative bodies and government officials and proceedings. The executive branch and courts are covered as well. Thus, speeches by the president or testimony of witnesses and arguments of lawyers in Court are protected.

The privilege also attaches to documents and publications by a public official directly concerning their *official duties*. Thus, legislative and presidential reports or any reports by a governor, mayor, or other department leader are protected. So too are court documents.

In fact, all such utterances and documents are protected absolutely as long as they are part of an official proceeding or concern official business.

The privilege, however, does not cover officials or other citizens when they are not engaged in official business. Therefore, a council member's comments during a city council meeting recess would not be privileged. Likewise, a citizen's testimony in court would be protected during trial, but his comments afterwards would not be. In some states, court documents are not privileged until they are introduced into the court process or addressed by a judge.

The Court has broadened the concept of privilege to include what it calls **qualified privilege**. Recognizing that the people have both a right and need to know what their government is doing, the Court has thus affirmed the news media's limited privilege to report on official matters.

Qualified privilege allows the news media to report about government proceedings and documents without fear of getting sued if such documents contain libelous material so long as the media reports them in a "fair and accurate" manner. Fair means that all sides of any dispute are reported. Accurate means that the report is an honest account of the matters being discussed.

Courts have also suggested that a report means just that—a report. It should not include commentary. If the report changes the substantial meaning of what happened at the meeting or what was in the document, the privilege will be lost. A report that is not fair or does not report the matter in context will not be protected. This does not mean the report must be a verbatim account of what happened. An accurate and balanced summary is sufficient. Most states follow the rule that the reporters don't have to believe the report or document, only that they report it accurately.

Qualified privilege then is just that; it is conditional. Where absolute privilege cannot be lost, qualified privilege may be. If a report or speech contains libelous material and the journalist gets the report wrong, he can be still be sued. On the other hand, if the report contains libelous material and he gets the report right, he is protected in spite of the libelous statement.

The reporter bears the burden of proving that privilege applies to any libelous material he reports. The judge will determine if privilege attaches to the proceeding or document. The jury will determine if the newsperson's report is fair and accurate.

The problem of what is and is not privileged can been confusing, and the law varies from state to state.

For example, police reports are protected; off-the-cuff hunches by an officer may not be. Official comments by government leaders are covered; comments by lesser officials may not be. At the same time, the

Restatement of the Law of Torts notes that if public meetings are open to the public and matters of public concern are discussed, the reports of those proceedings are privileged. On the other hand, if a lawyer tells you that he is filing suit against someone, it is generally better to wait until he does so before writing the story.

To illustrate the problem of trying to determine when something is privileged and when it is not, even in the case of absolute privilege, consider the case of *Hutchinson v. Proxmire*, 443 U.S. 11 (1979). Sen. William Proxmire, D-Wis, presented his "Golden Fleece of the Month Award" to various individuals and organizations wasting taxpayer money. One such award was given to Dr. Ronald Hutchinson, a mental health researcher, for using government grants to study the habits of monkeys under stress. Hutchinson sued, claiming the award damaged his professional reputation.

Proxmire had sent out press releases to the media notifying them of each month's winners. The Court said the privilege defense did not protect him from the libel charge in this case since he reported his award outside of official proceedings. Had he made them in the *Congressional Record*, the Court said that they would have been privileged, but since he sent out a press release that was not directly related to his official duties, privilege did not attach.

• Fair Comment and Criticism

Writers, artists, entertainers, teachers, ministers, owners of businesses, institutions, and anyone else who places themselves in the public eye invites public comment and criticism. As such the centuries-old common law defense of *fair comment and criticism* protects them.

Theater critics, art critics, and even restaurant patrons are free to express their opinions on the work of others so long as their comments are considered a matter of public concern, are based on true facts, represent the opinion of the speaker, and are not made solely for the purpose of harming someone. A distinction must be made between assaulting the work and impugning the creator's character, reputation, or competence.

This defense has been eclipsed largely by the broader First Amendment protection of opinion.

• Opinion

The U.S. Supreme Court ruled in 1991 that the First Amendment protects pure opinion. This constitutional defense makes it stronger and more effective than the common law defense of fair comment.

Even before the ruling, the Court noted that First Amendment protection is warranted because opinion is essential to the democratic process. As U.S. Supreme Court Justice Louis Brandeis noted nearly a century ago, "[F]reedom to think as you will and speak as you think are means indispensable to the discovery and spread of political truth."

The problem comes in trying to determine when something is a false fact, and therefore potentially libelous, and when it is just a bad opinion, and constitutionally protected. The Court said adding the words, "in my opinion," or "I believe" isn't enough to protect against libel. Rather, the question in every case is whether the statement made by the defendant can be proven true or false. The key question is whether a reasonable reader would conclude from the words that the writer was stating a fact. To say someone is a "liar" can be proven. To say someone is "beyond ignorant" cannot. Thus, to say, "I believe he is a liar," suggests the reporter knows a fact others do not. Adding the words 'I believe" makes no difference.

A lower court finally came up with a way to help determine fact from opinion in *Ollman v. Evans*, 750 F.2d 970 (1985). In that case, Bertell Ollman, a political science professor at New York University, sued syndicated columnists Rowland Evans and Robert Novak for libel after they accused Ollman of being a Marxist and using his position as a professor to indoctrinate students. In deciding the case, the Court used a four-part test. They asked the following questions:

1. Could the statement be proved true? This was critical. Facts can be proven; opinions cannot.
2. What words were used and what was their ordinary meaning? Calling someone a jerk is obviously meant to be an opinion. Was it a matter of **rhetorical hyperbole**, an exaggerated statement not to be taken seriously or literally? (Such statements as "he must be out of his mind" and "he's an idiot" are protected as opinion.) Likewise, **satire** and **parody** are also protected.

3. **In what journalistic context was the statement made?** Was the
   offending statement in a news story, or was it in a column or letter
   to the editor where opinion would expect to be found?
4. **In what social context was the statement made?** Was the statement
   made at a political convention, or was it made in a scientific article?
   One contains heated debate; the other contains verified facts.

The U.S. Supreme Court emphasized the importance of determining
fact from opinion in *Milkovich v. Lorain Journal Co.*, 497 U.S. 1 (1990).
In Milkovich, the Court held that a statement in a sports column, normally a place for commentary, could be construed as a fact because of
the way it was written. The sports columnist had accused a wrestling
coach in Ohio of lying under oath following an investigation of a disruption at a wrestling match. The Court ruled that just because facts
are imbedded in a column would not make them opinion.

Furthermore, the facts on which the opinion is based must be accurate.
To comment that a teacher grades unfairly when the facts say otherwise
would be troublesome. Also, leaving important facts out of a story so
that it changes the meaning will not insulate the defendant from an
effective libel suit.

• Jurisdiction

Generally speaking, publishers may be sued in any state where they
circulate the defamatory material. Thus, a resident of New York can sue
an Ohio publication in New Hampshire if the publication distributed
damaging information about the resident in New Hampshire. The U.S.
Supreme Court held such action was permissible in *Keeton v. Hustler*,
465 U.S. 770 (1984). The Court noted that defamatory information
"harm(s) both the subject of the falsehood and the readers of the statement." Therefore, the state where the defamatory information was
circulated "may employ its libel laws to discourage the deception of
its citizens."

Consequently, a journalist who defames someone in another state may
have to defend himself in that state's courts.

When it comes to libel suits in foreign countries, journalists and others now have a bit more protection. President Barack Obama signed
the SPEECH Act (Securing the Protection of our Enduring and

Established Constitutional Heritage) in 2010. The law, which applies to both state and federal courts, protects Americans from foreign libel judgments if such actions would fail in the United States because of First Amendment infringement or a constitutional violation of due process rights.

Defamation on the Internet is treated much the same as defamation elsewhere, holding *originators* of defamation liable.

When it comes to Internet service providers such as YouTube, Facebook, or Twitter, however, the law offers more protection. *Section 230 of the Telecommunications Act of 1996* provides that these and other interactive computer service providers are not liable for the content of a message they carry on the Internet from someone else.

The law differs from what is required of traditional media by giving online providers broader protection. Newspapers and magazines are responsible for repeating a libel under the common law republication rule. Broadcasters, too, can be held liable for libelous statements made by callers on talk shows.

If the online provider *creates* the libelous content, however, the law does not grant them immunity.

• Neutral Reportage

Despite the republication rule, a limited number of courts have recognized the *neutral reportage* defense, which provides that responsible news reporting done fairly, evenly, and objectively should be protected under the First Amendment principle that the free flow of information is important. Thus, if someone in the news makes libelous accusations against another and the media publishes them neutrally, the publisher should be protected from libel. This holds even if the publisher had serious doubts about their veracity.

Courts that accept the defense look to see if the defamatory statements are 1. newsworthy and about a public controversy; 2. made by a prominent source; 3. reportedly objectively, neutrally, and accurately; and 4. about a public official or person.

This rule is not widely accepted because it eliminates the publisher's responsibility of making sure the report is accurate.

• Wire Service Defense

The republication issue is also at the heart of the *wire service defense*. Newspapers, TV, and radio stations and other media often contract with wire service companies to provide them with news from across the country and abroad because it is too expensive for most media to send their own reporters. However, verifying information from half-way around the world is difficult. Mistakes that lead to libel could be imbedded in a story, and the news organization that received it would have no way of knowing.

Again, a limited number of Courts have held that if the news organization republishes the wire report accurately, the organization is not at fault. This defense is available if 1. The wire service is reputable; 2. The news organization that received the information did not know it was false; 3. There was nothing on the face of the report that would indicate it was false; and 4. The wire report was published without major changes.

• Single Publication Rule

The single publication rule holds that once a matter has been published republication does not mean a new libel has been committed. The entire edition of a newspaper or other publication is a single publication, and reissues are not republications. This applies to Internet publications as well unless the content changes and new libel is published.

• Libel-Proof Plaintiffs

In some cases, a libel plaintiff's reputation may be so bad that his reputation cannot be damaged any more. But courts also have noted that just because someone holds a bad reputation in one area doesn't mean their reputation is impugned in other areas. For example, just because someone is a drug user doesn't mean calling him a thief couldn't damage his reputation further. Thus, the defense will depend upon the circumstances of each case.

• Section 315 of the Federal Communications Commission Act

The difference between print and broadcast libel is minimal. However the U.S. Supreme Court has exempted broadcasters from libel claims generated by political advertising. Under the *Section 315 rule of the*

Federal Communications Act, broadcasters are forbidden to censor political ads. Thus, the Court will not hold them responsible for libelous statements made by candidates. However, this does not prevent the candidate from being sued.

• Consent

Those who *consent* to defamation will find it difficult to come back later and sue. Obviously, this rarely happens. Nevertheless, if Bill tells Mary he has heard rumors that she is involved in prostitution and asks if he can publish them in the newspaper and she consents, she likely will not be able to win a libel suit later. The consent will not be valid unless the defamed party understood the full extent of the defamation in advance.

• Right of Reply

Another rare defense is *right of reply*. Often referred to as the right of self-defense, it allows people to reply to a defamatory statement with a defamatory statement of their own and not be sued. The catch is they can't increase the provocation.

The defense only helps the mass media if it was not involved in the defamation. In other words, it merely served as a communication platform for both adversaries. If one of the defamed parties sues the media, the media can plead right of reply in that both parties responded to the libel equally.

• Retractions

Retraction statements usually do not eliminate a charge of libel, but they may be effective in mitigating the damages caused by one. A retraction is an apology for libeling someone and an attempt to set the record straight. Thirty-three states have retraction statutes.

Typically, the statutes require that those who are defamed ask the publisher or broadcaster of the libelous statement for a retraction before the state will allow them to proceed with their lawsuit. If the retraction is granted promptly and the apology and correction are prominently displayed according to the provisions of the statute, the right to sue may be denied, or if the matter is allowed to proceed to trial, any award of damages may be limited.

Retraction statutes vary from state to state. Media professionals should familiarize themselves with the laws of the state in which they work.

DEFAMATION FLOW CHART

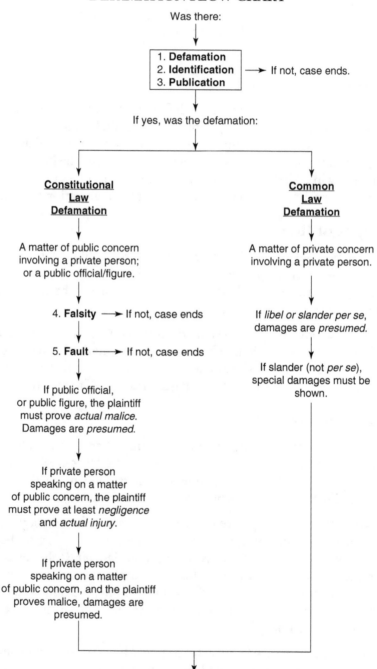

Was there:

1. **Defamation**
2. **Identification** ———► If not, case ends.
3. **Publication**

If yes, was the defamation:

Constitutional Law Defamation

A matter of public concern involving a private person; or a public official/figure.

4. **Falsity** ———► If not, case ends

5. **Fault** ———► If not, case ends

If public official, or public figure, the plaintiff must prove *actual malice*. Damages are *presumed*.

If private person speaking on a matter of public concern, the plaintiff must prove at least *negligence* and *actual injury*.

If private person speaking on a matter of public concern, and the plaintiff proves malice, damages are presumed.

Common Law Defamation

A matter of private concern involving a private person.

If *libel or slander per se*, damages are *presumed*.

If slander (not *per se*), special damages must be shown.

Punitive damages may be awarded where permitted.

CHAPTER 7

Invasion of Privacy

The Need to Be Let Alone

If reputation is important to the concept of ordered liberty, so too is the need for privacy. Privacy gives us the quiet time we need to discover ourselves. It insulates us from the everyday crush and noise of humanity. It gives us rest and allows us the secrecy of our own thoughts. Psychologists tell us it is necessary to mental health. Without the chance to escape inward to the sanctuary of solitude we would literally go crazy. As such, it is important to the maintenance of a civilized society.

Although people have long understood the value of privacy, the courts have only recently recognized it as something that deserves legal protection. Where libel law has been around for centuries, the idea that privacy should be a legal right was suggested in the late 1800s.

With population growth, the exodus from rural towns to big cities, the development of technology, and the increased power of business, the Press and government became forces of change at the end of the 19th century. Newspapers in particular began to focus on sensational stories about crime and scandal, and their technologically advanced presses could print enough copies to reach into the homes of millions. These combined forces were enough to change the culture. The country had entered into a new era that threatened a human condition people had taken for granted for thousands of years—the right to be let alone.

The beginnings of modern privacy law began in 1890 when two Boston lawyers, Samuel D. Warren and future U.S. Supreme Court Justice Louis D. Brandeis, published an article in the Harvard Law Review first suggesting that the courts recognize a right to privacy. Warren's prominent Boston family had occasionally been the focus of unflattering news columns. Noted the two:

> *Instantaneous photographs and newspaper enterprise have invaded the sacred precincts of private and domestic life; and numerous mechanical devices threaten to make good the prediction that 'what is whispered in the closet shall be proclaimed from the house-tops.'*

The two lawyers proposed in their article, "The Right to Privacy," that citizens should be able to get the courts to stop such invasions and also sue for damages. They argued that the basis for such action could be found in the common law.

> *The common law has always recognized a man's house as his castle, impregnable, often, even to its own officers engaged in the execution of its commands. Shall the courts thus close the front entrance to constituted authority, and open wide the back door to idle or prurient curiosity?*

Sources of Privacy Law

Although the courts initially were reluctant to find such a right, today the federal government and all but three states recognize some kind of a right to privacy. The courts have found it in the U.S. Constitution as well as in statutory, administrative, and common law.

The U.S. Constitution does not specifically mention the word "privacy," yet the U.S. Supreme Court has ruled that there is an *implied right* to privacy within the document. The Court has found it in the

Fourth Amendment that protects people from unreasonable searches and seizures in their homes, papers and effects. It is implicit in the Fifth Amendment that protects against self-incrimination. The Third Amendment prohibits the government from quartering soldiers in people's homes. And the Court has said that the word "liberty" in the 14th Amendment includes personal privacy. Therefore, although not specifically mentioned, the Court said that the evidence of it exists all through the document.

So why didn't the Founders note such an important concept in the document that was to be the law of the land? Perhaps it seemed too obvious to note. The Court has likened the right to privacy to the example of a penumbra—the ring of light that shines out from behind the moon during an eclipse of the sun. Although we can't see the sun, we know it is there because we see its effects. Likewise, the Court has said the effects of privacy are everywhere.

Too, since western law is based upon the concept of personal autonomy where people are legally responsible for their own actions, it seems logical that autonomy includes the characteristic of privacy. If we have rights and responsibilities as individuals, then we must have the right to private thoughts and actions.

Brandeis was to return to the issue of privacy later as a Supreme Court justice. In *Olmstead v. U.S.*, 277 U.S. 438 (1928), the Court ruled against suspected bootleggers during the era of prohibition in a case involving government eavesdropping to gain evidence. A majority of the Court said there was no privacy violation unless the government had physically trespassed to get the information. Brandeis dissented. He said the framers of the Constitution had intended for there to be a right to be let alone "to protect Americans in their beliefs, their thoughts, their emotions and their sensations. . . ."

Speaking of the Founders, Brandeis said, "[t]hey conferred, as against government, the right to be let alone—the most comprehensive of rights and the right most valued by civilized man."

The *Olmstead* decision that allowed government eavesdropping without physical trespass was reversed just over 40 years later in *Katz v. U.S.*, 389 U.S. 347 (1967). In that case the government had used electronic listening devices to gather information about illegal bookmaking. The Court extended the right to privacy by noting that the right extended to all areas where there was a *justifiable expectation of privacy*. No longer were privacy problems limited to matters of physical trespass. Electronic listening devices and other emerging technologies could violate the right as well.

The Court reaffirmed its decision in *Kyllo v. U.S.*, 533 U.S. 27 (2001), when it ruled against federal agents using heat-sensing equipment to find where marijuana was being grown. The Court said that use of the technology without a search warrant violated the Fourth Amendment right to privacy.

The Court has used the right to privacy in matters of contraception, abortion, and homosexuality as well. In *Griswold v. Connecticut*, 381 U.S. 479 (1965), the Court overturned a state law barring the use of contraceptives. Justice William Douglas declared that a couples' decision to use contraceptives was not the business of the state, but a matter of personal privacy.

In *Roe v Wade*, 410 U.S. 113 (1973), the Court also declared that abortions were a private matter, at least during the first six months of pregnancy. In a case that has generated decades of national debate, the Court drew a line between private and public concerns by holding that a woman's right to decide to have an abortion extended until the time the fetus became viable, that is, able to live outside the womb. At that point, the state's interest in protecting a citizen's right to life superseded the mother's right to an abortion.

As a result of the ruling, some states passed laws making it more difficult for a woman to get an abortion. Although the Court upheld some of these restrictions, it reaffirmed the right in *Planned Parenthood of SE Pennsylvania v. Casey*, 505 U.S. 833 (1992), noting that states could not place *undue burdens* on a woman's right to choose to have an abortion.

The Court also looked at privacy concerns in its rulings regarding homosexuality. In *Bowers v. Hardwick*, 478 U.S. 186 (1986), the Court upheld a Georgia law that prohibited sodomy. It ruled that even though privacy rights protected matters of contraception and abortion, they did not protect the rights of homosexuals to engage in private sexual acts. The Court changed its mind on the issue 17 years later. In *Lawrence v. Texas*, 539 U.S. 558 (2003), the Court voted 6–3 to overturn a similar Texas sodomy law, thus invalidating the *Bowers* ruling.

Federal and state statutes also protect privacy. For example, the Family Educational Rights and Privacy Act (FERPA) protects student educational records, and the Health Insurance Portability and Account-ability Act (HIPPA) protects health records. States have passed laws protecting the publicity rights of dead celebrities, autopsy photos, and other matters.

Under administrative law, the Federal Trade Commission has settled claims alleging privacy concerns on the Internet and problems regarding facial recognition technology.

The common law in the great majority of states recognizes four areas of privacy law—intrusion, disclosure of private facts, appropriation, and false light. Many cases today fall into one of these areas.

Contrasting Libel and Invasion of Privacy

Like libel, invasion of privacy is a tort. Both are largely a matter of state law though, as with libel, the federal courts have addressed constitutional concerns. For example, they have adopted the *New York Times v. Sullivan* principle in certain privacy cases of false light (which will be discussed later). The Court also has recognized that the media have a constitutional right to publish public records about people without fear of an invasion of privacy suit if those records are open to the public.

As with libel, only living individuals may sue for invasion of privacy; the dead have no personal rights, though a *right to publicity* does exist for deceased famous people. (The right enables the famous to continue to earn money off of their fame after death, thus benefiting their heirs.) Also, since invasion of privacy is a personal right, businesses, unions and other groups generally are unable to sue for invasion of privacy.

Yet, the two areas of law are also different in that they protect different property interests. Where libel laws protect one's reputation, privacy laws protect one's peace of mind. The defenses are also different. Truth is the ultimate defense against libel. In invasion of privacy cases, apart from the constitutional protections, the defenses are usually consent and newsworthiness.

The Growing Privacy Problem

Invasion of privacy promises to eclipse libel as the premier media concern and create greater problems for government and business as well. Today, the problem of privacy has grown so acute it has pushed many other issues aside and taken center stage in the national debate. Privacy concerns include the important issues of Internet hacking, government spying, identity theft, protection of minors, and continued concerns about personal rights regarding birth control and abortion. And the technological and societal changes that first created the problem have only grown to make it worse. Technology continues to make it easier to invade the space of others. And political events, some argue, have made it all but necessary.

As throughout American history, fundamental liberties often suffer during times of national crises. In fact, privacy rights have diminished since the September 11, 2001, attacks on the World Trade Center Buildings in New York City. Concerns over national security have led to the *Patriot Act*, which allows the government to obtain information about citizens from libraries, businesses, hospitals, Internet providers, and other places. This zeal to gain information also has led to a massive government surveillance of private citizens' phone records. As a result of these efforts, the United States has reportedly gathered personal information about millions of Americans from numerous sources.

Privacy has become a problem in the commercial world as well. Hacking of corporate computers has threatened business security. Businesses have found their financial records compromised.

Personal privacy is also at risk. Popular websites have installed tracking devices that enable data gathering companies to analyze the personal habits of citizens. Many smartphone applications send personal data to advertisers. The spread of such personal information has led to a national identity theft crises.

Meanwhile, many citizens seem oblivious to the dangers associated with the loss of privacy. They are willing to post personal information on numerous Internet sites that can be used by thieves and predators to create havoc.

All of these trends promise to make the problem of privacy worse.

Since the law of privacy is largely a matter of state law and generally falls within the four distinct areas of intrusion, disclosure of private facts, appropriation, and false light, it makes sense to review each of them separately.

• Intrusion

When Warren and Brandeis first suggested people should have a right to privacy, it was because of the prying eyes of a sensational Press. Although surreptitious investigations by the news media have led to important stories, interfering with another person's solitude and privacy with or without good cause can often be illegal. Snooping, eavesdropping, trespassing, and the like can result in both civil and criminal penalties.

The courts have ruled that **it is illegal to intrude physically or otherwise upon the privacy of another if the person has a reasonable expectation of privacy and the intrusion would be highly offensive to a reasonable person**. Only New York and Virginia don't recognize the tort. The intrusion can be by physical trespass or through the use of technology.

In all cases, the Court's main question will always be: "Did the plaintiff enjoy a reasonable expectation of privacy?"

To win a suit for invasion of privacy, the plaintiff must show that:

1. The defendant intruded into the affairs or seclusion of the plaintiff.
2. The intrusion would be objectionable to a reasonable person—that is, an average person in the community would be offended because the intrusion goes beyond the realm of ordinary decency, and
3. The intrusion was into something that was private.

Not all intrusion is illegal. The courts consistently have held that there is no right to privacy in those things that are already public. Thus, publishing the contents of public records that contain private information but are open to the public is not an invasion of privacy. Neither is taking someone's picture in a public place, such as a park or on a sidewalk (unless you are doing it for commercial gain, which will be discussed later). Generally, if the person can be heard or seen from a public place without the benefit of technological help, no expectation of privacy exists.

It would not be an invasion of privacy, therefore, to eavesdrop at a restaurant on a conversation that could be overheard by others, so long as it was done without the aid of a listening device. But even in a public restaurant, it would be an invasion if the listener bugged the centerpiece on the table. Likewise, using a ladder to look over a seven-foot fence to take someone's picture would be an invasion. Using a telephoto lens also might be an invasion if it intruded into an area not visible to the naked eye. Taking someone's picture when they are in plain view of a public street, however, is not.

Copyright © of Mark Zimmerman. Reprinted by permission.

Also, it is sometimes difficult to know what is public and what is private. Just because taxpayers own government land, does not make it open to the public. Trespassing onto a military base without permission will result in arrest. It is permissible to enter a business to buy products and services, but it is not always permissible to enter for other reasons.

Consent is the main and sometimes only defense in all invasion of privacy cases. The consent should be explicit. The Press and others often rely upon something called *implied consent*, but just because a reporter begins asking questions and the interviewee answers does not mean the person has given their consent to have their comments recorded or published. In the majority of cases, the defense may well work, but implied consent is weak at best. Some states require consent regarding certain matters to be in writing. Newsworthiness is generally not a viable defense, though in some instances it can mitigate the harm by negating the offensiveness of the intrusion.

Also, in the matter of secret recordings, most states and the federal government require that at least one party to the conversation consent to the recording, but in others, such as California, all parties must consent to the conversation. If a person consents, they cannot come back later and claim an invasion has occurred.

Invasion of privacy occurs with the intrusion; unlike in a case of libel, publication is not required. Just entering someone's home without the occupant's permission is enough to violate the law. It is how the information is gathered that matters, not whether it is published.

Intrusion Cases

Invasion of privacy cases are varied. To add to the problem, different courts in different states often view the same matter differently. As such, the decisions are somewhat inconsistent, and finding a general rule to follow is difficult. The following cases are representative of the different subject areas that confront the Court.

Ride-alongs. Just because police can enter someone's home with a search warrant doesn't mean that they have the authority to invite news people inside with them. In *Wilson v. Layne*, 526 U.S. 603 (1999), the Supreme Court held it is a violation of the Fourth Amendment for journalists to enter a home with police without the consent of the residents.

In this case, the police had entered the home of Charles and Geraldine Wilson early in the morning to arrest their son, who was, as they later discovered, no longer living there. A reporter and photographer, who were accompanying the police during a ride-along to watch law enforcement at work, entered the home with them. The Wilsons sued despite the fact that photographs taken at the scene were never used. The Court said that the police violate the law when they allow the media to join them on private property to conduct a search or make an arrest. The Court stopped short of saying the officers could be sued in this case because the law about ride-along liability might not have been clear before, but in future cases such lawsuits would be permitted.

Subsequent cases involving the media working with law enforcement and emergency personnel have found that the media may also be held liable for the trespass.

For example, in *Shulman v. Group W. Productions*, 18 C.4th 200 (1998), the California Supreme Court held that an accident victim could sue a TV producer for shooting video of an accident victim being rescued from a car and receiving medical care while being transported in a helicopter. The Court was concerned that the paramedics had been wired and recorded private medical conversations with the victim.

Shi Yali/Shutterstock.com

Harassment.   Photographing people in a public place is one thing, but harassing them to get the photo is something else. In the case of *Galella v. Onassis*, 487 F.2d 986, 2d cir. (1973), the Court found freelance photographer Ron Galella had gone too far in photographing the late Jacqueline Kennedy Onassis and her children by generally being underfoot at all times to get the pictures.

Paparazzi.   Photographers who chase celebrities to take their pictures and sell them for exorbitant sums have given traditional journalists a bad name and prompted fed-up legislators to write laws protecting famous people from unwanted intrusion. California, which is home to the entertainment industry, has led the way in such laws. Those who photograph, videotape, or record people who are in personal or family activities may be held liable for invasions of privacy. Damages can also be assessed against those media outlets that buy the photos and recordings.

Secret Recordings.   In *Desnick v. American Broadcasting Co.*, 44 F.3d 1345 (1995), the Court held that it was not an invasion of privacy when ABC's *Prime Time Live* put hidden cameras on seven people and had them pose as patients at a cataract clinic. The story that followed suggested the clinic was doing unnecessary cataract surgeries for Medicare patients. The Court said that even though deceptive measures were used to get the information, the clinic was open to anyone who wanted an eye examination, which the "patients" received.

Courts have also held that restaurant critics may enter a restaurant for purposes of doing reviews without announcing their intentions. The restaurant is open for the purpose of serving food and the critic has entered the business establishment for the purpose of eating it. However, someone who enters a place under false pretenses with no substantive reason for being there, as in the case of someone posing as a meter reader for the sole purpose of gaining entry to a person's home, would not be protected from an invasion of privacy suit.

In fact, when it comes to intrusion of a person's private homes, the Court often looks at the situation differently. In *Dietemann v. Time, Inc.*, 449 F.2d 245 (1971), two reporters for *Life* magazine investigated a man suspected of practicing medicine without a license out of his home. The reporters went to the man's house, secretly took photographs and wore hidden microphones so police could monitor the conversation. A subsequent story accused the man of medical quackery. He sued for invasion of privacy. Although the Court found the story newsworthy, it said that the reporters did not have a right to violate the man's privacy in his home.

Using Stolen Recordings.   The U.S. Supreme Court ruled in *Bartnicki v. Vopper*, 532 U.S. 514 (2001), that under the First Amendment, a broadcaster could air a newsworthy but pirated tape of a cellphone call. The Court said that it was not a violation of the federal wiretap law.

In that case, someone had secretly taped a conversation between two teachers' union officials and gave it to an anonymous anti-tax crusader who then passed it on to Frederick Vopper, a Pennsylvania broadcaster, during a controversy over teachers' salaries. Vopper aired the tape, which contained fiery rhetoric against local school leaders. Bartnicki and another union leader sued.

The Court said that the tape involved an issue of public concern and since the media got it lawfully from a third party and did not participate in the illegal taping, the media had a right to air the tape. The Court relied on the Pentagon Papers case in its ruling. Some members of the Court, however, said that the right would not extend to a secret tape of a private conversation regarding a non-public controversy.

Also, had the broadcaster in some way aided or cooperated with the illegal taping, he would have been liable.

Recording the Police. The Court has held that a citizen has a right to record government officials, including police and other law enforcement officers, in the discharge of their duties in a public area.

In *Glik v. Cunniffe*, 655 F.3d 78 (2011), the Court upheld the right of Simon Glik to use his cell phone to record three police officers arresting someone in Boston. Glik was charged with violating wiretapping law, disturbing the peace, and aiding the escape of a prisoner. The Court dismissed the charges, and an appellate court said that the First Amendment protected Glik's actions. It noted that the wiretapping law did not apply since there was no secret recording, and he did not interfere with the police.

• Disclosure of Private Facts

The "keyhole" journalism of the 19th century, which involved journalists indiscriminately invading people's privacy, gave rise to another tort that is recognized in many, but not all states, today. Unlike the intrusion tort, which involves physical trespass or the use of technological devices to violate the solitude of another, this tort results from the disclosure of truthful, but private, facts. In those states that recognize the tort, juries may award monetary damages to compensate those who have suffered emotional injury as a result of having intimate information about their lives publicized.

Put simply, one can be successfully sued for **publicizing truthful, but private, information about another if the Court finds that disclosure of the information would be highly offensive to a reasonable person and it has no legitimate public concern.**

In such cases, the plaintiff must prove:

1. Private, intimate facts about the plaintiff were involved. This need not be about illegal or reprehensible matters. It might include financial situations, medical information, domestic problems, or sexual habits. Generally, information that is in a public record, open to the public, is not private. Neither is information the plaintiff has made public, assuming it has been made to more than a few close friends.

2. The information would be highly offensive to a reasonable person. The information would be more than just embarrassing. It would be the kind of information that the plaintiff would not want the community to know. If publishing the intimate details would outrage the community, it would be deemed highly offensive. The *reasonable person standard* requires that the information be viewed from the perspective of a typical person in the community, not from the viewpoint of someone overly sensitive or overly callous.

3. The intimate facts were publicized. Unlike the libel tort, publication is not enough. Publication means a third party other than the plaintiff and defendant has seen the libelous material. The publication of private information tort requires *publicity*. A large number of people must have seen the private information.

4. The information is not of legitimate public concern. Private facts are permissible if they are newsworthy or about a legitimate public concern—such as an issue before the community. The Court will look to see whether there was some logical reason that connected the news events to the private facts. Stories about crimes, suicides, and other topics that find their way into the news are newsworthy even though people may not want them published. Generally, it doesn't matter how offensive or embarrassing the material is.

Because of First Amendment concerns, judges give the media wide latitude in what is considered newsworthy. The Court does not want to get into the business of second-guessing the media.

Sometimes people can find themselves in the public eye even though they didn't want to be there. The Court has ruled that for purposes of privacy law involuntary participants cannot win a private facts case if the event in which they found themselves is newsworthy and there is some logical connection between the news event and the private facts about them used in the story.

Also, people who are closely related or associated with newsworthy individuals can lose some of their privacy rights as well. Still, the media should be able to show some legitimate reason for revealing the information, something other than just for morbid curiosity.

Even celebrities have a right to keep certain matters private unless they drag them out for public display. For example, a recording of celebrities having sex in their home would likely not be of *legitimate* public concern.

Defenses to a publication of private facts case include the *First Amendment, consent and newsworthiness.*

The Supreme Court has said that the First Amendment protects the publication of truthful information if it is of legitimate public concern, lawfully obtained from public records and there is not a compelling state interest that overrides the right to publish. So far, the Court has not noted a compelling interest in private facts cases.

When the Court focuses on newsworthiness, it looks to the subject of the story and not to the individuals named in the story. A story about a robbery is important enough to overcome the victim's privacy.

Private information in public records is not private. Neither is information revealed in public meetings. Thus, some of the defenses associated with libel, namely absolute and qualified privilege can apply. But some records are not public, such as tax records. And some places are not public, such as hospital rooms.

The passage of time does not eliminate newsworthiness. "Where are they now?" stories that simply document what happened to someone in the news long ago are permissible so long as they are not used to embarrass the person or reveal something that has nothing to do with their newsworthy past.

Sensational treatment of the story generally does not eliminate the newsworthiness defense, though it may well prompt the Court to look closely to see if the intimate facts have anything to do with the subject matter.

Those who consent to have their privacy invaded cannot claim later that it was unwarranted. Nevertheless, for the consent to be valid, the person:

1. Must have the legal capacity to consent.
2. Must understand the consequences of their actions, and
3. Must be fully informed about what is going to be revealed.

It should be noted that privacy law applies as well to stories on the Internet. The Court treats online stories the same as those in the newspaper or TV.

Disclosure of Private Facts Cases

The following examples illustrate the various private facts cases that have found their way before the Court.

Public Records. In *Cox Broadcasting v. Cohn*, 420 U.S. 469 (1975), the U.S. Supreme Court held a constitutional right exists to publish information from most public records that is truthful. The decision came from a case involving a news broadcast that identified a rape victim. A state law in Georgia made it a crime to publish or broadcast the names of rape victims, but a reporter was given a copy of a court record containing the name during trial. The Supreme Court ruled the report was a truthful account of an open court record.

Limitations on Public Records. The right to publish truthful information from public records is limited. First, the record must be open to the public. Second, courts have created exceptions to the rule. In *Times Mirror Co. v. Superior Court of San Diego County*, 198 C.A. 3d 1420 (1988), the Court said that the media went too far when it published the name of a woman who was a material witness to a murder and the murderer was still on the loose. Despite the fact her name was listed in the coroner's report, a public record, the Court said that the First Amendment did not necessarily apply.

Newsworthiness. The newsworthiness defense is often effective if the facts are indeed newsworthy. In *Virgil v. Time, Inc.*, 527 F.2d 1122 (1975), a colorful surfer was profiled in an article in *Sports Illustrated*. The article revealed accurately that he put cigarettes out on his tongue, ate bugs, and dived headfirst down stairs. He sued. The Court said that the article was newsworthy and found for the magazine. The Court said: "In determining what is a matter of legitimate public interest, account must be taken of the customs and conventions of the community." The Court further noted that the subject must be newsworthy or the First Amendment will not protect the publishing of private facts.

Outrageous Acts. Typically, only those whose privacy has been invaded can sue. However, in some situations the outrageousness of the information may lead to an extension of the privacy tort or to another different tort. In *Catsouras v. State of California Highway Patrol*, 181 Cal. App. 4th 856 (2010), the Court said that the family members of the deceased can have their privacy invaded in outrageous cases. In this case, a woman was decapitated in a horrible car accident. The California Highway Patrol took photos of the accident that were later leaked online. Family members sued. The Court said that no Press freedom issues were at stake in the case. Said the Court:

> *The dissemination of death images can only affect the living. As cases from other jurisdictions make plain, family members have a common law privacy right in the death images of a decedent, subject to certain limitations.*

Thus, at least in some circumstances, the courts appear to be expanding the right of privacy, though such cases generally fall under the tort of *intentional infliction of emotional distress*, which will be discussed at the end of this chapter after the four areas of privacy law have been reviewed.

Finally, many courts find the tort of publication of private matters suspect because it punishes the press for publishing truthful information—a concept contrary to both the First Amendment and the hallmarks of a free press. Nevertheless, a majority has decided that some information should remain private, even if it is accurate. Some information, they hold, is nobody's business, and publicizing such information goes beyond the bounds of ordinary decency. Still, most publication of private facts cases fail because of the First Amendment right to print and broadcast what is newsworthy or because of the existence of a public record containing the information.

A great many private facts lawsuits could be avoided if those in the media paid more attention to ethics. Often the cases point to bad decision-making on the part of editors and producers. Perhaps in most cases, the lawsuits could have been avoided altogether if the stories had been told without delving into sordid and sensational details. A question all of those in the media should ask is: "Why am I publicizing this?"

• Appropriation

Taking someone's picture and putting it in an advertisement without their permission or using the voice of a famous dead actor without the consent of whoever is in control of their estate is illegal. **Appropriation means using someone's name, likeness, or some other aspect of their personality for commercial or trade purposes without their consent.**

Of all the privacy torts, appropriation is the oldest. The first law dealing with the matter dates to 1903. And unlike other privacy torts, this one is widely recognized.

Appropriation is really a tort that covers two interests—a *right to privacy* and a *right to publicity*. The first protects a person's dignity and peace of mind; the second protects the commercial value of their identity. The first right dies with the individual, as in the case of the other privacy rights. But the right of publicity can live on after death and be transferred to others, like any other property interest. The right can last for years, depending upon the laws of the state where the person resided when he died.

A federal appeals judge first used the phrase "right of publicity" in *Haelan Laboratories v. Topps Chewing Gum*, 202 F.2d 866 (1953). The case upheld the right of baseball players to commercially control their names and photos on baseball trading cards.

Although everyone has a right to keep others from using their name, likeness, or image for commercial gain without their permission, not everyone may have a right to publicity. Usually, only someone famous whose name or image has commercial value can claim such a right. The number of right to publicity cases has increased in recent years due to the media's attention to celebrity and business recognition that a celebrity's name can be an important advertising tool.

To win a case for appropriation, the plaintiff must prove:

1. The plaintiff's name, likeness, or some other aspect of his persona or personality was used for commercial gain or trade purposes by

another without the plaintiff's permission. Thus, the plaintiff must prove each aspect of the statement, including,

a. that the use involved some aspect of the plaintiff's identity,;
b. that the defendant used it for commercial gain,; and
c. that the plaintiff did not grant permission for his identity to be used in such a manner.

Use of a person's name may not be enough. Many names are alike. What is important is to show that the name, likeness, or some other aspect of the person was used in such a way as to indicate a specific individual. This does not mean that a mistake couldn't lead to a claim of appropriation. If the defendant intends to use a fictitious name, but a real person in the community can show that enough people believe the ad in which his name appeared belonged to him, he may have a case. The key will be to show that enough similarities exist between the real person and the fictitious character to lead a reasonable person to believe the two are one and the same.

Generally, just hinting will not be enough. For a defendant to show an image of someone's back and the plaintiff to suggest it's his back probably won't be enough unless there is something distinctive about the person's back. Yet if the defendant mimics someone's vocal style, makeup, costume, body movements, or some other aspect to suggest it is someone famous, they may be inviting a lawsuit.

Also, a person can be identified by their name, photograph, drawing, pen name, pseudonyms, or in any other way that leads people to believe that the plaintiff is the subject of the appropriation. The Court will look for a "clear representation" of "identifying features."

The right extends to look-alikes and sound-alikes. Thus, someone who impersonates a famous actor or singer without the person's permission may be sued. In some cases, courts have allowed actors to retain the right to sue when someone exploits a character they portrayed.

Advertising and trade purposes can include taking a person's picture in the park and then using it in an advertisement without permission, falsely suggesting that they endorse a product, or using their identity in a feature film, TV show, or novel without getting a release.

Several defenses are available to an appropriation claim.

Consent is the best defense. Some states require the consent be in writing. Oral consent will work in others, but the defendant may have difficulty proving he received it. In some instances, consent may be implicit. Permission may be implied if people decline to leave a location after being told a photographer is going to take a photo of where they are sitting.

Not all can give their consent. Those who are mentally ill, under age 18 years, or incarcerated in prison usually cannot consent. Also, the consent may become invalid over time. Nor is it valid if the matter consented to is materially altered, as in a photo being substantially changed. Minor retouching usually will not invalidate the consent.

More often, *newsworthiness* is used as a defense. The news media may publish photos and stories about people without their permission if they are involved in a news story. Despite the fact that the news media must make a profit to stay in business, the courts have ruled that the overriding purpose of the Press is news and information, not profit.

Nevertheless, there are limits to what the Press can do. The U.S. Supreme Court permitted a state court to rule in *Zacchini v. Scripps-Howard Broadcasting*, 433 U.S. 562 (1977), that when a TV station broadcast an entire human cannonball act, it denied the performer the ability to make money off of his performance since the viewers would no longer need to go to the circus to see the act.

Generally, information that is widely available in the *public domain* is immune from an appropriation suit. Thus, the use of ballplayers names and statistics can be used without payment.

The First Amendment also offers some protection against an appropriation claim. Selling posters of newsworthy people or events generally is permitted since courts make a distinction between what is news and what is exploitation.

The media also may be protected when they use a famous person's name or image from one of their stories as part of an advertisement to promote the publication. As long as they do not claim the person endorses the publication or station, the use does not constitute appropriation. The defense is known as the *Booth Rule* and comes from *Booth v. Curtis Publishing*, 182 N.E. 2d 812 (1962).

In that case, the Court said that *Holiday* magazine could use a previously published photograph of actress Shirley Booth to promote its publication. Booth had consented to the story and photo but not the ad. The Court said that the ad did not state or imply that she endorsed the publication. Rather, it was designed to provide an example of the content and quality of the magazine.

Some courts have also acknowledged that a fleeting glimpse of a person's name or likeness may not be enough to warrant an appropriation claim. The question is whether the use is really incidental to the purpose for which the name and likeness are being used. For example, someone pictured in a large group of people would have a hard time arguing that the ad was ultimately successful because he was in the shot.

Sometimes, courts will use other tests to help them decide if the material being used has been appropriated and falls outside First Amendment protection. The tests are called the artistic relevance test, the transformative test, and the predominant use test.

The artistic relevance test looks to see if the use of a celebrity's name or picture is artistically relevant to the purpose of the art. The Court said that the First Amendment allows the use of someone's name, either journalistically or artistically, without permission. In other words, the name is used as part of some artistic expression. If the name is just used to generate interest and money, then the defendant will lose.

The transformative test means the defendant transformed the original celebrity name or likeness by adding his own creative elements, such as when an artist draws a caricature of someone. The work becomes a new creation and is therefore not an appropriation. Satires, critiques, news stories, or works of fiction fall into this category.

Under the predominant use test, the Court asks if the purpose of the work is predominantly to make the plaintiff money or to allow the plaintiff to express himself. If it's the latter, the Court is more inclined to find that it is not an appropriation.

Finally, a disclaimer often will prevent a successful suit, but the disclaimer must be prominent enough to be effective. Small type will not work. Nor will one be effective if it is hard to hear or drowned out by other voices or music.

Appropriation Cases

Celebrities   In *Carson v. Here's Johnny Portable Toilets Inc.*, 698 F.2d 831(1983), the Court ruled that a company that used entertainer Johnny Carson's signature line "Here's Johnny" had appropriated an important element of Carson's personality for commercial gain. The company had used the line to help market a toilet. The Court held the use would confuse the public into thinking Carson was somehow endorsing the product.

Singer Bette Midler sued Ford Motor Company and the Young & Rubicam ad agency in *Midler v. Ford Motor Company*, 849 F.2d 460 (1988), for using a sound-alike singer to sell a car. The Court held that listeners would think it was her singing.

The Court was criticized for a case that some say went too far. In *White v. Samsung*, 971 F.2d 1395 (1992), game show hostess Vanna White sued Samsung Electronics and its advertising agency for an ad that used a blond robot wearing a gown and jewelry similar to those White wore on the TV show. One judge said that there could be no confusion that the robot was not White, but two other judges ruled that there was a misappropriation. Critics have argued that as a result of such rulings anything that even *reminded* the public of a celebrity would be illegal. One judge called it "bad law." The Supreme Court refused to hear an appeal.

• False Light

When someone libels another with a false statement, they are not only harming their reputation, they are also putting them in a false light. **That is, they are making them out to be something they are not.** As a result, they may suffer emotional harm as well as reputational harm. Consequently, when a lawyer files a lawsuit against a libel defendant, often the lawyer will include a separate false light cause of action.

As with other privacy areas, some states refuse to recognize a false light claim. Courts in those states argue that false light is too similar to libel, and therefore redundant. Others say it interferes with First Amendment rights of the Press. Nevertheless, more states recognize the tort than do not.

To win a false light claim, the plaintiff must prove:

1. The matter was widely published. Any material published in the mass media meets the publicity test.
2. The false, offensive facts were about the plaintiff. Furthermore, a large number of people must believe the information is about the plaintiff.

3. <u>The information about the plaintiff must be false or imply false things</u>. Generally, more than minor errors are required. A false light fact would include attributing to him views he doesn't hold or actions he didn't take.

4. <u>The published material would be highly offensive to a reasonable person</u>. Adding facts, eliminating facts, taking facts out of context, or simply making them up could result in a statement being both false and offensive. Problems arise when docudramas jazz up the story by adding untrue material. And just because a novelist adds a disclaimer that all characters in the book are fictitious doesn't shield him from liability if enough similarities in the story match a real person. Perhaps, the biggest problem for the news media is the use of photographs and video for stories other than the ones they originally illustrated. Using a picture of the wrong person in a crime story can result in a lawsuit.

5. <u>The publisher or broadcaster of the false light statement was at fault</u>. The fault requirement is the same as in the *New York Times v. Sullivan* case. The plaintiff must prove actual malice. That is, the falsehood was published knowingly or with reckless disregard for the truth. As in the case of libel, the First Amendment protects the media when reporting on stories of public concern. Yet, unlike in the *Times'* case, even a private person speaking on a matter of public concern must prove malice. Courts are split on this issue. Some require that, as in *Gertz v. Welch*, the private person need only prove negligence.

The defenses to a false light claim are the same as those in libel. Thus, truth, privilege, consent, etc., are among those available to the defendant.

False Light Cases

The U.S. Supreme Court has decided two main false light cases.

The first is *Time, Inc. v. Hill*, 385 U.S. 374 (1967), which involved a family that was held hostage by three escaped convicts in 1952. The next year Joseph Hayes published *The Desperate Hours*, a similar story about a family taken hostage by escaped convicts. The story differed from the real event in many ways, nevertheless, the family sued for invasion of privacy after an article was published in *Life* magazine stating that the book was based directly on the family's experiences.

The family said in their suit that the story gave people the false impression that it was about their ordeal. The Court, however, applied the *New York Times v. Sullivan* rule, noting that those who are involved in a matter of public interest could only win a false light suit if they proved actual malice.

In the second case, the Court ruled in *Cantrell v. Forest City Publishing Co.*, 419 U.S. 245 (1974), that an invasion of privacy judgment was justified because of "calculated falsehoods" and "reckless untruth."

The case stemmed from a bridge collapse into the Ohio River. Melvin Cantrell was among the victims who died, and a reporter for the *Cleveland Plain Dealer* did a follow-up story about how the man's family was coping with the tragedy. Yet the reporter did not talk to the widow and relied instead on information from the children. The Court said that the story was filled with inaccuracies and falsely described the widow's mood and attitude, and that the false light judgment was justified.

Privacy and the Internet

Unlike the European Union, the United States has not passed an Internet or data privacy law. If American businesses want to do business in Europe, they must comply with the EU law that requires data-protection safeguards to prevent the use of unauthorized personal information from the Internet.

Meanwhile, the Supreme Court has held that employers may monitor employees' e-mail and text messages on company equipment for work purposes. The concern over Internet and social media privacy has been heightened by the disclosure of government surveillance to thwart terrorism.

In terms of appropriation problems, the courts generally have held that the unauthorized use of someone's name or likeness from the Internet is illegal unless it is a matter of news coverage. If a website is concerned with the gathering and reporting of news, it can use the names and likeness of others just as any other publication could. This, however, would not necessarily cover potential copyright infringement (which will be discussed later.)

Congress has been working to write laws to protect data privacy. Most are still in committee.

Infliction of Emotional Distress

Given the fact that privacy lawsuits are personal and can only be brought by the person whose privacy was harmed, courts dismiss lawsuits from parents or other relatives over the disclosure of intimate or gruesome information concerning the death of a loved one. Yet, some relatives are able to pursue a tort often associated with libel cases—*intentional infliction of emotional distress.*

The law allows for recovery of damages in those instances where the defendant has inflicted distress so severe that it is beyond what should be tolerated in a civilized society. Such distress sometimes results in emotional and psychological damage so problematic that it requires a physician's care.

The plaintiff must prove four elements to establish a prima facie case:

1. The defendant's actions were reckless or intentional.
2. The defendant's actions were extreme.
3. The defendant's actions caused emotional distress.
4. The distress was severe.

IIED cases are usually associated with libel suits on the theory that the defamatory statement not only damaged the plaintiff's reputation but also caused severe emotional turmoil. This, despite the fact the tort has more in common with the emotional harm associated with invasion of privacy.

Perhaps, the most famous IIED case almost led to an undoing of the *New York Times v. Sullivan* rule and the possible elimination of parody and satire in the United States.

In *Hustler Magazine v. Falwell*, 485.U.S. 46 (1988), evangelist and Moral Majority leader the Rev. Jerry Falwell sued *Hustler* magazine for libel, invasion of privacy and intentional infliction of emotional distress over a parody ad in the magazine that implied that Falwell's first sexual experience was an incestuous relationship with his mother.

Despite a disclaimer at the bottom of the ad, both the trial court and the appellate court found for Falwell. As a result, the magazine appealed to the U.S. Supreme Court. In a unanimous decision, the high Court overturned the decision. Noted Chief Justice William Rehnquist:

> *Were we to hold otherwise, there can be little doubt that political cartoonists and satirists would be subjected to damages awarded without any showing that their work falsely defamed its subject.*

In short, because of his position as leader of the Moral Majority, Falwell likely would be considered a public person and have to prove malice in a libel suit, but he could effectively circumvent that Press protection by filing an IIED claim which doesn't even require a showing of negligence. As a result, any cartoonist, political satirist, comedian, or other pundit could be silenced by a mere accusation that what they said hurt someone's feelings.

Despite the obvious outrageousness of the ad, the Court added:

> *The appeal of the political cartoon or caricature is often based on exploration of unfortunate physical traits or politically embarrassing events—an exploration often calculated to injure the feelings of the subject of the portrayal. The art of the cartoonist is often not reasoned or evenhanded, but slashing and one-sided.*

What then constitutes an effective IIED case?

CNN's Nancy Grace interviewed Melinda Duckett, the mother of a two-year old child who was reported missing and intimated during the interview that Duckett killed the child. Just before the interview was broadcast, Duckett killed herself. Despite this, the network aired the interview anyway. The family sued. The Court denied CNN's motion to dismiss. The Court said that the plaintiff had listed all the elements of an IIED case; therefore, the case would need to go to trial. Grace later reached a settlement with the woman's estate.

In some cases, the media may be sued for *negligent infliction of emotional distress.*

To bring a suit for negligent infliction of emotional distress, the plaintiff must prove:

1. The defendant owed a duty of care to the plaintiff.
2. The defendant breached the duty.
3. The breach was the direct cause of the plaintiff's injury.
4. The defendant was negligent.

An example of negligent infliction of emotional distress is *Times Mirror Co. v. Superior Court of San Diego County*, 198 C.A. 3d 1420 (1988). In that case, the Court said that the media went too far when it published the name of a woman who was a material witness to a murder and the murderer was still on the loose. The Court said that the First Amendment did not necessarily apply to prevent her suit of negligent infliction of emotional distress.

CHAPTER 8

Open Records and Meetings

A popular Government, without popular information, or the means of acquiring it, is but a Prologue to a Farce or a Tragedy; or, perhaps both. Knowledge will forever govern ignorance; And a people who mean to be their own Governors must arm themselves with the power which knowledge gives.

—*James Madison*
Father of the U.S. Constitution
Author of the Bill of Rights
4th President of the United States

The Need for Information

Without access to information, freedom of Press means very little. Credible information is the lifeblood of a healthy Press. Without it, the media become nothing more than a series of rumor mills churning out undocumented opinions. More, the Press needs information to fulfill its role of keeping the people informed. For without an informed electorate, democracy dies.

James Madison, Thomas Jefferson, Benjamin Franklin, and the other Founders understood well the essential role of the Press in maintaining the American Republic. Yet, for whatever reason, the First Amendment makes no mention of the right to access information about the government, only the right of the Press to publish whatever information it can get. Was this an oversight? Did the Founders assume that a free Press naturally meant a right of access? Or did they intentionally leave

yurchello108/Shutterstock.com

Benjamin Franklin

it out? Were they, like politicians everywhere, making it difficult for a nosy Press and public to find out what they were doing?

Given the times, it was probably nothing that nefarious. The Press in the 18th century was more of a sounding board for ideas and commentary than a repository of factual information. The country was small. It was relatively easy for Americans to find out what their elected officials were doing. They just asked them.

But the world has changed drastically, and so too the government that serves us. The original, small system has become a monolith of departments, commissions, and bureaucracies, all of them producing thousands of documents a year, all of them meeting and making decisions that affect every American. How can average citizens make decisions about their government today if they can't find out what it's doing?

Even some of those on the high Court have recognized the importance of access to information. Former U.S. Supreme Court Justice Lewis Powell noted in *Branzburg v. Hayes*, 408 U.S. 665, 728 (1972), that a right to gather news is crucial.

> *News must not be unnecessarily cut off at its source, for without freedom to acquire information the right to publish would be impermissibly compromised. Accordingly, a right to gather news, of some dimensions, must exist.*

Yet the Court, as a whole, asserted in the same case that while some protection to gather the news might exist, "the First Amendment does not guarantee the press a constitutional right of special access to information not available to the public generally."

As a result of government secrecy during World War II and the growth of government bureaucracy during the same period, and perhaps because they were unable to rely on the First Amendment, some in Congress, and the Press in particular, pushed for a law that would provide more openness. The Society of Professional Journalists and the American Society of Newspaper Editors lobbied hard for legislation that would provide greater government access and transparency.

The law was needed, they said, because it was becoming impossible for citizens to understand and use their own government. If people wanted to know what was going on, they had to read the *Congressional Record*, which published the day-to-day business of Congress. But as more agencies were being created, it was becoming more difficult for concerned citizens to learn what their government was doing, especially outside of Congress.

The Freedom of Information Act

As a result, Congress passed the *Freedom of Information Act* (FOIA) in 1966. The Act opened records held by all the executive agencies of the federal government, in essence providing all citizens the right to get information from the executive branch of government. Although the Press lobbied for the bill, academics, corporations, and average citizens have used it the most.

The act requires each agency to appoint someone who can help citizens get records from that agency. It also requires each agency to publish in the *Federal Register* a description of the agency and the procedures one can follow to obtain records. The law does not apply to Congress or to the courts.

The act was amended in 1974, 1976, 1986, and 1996, and again in 2007 with the passage of the *Open Government Act*. Records under the FOIA are presumed to be open and any exemptions to the act are to be construed narrowly, providing citizens with the most access to information.

Millions of documents have been made public since passage of the act. They have, in turn, led to other efforts to open the government. Data. gov increases public access to datasets of the executive branch. Other websites such as USAspending.gov and Recovery.gov also have been adopted to help citizens get information.

The FOIA has enabled journalists and researchers to uncover all manner of information and news. The law helped disclose the fact that the Central Intelligence Agency spied on Martin Luther King, Jr. during the civil rights movement. It revealed design deficiencies in the Hubble space telescope, dangers of nuclear weapons plants, and even hazardous levels of lead in imported wine. It exposed safety hazards in the Ford Pinto gas tank, and it was used to discover the health hazards of Agent Orange used during the Vietnam War.

The FOIA enables citizens to inspect agency documents and to copy them at a reasonable cost unless they fall into one of nine exemptions.

The law defines an "agency" as "any executive department, military department, Government corporation, Government controlled corporation, or other establishment in the executive branch of the Government, including the Executive Office of the President, or any independent regulatory agency." The Executive Office of the President includes the Office of Management and Budget, the Office of Policy Development and the Office of Science and Technology Policy.

Congress did not include the White House Office, so the president's advisors and their staffs are not covered by the act. Groups that receive federal funding but are not directly under government control—such as the Corporation for Public Broadcasting—are also not covered by the act. But all Cabinet level offices, such as Justice, Defense, State, and Treasury, are subject to the law, as are such agencies as the Federal Communications Commission, the National Space and Aeronautics Administration, the U.S. Postal Service, the Federal Trade Commission, and the Securities and Exchange Commission.

"Records" include all items that document government actions that can be reproduced. The record must already exist. The act does not require that the government create a record to fulfill a specific request for information. A record would include computer files, paper reports, films, tapes, photographs, and any other item that documents government action.

Agency records usually are defined as those documents created and kept by a particular agency. If an agency has a record but did not create it, it probably isn't an agency record. An agency is not required to go to

Copyright © of Mark Zimmerman. Reprinted by permission.

another agency to get a record not in its control. The record must be part of its official duties.

Internet Access to Information

The Internet has, by some accounts, made it easier to get information from the government, but ironically it has also prompted the public to demand more secrecy. Personal information that was once only available to an individual requesting a paper document is now available to anyone with a computer. As a result of public complaints, some agencies have removed information from their databases that had been routinely available.

Furthermore, the original paper records may have been destroyed once the information was transferred from a paper version to an electronic version. To make matters worse, those companies who won contracts to computerize government records may now charge higher fees for the public to get them. Thus, a system that was designed to make getting information easier has, in some cases, made it harder. Journalists complained that these changes were not working.

In response to the complaints, the *Electronic Freedom of Information Act of 1996* mandated changes in the way federal agencies respond to FOIA requests. The agencies had to make it easier for the public to identify and get information. The act established that electronic records are subject to the FOIA. And it stipulated that records requests could not be used to create new records, thus making it easier to hide information.

As a result of the law, agencies had to establish indexes and guides to help explain what records are available and where they can be located. The act established three categories of documents: those that had to be published, those that had to be released on request, and those that had to be placed in agency electronic reading rooms or online even if no one had requested them.

The law also required that the record be provided in whatever format is chosen by the person requesting the document. The agency is required to provide the document in the format requested if the agency keeps records that way.

The law also addressed the problem of redactions. Passage of the act required agencies to indicate where documents had been censored and how much had been censored so long as doing so would not reveal confidential information. In addition, the act gave agencies 20 working days to respond to requests instead of 10 days, though journalists and a few others could have their requests expedited.

Agencies were also required to identify routinely requested information and put it in a place where the public could get to it quickly, often without filing an FOIA request.

All of these changes increased public access tremendously.

Using the Freedom of Information Act

Asking for a record is fairly easy. Getting one may not be. The Reporters Committee for Freedom of the Press offers a helpful guide, *How to Use the Federal FOI Act*, at http:// www.rcfp.org/federal-open-government-guide. The guide includes U.S. government agency directories, fee schedules, fee waiver requests, request letter samples, appeal letter samples, and legal documents to file should one need to sue to obtain information. It also includes general instructions. Interested persons also can go to the government website, FOIA.gov. Also, the agencies now have their own websites to help guide requests.

It is generally better to use the FOIA as a last resort rather than a first effort. Formal requests take time. Journalists have long known that the best way to get information is by cultivating personal sources. If the requester knows someone, or he knows someone who knows someone, that may be the better route to take, at least early on.

Also, it is recommended that one look to other documents before using the FOIA. Court records and other traditional sources are often quicker and easier to use.

Those who do decide to use the FOIA to get information from the government should do their homework before filing a request. Requesters should understand in advance just what they want. Be specific. The narrower the request is, the better the chance of getting a productive response.

Requesters can contact the agency by telephone, email, or letter. In some cases, it may be better to inquire first by phone to get an idea of how difficult it may be to get the information, and then follow up with a letter that shows the date of the request and the records sought. That way an evidentiary record has been established to use in court should one need to sue to try to get the information.

The FOIA allows agencies to charge fees to search and/or copy documents. But fee waivers may be available. For example, the news media, educational institutions, and nonprofit organizations may be able to get the information for next to nothing. If the request is for commercial purposes, a fee likely will be charged. Even then, it may be better in some cases to pay the fee. Sometimes requesting a fee waiver will result in longer delays to get the information since agency personnel have to spend time determining the requester's fee status.

The law gives agencies 20 days to respond to an FOIA request. This does not mean the agency must produce the document in that time. The Court has said the agency must indicate, "the scope of the documents it will produce" and those "exemptions it will claim with respect to any withheld documents." If the time delay for producing the document appears too lengthy, the requester may file an appeal. If the agency refuses to produce the document, the requester may file suit in federal district court. If the lawsuit is ultimately successful, the FOIA requires the government to pay for the requester's attorney fees and court costs. Disciplinary actions may also be brought by the Civil Service Commission against the person who denied the request if that person acted capriciously.

The burden of proof is on the government to justify any delay or non-disclosure. If the government claims the request falls under a specific exemption, it must cite the exemption. If the agency withholds portions of the document on the basis of an exemption, it may only withhold those portions the law allows it to exempt. Again, the exemptions must be construed narrowly, that is, the agency can only black out or redact those portions necessary to comply with the exemption. Redaction poses another FOIA problem, however. It often takes an agency months or even years to go through a document line by line to eliminate exempted information.

In some instances, the agency may not even have to give an answer to an FOIA question. They can offer a *Glomar response*. In 1986, Congress said that the FBI and other federal law enforcement agencies could answer an FOIA request by neither confirming nor denying they had the document. Congress authorized the move because in some situations if an agency admitted it had a document it would tip off suspects that they were under investigation. The phrase was taken from the name of a ship called the *Glomar Explorer*, a Howard Hughes vessel used in an attempt to recover a lost Soviet submarine. The CIA would not confirm or deny ties to the operation.

Freedom of Information Act Exemptions

Nevertheless, the nine exemptions pose the biggest barrier to getting information under the FOIA. They include 1. matters of national security, 2. documents regarding internal agency rules and regulations, 3. statutory exemptions, 4. trade secrets, 5. agency memos, 6. information concerning personal privacy, 7. certain law enforcement records, 8. financial records of banks and other financial institutions, and 9. oil and gas exploration data.

1. Those records regarding **national security**, national defense or foreign affairs that have been classified as confidential, secret, or top secret are off limits under the FOIA. Agencies must justify the classifications to meet the FOIA exemption. If requested materials are thought to fall under the exemption, a federal judge has the authority to examine the materials in private to determine if their release could damage national security. The agency objecting to the release of the materials must provide affidavits justifying the nondisclosure and proving that the material falls under the national security exemption. Judges usually rule in favor of nondisclosure.

2. Documents relating to the **internal rules and regulations of an agency** are often referred to as "housekeeping matters." Congress authorized the exemption on the theory that it would not be worth an agency's time and expense to gather and release documents that pertained to vacation policies, lunch break rules, assigned parking spaces, and other similar matters. However, this does not mean that the agency can use the exemption to hide all internal agency practices. The U.S. Supreme Court has ruled, for example, that the exemption cannot be used to hide information or practices that would be of genuine public interest, as in the case of where Air Force Academy records were being sought regarding honor and ethics hearings.

3. Sometimes Congress will pass a law that specifically prohibits the release of information about a particular subject. Thus, this **statutory exemption** will override an FOIA request. The exemption is used increasingly to get around the FOIA. Still, the Court requires the government to show 1. that the statute cited covers the information sought and prohibits its release, and 2. nondisclosure is mandatory under the statute.

4. Businesses often must share lots of sensitive information with government agencies, including **trade secrets**, market-share information, formulas, and the like. The information must be confidential or privileged to be exempt. Such information was not generated by the government agency; it was merely collected to enforce other objectives, such as copyright, trademark, and patent laws. Were the information to get into competitors' hands, it could harm the business. Thus, such matters are not released.

5. The attorney-client privilege also applies to government agencies and their lawyers. Therefore, **inter-agency and intra-agency memos** and other correspondence regarding litigation are not open. Neither are studies that are used to create final reports. These are often referred to as "working papers." These are often used in an agency's initial decision-making process.

6. Personnel and medical files that fall under **personal privacy** laws are also exempt under the FOIA. The exemption applies to people and not corporations. Courts faced with FOIA requests that fall under the exemption usually will try to weigh the need for secrecy against the need to inform the public about government activities. The Court is often ultimately interested in how the

information is going to be used. The question also is how personal is the information. Medical matters are strictly personal, but other information might not be as sensitive. The Court looks to see if release of the information would be "clearly unwarranted."

7. Some **law enforcement records** are not open under FOIA; others are. Records that are exempt include those that if disclosed would interfere with enforcement proceedings, violate privacy laws, prevent a person from receiving a fair trial, reveal the identity of a confidential source, disclose law enforcement techniques that could be used to circumvent the law, or endanger the life of another. The trend is toward more secrecy. Daily police logs are open, but files of an open investigation are not.

OFFENSE/INCIDENT REPORT	1. TYPE			
INSTRUCTIONS ARE PRINTED SEPARATELY. IF ADDITIONAL SPACE IS NEEDED, USE REVERSE OF FORM; IDENTIFY ITEMS.	☐ a. ORIGINAL	☐ b. CONTINUATION	☐ c. SUPPLEMENT OR FOLLOWUP	

2. CODE NO. | 2a. SORT | 3. TYPE OF OFFENSE OR INCIDENT | 4. CASE CONTROL NUMBER

5. BUILDING NUMBER | 6. ADDRESS

7. NAME OF AGENCY/BUREAU | 8. AGENCY/BUREAU CODE | 9. SPECIFIC LOCATION | 10. LOCATION CODE

11a. DATE OF OFFENSE/INCIDENT | 11a. TIME OF OFFENSE/INCIDENT | 12. DAY | 13a. DATE REPORTED | 13b. TIME REPORTED | 14. DAY

15. JURISDICTION (X) ☐ EXCLUSIVE ☐ CONCURRENT ☐ PARTIAL ☐ PROPRIETARY | 16. NO. OF DEMONSTRATORS | 17. NO. EVACUATED | a. TIME START | b. TIME END

	ID CODE (a)	NAME AND ADDRESS (b)	AGE (c)	SEX (d)	RACE (e)	INJURY CODE (f)	TELEPHONE (g)
18. PERSONS INVOLVED		Last Name, First, Middle Initial					HOME
		Number, Street, Apt. No., City and State					BUSINESS
		Last Name, First, Middle Initial					HOME
		Number, Street, Apt. No., City and State					BUSINESS

Form GSA 3155. Created by the U.S. General Services Administration.

8. **Financial reports** or audits **of banks and other financial institutions** are exempt from disclosure. The burden again is on the government to show that release of the records would undermine the public's confidence in the institution. The law is designed to prevent a financial panic. Despite the fact that financial institutions are federally insured as a result of the 1929 stock market crash that led to the Great Depression, rumors of insolvency could threaten the financial sector and undermine the economy. The exemption is used mostly during times of financial crises.

9. Like trade secrets, this exemption is designed to prevent competitors from gaining an unfair advantage. Oil and gas companies involved in exploration must file information about their discoveries with federal agencies. This **geological data**, were it released, would give speculators an unfair advantage.

Freedom of Information Act Limitations

The Freedom of Information Act works only if those in government see its value and try to comply with the law. Unfortunately, even though the law has opened up part of the federal government, given the number and breadth of exemptions and other limitations, agencies often can circumvent the act's intent. Theoretically, an agency could destroy or conceal a record and those outside the agency might not be able to prove that the document ever existed.

And what if officials just take the records home? In *Kissinger v. Reporters Committee for Freedom of the Press*, 445 U.S. 136 (1980), the Supreme Court said former Secretary of State Henry Kissinger could keep secret his diary and official telephone calls because he took them home with him. The Court said the items could remain confidential unless the government required him to return them. Those who opposed the ruling warned that the decision would allow government officials to get around the FOIA by taking documents out of the office.

In addition, in *Forsham v. Harris*, 445 U.S. 169 (1980), the Supreme Court said that private organizations doing research under government grants did not need to reveal their data to the public because such information did not fall within the meaning of "agency records."

Other limitations also restrict information access.

• Interviewing Government Officials

Do reporters have a right to interview a public official? Can they require an elected official to talk? No. The U.S. 4th Circuit Court of Appeals held in *Baltimore Sun v. Ehrlich*, 437 F. 3d 410 (4th Cir. 2006), that Maryland Gov. Robert L. Ehrlich Jr. did not violate the First Amendment when he denied interviews to two *Baltimore Sun* reporters. The Court added:

> "[I]n the ongoing intercourse of government and press, a reporter endures only de minimis inconvenience when a government official denies the reporter access to discretionary information or refuses to answer the reporter's questions because the official disagrees with the substance or manner of the reporter's previous expression in reporting."

However, another Court noted that government officials cannot single out specific reporters and deny them access to press conferences when such meetings are open to all members of the Press. In *Citicasters v. Finkbeiner*, Case No. 07-CV-00117 (N.D. Ohio 2007), the judge ruled that a press conference is a public event. The case involved a mayor alleging a radio personality was an entertainer and not a news reporter and therefore should be excluded from the press conference.

• Executive Privilege

Under the concept of executive privilege, presidents and some state and local leaders have invoked the right to keep certain information from the Congress, state legislatures, courts, and the Press. The legal basis for the act is somewhat uncertain. It largely developed over time to give presidents and other leaders the right to keep working papers covering military

and diplomatic matters secret. It has come to include other internal documents produced in the executive branch as well. The courts have not challenged the overall concept, though they have ruled presidents can't use it to hide illegal activities. In *U.S. v Nixon*, 418 U.S. 683 (1974), the Supreme Court ruled that President Richard Nixon could not invoke executive privilege to protect incriminating tape recordings that were part of the Watergate scandal.

The court unanimously ruled that executive privilege is only absolute when it comes to military and diplomatic information regarding matters of national security. Otherwise, it had to be balanced against other interests.

Richard Nixon

JStone/Shutterstock.com

In the *Nixon* case, the Court said that the president was withholding evidence of a possible crime involving his aides. The Court, therefore, ordered that he turn over the tapes. Nixon complied. As a result, several aides were convicted and the president ultimately resigned from office.

• The 1974 Privacy Act

The growth of privacy concerns led Congress to pass the *1974 Privacy Act*. The act was designed to prevent government disclosure of American's personal information.

The American Civil Liberties Union had argued that as government agencies collected more information in computerized systems, some of it was bound to leak into the wrong hands. Journalists, meanwhile, feared such secrecy would enable the government to abuse its power. The Privacy Act represented a compromise between the two concerns.

The act strictly limits what government can do with the information. Also, the government is required to get permission from an individual before information about them is released or transferred to another agency. It gives individuals the right to inspect personal records and correct any errors. Officials that violate the law may be sued.

Unfortunately for journalists, the act encourages secrecy. Officials that release too little information, face no penalties.

In 1988, Congress provided even more protection by passing the *Computer Matching and Privacy Protection Act*, which helped individuals cross-check information so they would not lose government benefits.

• The Buckley Amendment and Clery Act

The Family Educational Rights and Privacy Act (FERPA), otherwise known as the *Buckley Amendment*, prevents schools that receive federal funds from disclosing permanent student records, including disciplinary records and proceedings, without written consent from the parent or guardian. If the student is at least 18 years old, the student must give permission. Public school systems that fail to follow the law can be denied federal funds.

The law does not forbid the disclosure of directory information, such as name, address, field of study, etc. Nor does it prevent the release of newsworthy information about a student involved in athletics or other extra-curricular activities.

Yet, school administrators often have used the Buckley Amendment to deny information that can be released, such as police incident reports of campus crime. Congress addressed the issue in the *Higher Education Act of 1998*, which requires all colleges and universities that receive federal funds to keep a log of incidents of crime on campus and make it open to the public. The log must include the nature of the crime, the date, time, location, and disposition of each incident. It must be made public within two business days. Information that would identify a victim or jeopardize an investigation is exempted.

In an effort to gain more information about campus crime, the federal *Crime Awareness and Campus Security Act*, otherwise known as the *Clery Act*, now requires schools to publish campus crime statistics annually. The Student Press Law Center offers advice about how to cover campus crime at www.splc.org.

• The Federal Advisory Committee Act

In an attempt to control an increase in the number of secret advisory committees in the executive branch of government, Congress passed the *Federal Advisory Committee Act in 1972*. The act mandates that those non-government organizations that advise the president and agencies of the executive branch hold public meetings and keep public records.

The U.S. Supreme Court ruled in *Public Citizen v. Dept. of Justice*, 491 U.S. 440 (1989), that the law does not cover privately-funded organizations like the American Bar Association, which review qualifications of potential federal judges. The ruling eliminated several private organizations from the reach of the law despite the fact their advice helps shape government policy.

• Criminal History Information

The now defunct federal Law Enforcement Assistance Administration issued guidelines in 1976 designed to restrict the release of personal information of people arrested or charged with a crime. Although not mandated, as a result of the directive, some law enforcement agencies stopped releasing police blotter information and conviction histories. Most states now restrict the release of criminal history records.

Civil libertarians had argued that public access to someone's police record could stigmatize them. Journalists countered that the practice could lead to police abuse, including secret arrests. They also argued that the public was entitled to know the information to protect themselves from people with a criminal history.

• The Federal Driver's Privacy Act

The 1994 federal *Driver's Privacy Protection Act* makes it illegal for states to disclose information from driver's licenses and vehicle registration records to the public. Insurance companies and private investigators still can access them. Such records often were useful to journalists doing automobile safety stories. After the law was challenged, the U.S. Supreme Court held in *Reno v. Condon*, 528 U.S. 141 (2000), that the Congress had the authority to pass the law under the Commerce Clause of the U.S. Constitution since some states were selling the information to insurance companies.

• The Health Insurance Portability and Accountability Act (HIPPA)

The *Health Insurance Portability and Accountability Act* (HIPPA) protects patients' medical records from being released without written consent from the patient. But the act makes it more difficult for journalists and others to find out the names and conditions of those who have been admitted to the hospital after an auto accident.

Government in the Sunshine Act

Getting documents is only part of the problem of government access. Theoretically, a people who would be their own governors also ought to be able to attend meetings where public officials are making decisions in their name with their money affecting their lives. Yet since the beginning of the Republic, officials have found it much easier if people are kept out, since it makes their job more difficult if people get to see and criticize what they do.

Journalists have long struggled to persuade, cajole, or otherwise pry their way into ostensibly public meetings to fulfill their watchdog role of government and report back to the people what officials are doing. After years of campaigning, they finally persuaded Congress to enact the *Government in the Sunshine Act* in 1976. Also known as the *Federal Open Meetings Law*, the act requires about 50 federal administrative agencies, commissions and boards to hold at least some of their meetings in public. Those organizations covered by the act must provide advance notice of when and where they are going to meet.

Closed sessions are still permitted if the subject matter falls under any of 10 exemptions. The agency must stipulate the legal reason for closing a meeting before doing so. The exemptions parallel the nine FOIA exemptions. The agency must vote to close a meeting before they can do so. The vote must be recorded, and minutes or transcripts of the meeting must be kept. If votes are taken in the closed meeting, a record must be made public of who voted and how they voted. The record must be made public.

Agencies that violate the law may be sued, and federal courts may order the agencies to open their meetings if they do not comply with the law. Those who sue the agency and win are entitled to attorney's fees and court costs from the government. Government officials who violate the law, however, are not subject to civil or criminal penalties. And any actions that were taken during the meeting are not invalid. Sometimes officials can also get around the law by sharing private policy memos among themselves and then deciding what to do in private before announcing their decision.

The act covers such agencies as the Federal Communications Commission, the Federal Trade Commission, Interstate Commerce Commission, the Consumer Product Safety Commission, the National Transportation Safety Board, the Civil Service Commission, the Securities and Exchange Commission, the Federal Reserve Board, and the U.S. Postal Service. It does not apply to cabinet-level departments or the National Security Council, which advises the president.

State Open Records and Meetings Laws

All 50 states and the District of Columbia have open record/open meeting laws, many of which follow the same guidelines as the FOIA. Most cover not only state government agencies, but also cities, school districts and other public bodies within a state. The laws provide varying degrees of access to records and public meetings.

For example, in some states records are presumed to be open; in others the presumption is that they are closed unless specified as open. As with the FOIA, state records concerning some topics such as personnel matters, law enforcement investigation files, and juvenile records are off limits. On the other hand, emails between government officials are often considered open records.

Generally, those seeking records are entitled to the information without demonstrating a need to know. The records are open by virtue of the fact that they are "public" records. In some cases, the common law covers openness. Those records concerning births, marriages, deaths, property transactions, etc., have always been open. As with the FOIA, state privacy laws also restrict access to certain information.

Laws usually allow meetings to be held physically or via a videoconference. State laws also require advance notice of when and where meetings are to be held and that minutes of the meetings be kept.

As with the federal FOIA, state laws generally allow for agencies to close their meetings or go into executive session for specific purposes. Each state specifies when and under what circumstances an agency may hold such a meeting. Again, many states follow the same guidelines as the FOIA.

State laws also often allow citizens to sue an agency that does not comply with the law and seek a court order requiring the agency to open its meetings and/or records. Unlike the Government in the Sunshine Act, any action taken by an agency in violation of the law is invalid in many states. Criminal actions also can be brought against officials who violate the law.

Some states have freedom of information organizations that help police state agencies. Some of these organizations have the ability to enforce the laws; others do not. Those who lack authority must turn to the state attorney general or local prosecutors for enforcement.

State laws generally provide greater access to state records and meetings than the FOIA does to federal government information. The Reporters Committee for Freedom of the Press (www.rcfp.org) provides an "Open Government Guide" that provide some guidance to various state open record/open meeting laws.

Additional Problems of Information Access

As already noted, free speech is often curtailed by time, place, and manner restrictions. Public access laws generally have no control over court records. And privacy concerns also limit what the Press may get and publish.

Officials do not have a right to prevent citizens from recording or taking pictures of police and other emergency personnel at news events so long as they don't interfere with the official investigation. Law enforcement officers do have a right, however, to prevent citizens and the Press from crime scenes or other areas of disaster where emergency officials are working. In most states, police do allow reporters access to such events, but it is considered a privilege and not a right, though the police and others may not arbitrarily grant access to some and not others.

Neither do reporters and others have a right to enter jails and prisons to conduct interviews. In *Saxbe v. Washington Post*, 417 U.S. 843, and *Pell v. Procunier*, 417 U.S. 817, both of which were decided on the same day in 1974, the Court held that reporters had no right to interview prisoners under the First Amendment. The Court said in a later case that a prisoner also had no right to request and be granted an interview with the media.

Some judicial documents and proceedings are open; others are not. Grand jury proceedings are closed, mostly to prevent those about to be charged with a crime from fleeing prosecution. Juvenile records are closed. Complaints and responses filed in lawsuits are usually open.

Access to information about privately held companies is usually confidential. But corporations whose stock is traded publicly must file certain public documents with the Securities and Exchange Commission as part of laws passed in the 1930s to prevent another stock market collapse, such as the one in 1929 that led to the Great Depression.

Sometimes lawyers will use other means to dissuade journalists from getting information. Those who misrepresent themselves to get information may be sued. Pretending to be someone else or failing to disclose to sources the nature of the story they are pursuing may result in legal action. When two reporters from ABC News used false names to gain entrance to the Food Lion grocery store chain in the 1990s and do a story on unsanitary practices, Food Lion sued. In the end, ABC got what amounted to a slap on the wrist, but not before spending a lot of money defending itself.

Trespass laws prevent information seekers from certain areas. Some public land is off limits, as is most private property. And those who continually make a nuisance of themselves to get information may be sued for harassment.

Although the world is becoming more addicted to social media, use of undocumented information from online and social media sources also can result in legal action, or at the very least—embarrassment. And state laws often restrict recording events and conversations.

Suggestions for Getting Information

Journalists and other media professionals should familiarize themselves with both the federal laws regarding open records and meetings as well as the laws of the state in which they work. Anticipate trouble. If one is seeking a document or preparing to attend a meeting that's likely to be closed, one should research the law before contacting the government agency for the document or showing up at the meeting. Know what the law provides.

Many journalists carry a copy of their state's open meetings and records act with them and refer officials to the specific passage that allows them public access. Being able to show officials the law moves the dispute from a personal confrontation to a legal conclusion. In every case, be polite and calm, but firm. Those who seek information should know their rights and make it known to officials that they will assert them.

If one works for a newspaper or other media outlet, it is wise to discuss in advance with management the possibility of denied access and whether the company will back an effort to gain the information in Court. If not, the reporter may have no alternative but to go it alone. That's a big step. Those who are willing to file suit should understand the consequences of such action. The federal Government in the Sunshine Act and many state laws require the government to pay the legal fees of those seeking records if they win, but if they lose, they will foot the bill themselves.

If officials are intent on going into executive session, demand to know the legal basis for closing the meeting. Ask to see minutes of the meeting or a transcript if one is made. Votes should be done in public. Interview as many people as possible that were involved in the meeting.

Finally, never underestimate the value of good sources. Those who know people often can schmooze their way in. Being knowledgeable about the law and firm in one's purpose is important. Confidence is an asset. Be persuasive. But never forget the adage that honey often works better than vinegar.

CHAPTER 9

Protection of Sources

The Need to Protect Sources

Sometimes, the truth is hidden from us, not because of concerns for national security or privacy, but because of more sinister reasons. Sometimes, the people we need to trust the most—those in government, industry, and other institutions—can't be trusted at all. Those who should be our champions to ferret out wrongdoing are themselves guilty of corruption.

When that happens, we often turn to the Press to expose what has been covered up. For the Press does more than report the news; it is a primary investigative tool of society, serving as a watchdog over the powerful.

To fulfill its mission, the Press often must rely on secret sources to provide it with the information needed to see into dark corners. In fact, without confidential sources, the watchdog would not have much of a bark, and those in high places would not fear its power to expose corruption.

Unfortunately, the sources that come forward with vital information are often in fear for their careers or their lives, and it is therefore necessary to protect their identities. Yet the Court has not recognized this practice of keeping sources secret as a fundamental right of the Press, and that has provided yet another problem for the media.

It's not that the law doesn't recognize and protect the sanctity of some relationships. The privilege of confidentiality developed under English common law and exists between a doctor and patient, a lawyer and client, a husband and wife, and a priest and a penitent. This means that a doctor or lawyer, for example, can't be made to reveal in court private conversations with their patients or clients. Secrecy in such cases is important to foster openness and trust in the relationship. The law, therefore, bolsters relationships that are necessary to maintain the health of the society at large.

Journalists have long argued that keeping the reporter/source relationship confidential is just as important. They contend that sources that are in fear for their jobs and lives and without protection will not talk. Furthermore, if reporters are forced to reveal their sources, it will have a chilling effect on the media, as fewer sources will agree to come forward with important information. And if they don't come forward, stories of corruption and waste will go unreported, harming society.

ostill/Shutterstock.com

Journalists and editors have argued the point since colonial times, noting as they did with public record access, that freedom of the press means little if sources can't be secured and protected. Therefore, they have long held that the First Amendment gives them that right.

Furthermore, they contend that the privilege belongs to them, not just their sources. In other privileged relationships, such as between a doctor and patient or lawyer and client, the privilege belongs to the patient or client and not the doctor or lawyer. Thus, the patient or client can release the doctor or lawyer from the privilege obligation. Journalists usually claim that they must keep the relationship confidential even if released from the obligation in order to protect the news process.

The Court, meanwhile, has not fully agreed that the Press has a complete right to any privilege of confidentiality. It has responded by noting that justice is best served when those with information important to a case are forced to reveal it. More than 60 years ago, the Court noted in *United States v. Bryan*, 339 U.S. 323, 331 (1950), that "For more than three centuries it has now been recognized as a fundamental maxim that the public has a right to every man's evidence."

In *Branzburg v. Hayes*, 408 U.S. 665, 710 (1972), the Court added "The obligation of all citizens [is] to give relevant testimony with respect to criminal conduct."

Thus, the Court has maintained that the Press often must reveal confidential information when ordered, especially in situations about crime, regardless of the reporter/source relationship. Those journalists who refuse to comply with the court orders are often found to be in contempt of court and jailed until they reveal the information.

Failing to Keep a Promise—When Sources Sue

As frightening as that may be to the journalist, giving up the information may result in an even greater problem. Those reporters who "burn" or reveal the identity of a source to avoid jail may find themselves facing a lawsuit. In addition to the ethical concerns of making a promise and then failing to keep it, the reporter may face a legal challenge from the source for breach of contract, or more accurately, *promissory estoppel*. That doctrine holds that a person can be found liable for making a promise to another if the second person relied on the promise to his detriment and it created an injustice that could be remedied by the Court.

The U.S. Supreme Court held just such a situation existed in *Cohen v. Cowles Media Co.*, 501 U.S. 663 (1991), when it ruled 5–4 that the First Amendment will not protect a journalist if he breaks a promise of confidentiality to a source. In that case, Dan Cohen, a public relations advisor to a Republican gubernatorial candidate in Minnesota, leaked information to the media just before the election about the Democratic candidate's past legal problems. The reporters had promised him anonymity, but their editors at the *Minneapolis Star Tribune* and *St. Paul Pioneer Press* disagreed and decided to name him in the story, believing it would be unfair to the other side not to do so. As a result, Cohen was fired, and he sued the papers for breach of contract.

The Court held that promissory estoppel is a "generally applicable law"—that is, it applies to everyone—and that the First Amendment will not protect anyone who breaks the law to get and publish information. The Court said that the papers did not obtain the information lawfully since they broke a legal promise of confidentiality. Noted Justice Byron White: "[T]he First Amendment does not confer on the press a constitutional right to disregard promises that could otherwise be enforced under state law."

Branzburg v. Hayes

In some situations, however, the Court has recognized a *qualified privilege* to keep sources confidential, eliminating the problem of making a choice between revealing a source and being sued or keeping the source confidential and being held in contempt of court.

(The concept of qualified privilege here is different from that discussed under libel law. Qualified privilege with regard to libel means the reporter under certain circumstances can publish information that is libelous and not be held accountable. Qualified privilege regarding confidential sources means the reporter in certain situations can keep sources secret from the Court.)

This qualified privilege to keep sources confidential developed from the U.S. Supreme Court case *Branzburg v. Hayes*, 408 U.S. 665 (1972). In that case, Paul Branzburg, a reporter for the *Louisville Courier-Journal*, wrote a story about illegal drug use, promising his sources he would not identify them. He was subsequently ordered to appear before a grand jury to answer questions about the story and his sources. He refused, claiming a First Amendment right to keep his sources confidential. (A grand jury is a group of citizens gathered to decide if enough evidence exists to charge someone with a crime.)

The Kentucky Court of Appeals ruled that the law did not protect him from testifying to the grand jury about events he personally witnessed. He appealed to the U.S. Supreme Court, which, consolidating that case with two others, upheld the lower court, ruling 5–4 that no one, including journalists, had a right to refuse to reveal information about a potential crime to a grand jury.

Four of the Supreme Court justices said that journalists must always comply when ordered to testify. Justice Byron White, writing for the four, noted that the purpose of a grand jury was to determine if probable cause exists to believe a crime has been committed and to protect citizens from wrongful criminal prosecution. Therefore, he said:

"Its investigative powers are necessarily broad, and the grand jury plays an important, constitutional role that outweighs any burden on newsgathering that might come from the occasional subpoena to reporters."

He added that if a reporter received a subpoena, it would only pose an "incidental burden" on newsgathering.

Justice Lewis Powell provided the fifth crucial vote upholding the lower court decision, but his concurring opinion left open the possibility that under certain circumstances the First Amendment might allow journalists to protect their sources. He noted:

The asserted claim to privilege should be judged on its facts by striking of a proper balance between freedom of the press and the obligation of all citizens to give relevant testimony with respect to criminal conduct. The balance of these vital constitutional and societal interests on a case-by-case basis accords with the tried and traditional way of adjudicating such questions.

Justice Potter Stewart wrote for the dissent, arguing that the First Amendment supported a qualified journalist's privilege. He and the other three dissenters argued that the government should have to justify requiring journalists to reveal their sources. Specifically, he said the government should be made to follow a three-part test:

1. The government should be required to show that a journalist has relevant information regarding a crime.
2. The government must show that the information cannot be obtained by some other means that doesn't tread on the First Amendment.
3. The government must show that it has a compelling and overriding interest in the information.

The *Branzburg* case made it clear that journalists must reveal their sources when called upon to do so by a grand jury. Nevertheless, the ruling was specific to grand juries. When it comes to other situations, lower courts have generally followed Justice Stewart's three-part test, providing journalists with at least a qualified privilege to keep sources secret.

After all, four of the dissenting justices voted in favor of allowing journalists to keep their sources confidential and a fifth—Justice Powell—agreed that journalists should have at least a limited privilege in some situations. Whether the Supreme Court would agree with such an assessment has not been tested.

The general question the Court seems prone to ask is whether the confidential information held by a journalist would ensure or detract from a person's right to get a fair trial. If one of the three factors supports the journalist's position, it is likely the journalist will be granted a qualified privilege of confidentiality.

Other Sources of Protection

In addition to the limited constitutional privilege from *Branzburg*, journalists have also found relief in court rules. The Federal Rules of Criminal Procedure, the Federal Rules of Civil Procedure and the Federal Rules of Evidence may not specifically note a reporter's privilege, but some federal courts have said a qualified privilege is inherent in them.

Rule 17(c) of the Federal Rules of Criminal Procedure notes that subpoenas may be issued in federal criminal cases for materials that are only admissible as evidence, thus the material must be relevant and necessary for trial. Therefore, the subpoena cannot be used for a "fishing expedition" to see what information may be available. Rule 26 of the Federal Rules of Civil Procedure prohibits judges from granting subpoenas if the burden required to obtain the information outweighs the benefit or if the information can be obtained somewhere else. Rule 501 of the Federal Rules of Evidence allows the Court to establish privilege for news people on a case-by-case basis.

The U.S. Justice Department also limits its attorneys in their quest to subpoena journalists or their notes. The department's guidelines require that First Amendment concerns be balanced against law enforcement needs, that reasonable attempts be made to find the information elsewhere, that Justice Department lawyers try to negotiate with journalists to get the information before issuing a subpoena, and that in criminal cases they make certain that a crime has been committed and that any information held by the journalists is vital to the trial before asking for it.

Nevertheless, just because a journalist receives a subpoena doesn't necessarily mean he will end up testifying in court. Thousands of subpoenas are issued each year to the news media asking journalists to appear to answer questions or provide story notes or broadcast out-takes. Journalists and others often fight such orders by filing a motion to *quash* the subpoena. Such a motion is a request that the judge set aside the order.

Often, judges will dispose of subpoenas because they are overbroad in their request for information because the information is not relevant or necessary to the case, or because there are other ways to get the infor-mation that won't involve offending the First Amendment.

Contempt and the Collateral Bar Rule

In any case, journalists who receive subpoenas or other legal mandates can't just ignore them; they are valid court orders to appear in court or bring some piece of evidence to court. Failure to appear or provide the requested information will result in a contempt of court ruling from the judge.

Those who receive a subpoena should inform their editor or publisher immediately and ask to talk to the company's legal counsel. One should never accept a subpoena for someone else.

If a subpoena asks for certain documents or information, those become official evidence once the subpoena has been served. Therefore, destroying the material will most certainly result in a contempt citation from the Court. The proper course of action is to gather the requested material in case the subpoena can't be quashed and the recipient of the subpoena must reveal it later. If one thinks that the material should be withheld, but his employer and his employer's attorney disagree and are unwilling to protect the information, the recipient may need to hire his own lawyer. Company attorneys work for the company, not the reporter.

Even those who think a court order may be illegal must still follow the order until a higher court overturns it. This is called the *collateral bar rule*. It prevents individuals from arbitrarily deciding for themselves which court orders to follow. Thus, a reporter who thinks a judge's order to turn over information is unconstitutional and disobeys it and is found in contempt will likely not have his contempt citation overturned on appeal—even if the original order is found to be illegal.

Contempt is a judicial rule that allows judges to maintain the decorum of the courtroom. The rule existed before the founding of the Republic. It gives the judge the power to punish those who show disrespect for the legal process by either physically disrupting the Court or by ignoring its rules or orders. Punishment can include time in jail or a fine or both.

Direct contempt usually involves some misconduct or disruption in or near the courtroom. It may also occur when someone refuses to obey a judge. For example, news photographers or journalists who fail to obey a judge's order to turn off a voice recorder or stop taking pictures will be found in direct contempt. Direct contempt also occurs when a reporter refuses to name sources. *Indirect contempt* occurs when a party fails to follow a rule or an order outside the presence of the Court.

Contempt can be civil or criminal. Criminal contempt is often cited when someone violates court rules or becomes physically unruly. It usually results in a fine or jail time or both. Civil contempt is used to force someone to comply with a court order. In some ways it can be more severe. For example, a judge may lock up a journalist for refusing to name a source until the journalist is willing to do so. Thus, the stay in jail may be indefinite.

A judge may not unilaterally impose a criminal contempt sentence that exceeds six months. The U.S. Supreme Court has held that the Constitution requires a jury trial in such cases. The requirement does not apply to criminal contempt citations of less than six months. Neither does it affect civil contempt citations. Therefore, reporters who refuse to reveal their sources on principle should be prepared to spend a long time in jail. Judges usually release journalists from jail when the information they have withheld is no longer necessary to the case. But cases may drag on for years.

Criminal Cases v. Civil Cases and Nonconfidential Information

Because of the Sixth Amendment right to a fair trial, the Court often is less likely to grant journalists the privilege in criminal cases than in civil cases. In civil cases, the Court will generally ask:

1. if the person seeking the information from the reporter has shown that it is relevant to the case;
2. if the information is critical to deciding the case; and
3. if there are no alternative ways to get the information.

If the questions are answered in the affirmative, the journalist will probably have to reveal the confidential information.

Courts are also less likely to protect nonconfidential information, such as broadcast outtakes. Photographers are routinely ordered to provide photos of fires and auto accidents. When nonconfidential information is involved, the Court generally treats the request for privilege the same regardless of whether it is a criminal or civil trial. Meanwhile, when journalists or others are eyewitnesses to an event, the Court will not excuse them from testifying about the matter.

In addition, courts are less likely to grant privilege when the journalist is a party to litigation—as when the reporter is being sued for libel and wants to keep sources secret. Sometimes, it is necessary to gain access to reporter's notes, sources, and other such information to prove that the journalist acted negligently or with malice. In other civil matters, courts are generally more lenient.

Yet, many state courts also have recognized a journalist's privilege based on the First Amendment—sometimes even in criminal cases if the information cannot be shown to help the defendant. The Court made such a ruling in *Zelenka v. Wisconsin*, 266 N.W.2d 279 (1978).

Telephone Records

In some cases, subpoenas have been issued for reporters' telephone records as a way to find their confidential sources. In *New York Times v. Gonzales*, 459 F.3d 160 (2d Cir. 2006), the Court said "whatever rights a newspaper or reporter has to refuse disclosure in response to a sub-poena extends to the newspaper's or reporter's telephone records in the possession of a third party provider." The Court said the telephone was an essential tool of journalists in gathering information and therefore the protection extended to that tool. The Court held that the privi-lege was qualified and could be overcome by a compelling government interest.

Mega Pixel/Shutterstock.com

Anonymous Online Posts

What happens if someone posts an anonymous message online that libels someone? Can the defamed party compel the online service pro-vider to reveal the name of the person who posted the message? Yes, sometimes.

Courts are grappling with the problem of when to allow such action, weighing the First Amendment right to engage in anonymous speech against the right to legally confront unlawful speech. The Court has held that the First Amendment right to anonymous speech is not absolute.

At least one appellate court has fashioned a four-part test to help judges decide when subpoenas should be issued to discover the identity of those who post anonymous, yet libelous, messages online. Known as the *Dendrite Test* from *Dendrite International Inc. v. Doe*, 775 A 2d 756 (N.J. Super. Ct. 2001), the Court said that the plaintiff first must be able to establish a prima facie case for libel before issuing a subpoena. The Court said:

1. The plaintiff first had to try to contact the anonymous poster and notify him that an application for disclosure had been made trying to identify him.
2. The plaintiff must identify the defamatory statements made against him.
3. The plaintiff must provide evidence to support all the elements of libel.
4. The Court must balance the First Amendment right to anonymous speech against the strength of the plaintiff's case.

As a result, the Courts have made clear that protections for anonymous online speech are not absolute.

State Shield Laws

In addition to the other protections, 39 states have passed laws recognizing some kind of reporter's privilege. Such statutes are called *shield laws,* and they give news people the right to keep sources confidential in certain situations. Some states have gone so far as to put their shield laws into their state constitutions to safeguard them from being overturned by the courts.

Shield laws vary widely from state to state. They generally fall into three different groups—1. those that provide absolute privilege, 2. those that offer privilege if the source's information is published or broadcast, and 3. those that are filled with numerous exceptions. In some states, for example, the law only allows protection if the information is relevant to a case, cannot be obtained elsewhere, and there is a compelling reason for making the reporter reveal them. (This is the rule that was suggested in the *Branzburg* case.)

Unfortunately, in some states journalists find shield laws so porous as to make them almost useless. For example, it is not unusual for a law to offer journalists the right to keep sources confidential only until officials have tried and failed to find the information elsewhere. At that point, they may return to compel the journalist to reveal the name of the source. Such "last resort" protection doesn't provide much comfort or protection for news people.

Journalists and others dealing with confidential information should read carefully the shield laws of the state in which they work. The Reporters Committee for Freedom of the Press has prepared an online source called *The Reporter's Privilege* listing the rules of each state. It can be found at the organization's website at http://www.rcfp.org/privilege.

Who Is a Reporter?

Another problem is that most shield laws only protect "news reporters." The question then is who is a "news reporter?"

Technically, the First Amendment gives all citizens the right to gather and publish or broadcast information. Therefore, one could argue that any citizen with a recorder and a cell phone camera could be a "journalist." Unlike doctors and lawyers, who must be licensed, journalists need not meet any qualifications. Most would argue that this is a good thing. Otherwise, the government could control who provides us with news and information.

Most shield laws have attempted to define who the law protects. Again, it varies widely from state to state. A broad definition might include those who are directly engaged in gathering, procuring, compiling, editing, or publishing information to the public—as does Minnesota's law. Other shield laws, however, protect only those who work for newspapers or broadcast stations. Freelance writers, book authors, magazine writers, and those who publish on the Internet, such as bloggers, are sometimes left out. In many states, the question of who is and is not a journalist remains unanswered.

In interpreting the term "journalist," courts often look to see how closely the reporter or writer resembles a traditional journalist. Questions include whether the "reporter" has a journalism education, credentials, or affiliation with a news outlet such as a newspaper or TV station, an adherence to journalism principles regarding editing and fact checking, as well as journalism ethics and other professional standards and practices, and whether the "reporter" was producing an independent news product for public consumption and benefit instead of promotional material for purely commercial gain. These questions are particularly useful when the Court is trying to decide if a blogger qualifies as a newsperson gathering and disseminating recent news rather than an activist or commentator.

This is not to say that nontraditional journalists are always left out in the cold. Filmmaker Ken Burns and his daughter were granted privilege in *In re McCray et al.*, 41 Media L. Rep. 1313 (2013) regarding materials used in the documentary *The Central Park Five* about five men's civil suit against New York City for wrongful imprisonment. And an investigative book author was granted privilege in *Shoen v. Shoen*, 5 F.3d 1289 (1993), when his notes and tapes of interviews for a book detailing the battle between U-Haul founder Leonard Shoen and his sons Mark and Edward were subpoenaed. In the Burns' case, as in others, the judge noted that the information was gathered for the purpose of sharing it with the public and not for other reasons.

Efforts to Pass a Federal Shield Law

Congress has proposed a federal shield law to protect journalists from being found in contempt for failing to reveal sources, but so far such legislation has not passed despite repeated efforts. Both houses of Congress as well as the president were on record in 2009 supporting such a measure.

The idea has been around since the 1970s. Numerous bills were proposed after the *Branzburg* decision, but Congress has been unable to agree on whether to grant privilege to journalists who witness crimes—as in the *Branzburg* case. Neither have they been able to agree on how to define a journalist. Limiting the criteria would cause First Amendment problems. And the advent of bloggers and Internet publishing has made the matter more difficult.

Zurcher v. Stanford Daily

Subpoenas aren't the only problem-facing journalists. Search warrants can also be a headache. A *search warrant* is a court order that gives law enforcement officials the right to search a specified place for specified materials or people. The authority comes from the *Fourth Amendment* to the U.S. Constitution. However, the search must be conducted reasonably and done only when there is probable cause to believe that information necessary to a criminal investigation is located on the premises.

Unlike subpoenas, which can be challenged at a later date in court, search warrants give authorities the immediate right to enter the location specified in the warrant. Thus, search warrants are used when police believe evidence will be destroyed or lost or suspects will flee.

Those authorities seeking a warrant must appear before a judge and give a valid reason for the search before receiving the warrant, but they pose a problem for journalists because of the lack of advance notice that police are about to invade their newsroom. As a result, the police may see other confidential information in plain view but not listed in the search warrant that journalists need to keep confidential.

The problem of search warrants in the newsroom reached the U.S. Supreme Court in *Zurcher v. Stanford Daily*, 436 U.S. 547 (1978), when the Court ruled 5–3 that it is not a violation of the U.S. Constitution when law enforcement officials conduct an unannounced search of a newsroom. The Court said such action was legal so long as the warrant was specific and reasonable. Although police could not rummage indiscriminately through the newsroom, they could search for specific evidence noted in the warrant.

The case stemmed from an incident in 1971 when demonstrators occupied the Stanford University Hospital and sheriff's deputies ejected them. The Stanford University newspaper covered the violent event, which injured several police. The newspaper published photographs of the conflict a few days later. The police then secured a warrant and searched the newsroom for more photos and other information that could possibly identify those who injured the police officers. Student journalists were present, though none were suspected of a crime. The police found nothing.

The newspaper staff subsequently sued in a federal civil action, claiming a violation of the First, Fourth, and 14th Amendments to the U.S. Constitution. The lower court and appellate court ruled in favor of the students, but the police appealed, and the U.S. Supreme Court reversed the lower court decisions.

The newspaper had argued unsuccessfully that searches of newsrooms threatened the ability of the Press to gather, analyze, and disseminate news. Their argument was based on the fact that a search would be disruptive to the timely news process, that it would dry up confidential sources out of fear that other information might be revealed, that it would discourage reporters from keeping notes and records, that it would inhibit internal editorial deliberations, and that it would prompt journalists to self-censor to conceal information potentially of interest to the police.

The Court rejected the arguments, noting that nothing in the Fourth or First Amendment prohibited the police from searching a newsroom. As a result of the ruling, the number of search warrants for newsrooms quickly increased.

Ironically, the Court noted that the Congress or state legislatures could pass laws forbidding newsroom searches. Such bills were introduced at both the state and federal level within days of the ruling, supporting the journalists' arguments in *Zurcher*.

The Privacy Protection Act

As a result of the *Zurcher* case, Congress passed *The Privacy Protection Act of 1980*. The law limits the use of search warrants against the media. It also effectively overruled *Zurcher*.

Under the act, state and federal officers are prohibited from searching and seizing a journalist's work product or documentary materials when investigating a crime. Work products include notes, outtakes, rough drafts, etc.. Documentary materials include photographs, tapes, films, manuscripts, and the like.

Instead of securing a search warrant, officers must issue a subpoena, except under very limited circumstances. The law allows officials to search and seize work products only when:

1. The person who has the material is suspected of a crime, or
2. The materials must be seized to prevent serious injury or death.

A search warrant also may be used to obtain documentary materials if either of the first two conditions exists, or

3. In cases where issuing a subpoena would give someone time to destroy, hide or change the evidence, or
4. The person holding the material has not responded to a subpoena or other legal requests and further delay would hamper the pursuit of justice.

Those officials who violate the law may be sued. Journalists who are successful can also recover court costs and attorney's fees.

What should journalists do if the police show up at the newsroom with a warrant instead of a subpoena? The *First Amendment Handbook* published by The Reporter's Committee for Freedom of the Press notes that staff members should take pictures and record the process. They also should call the company's attorney. Staff personnel may not interfere with the police search. However, staffers are not required to assist the police.

Consider Alternatives

Many, if not most, journalists are not aware of the legal ramifications of entering into reporter/source agreements. Far too often they routinely agree to matters that could land them in court. Given what can happen, it is best not to offer confidentiality to a source unless there is absolutely no other way to get the information and it is of such importance that the community will suffer harm without it. Even then, journalists should exercise care.

Journalists should consider carefully whether it's even necessary to enter into a promise with the source to get the information. They should first determine if it's possible to get it somewhere else. Journalists should always talk to their editors before offering confidentiality. The news organization may not be willing to back up the reporter. Also, never talk to anyone else outside the news organization—not even a spouse or best friend—about the source or confidential information. The Court may rule that such outside discussions constitute a waiver of the privilege since the reporter has not attempted to keep the source or information secret.

It is a better practice to try to persuade the source to come forward without offering anonymity. Appealing to the source's concern for country or community may be enough to convince him to go on the record.

If that fails, some journalists will urge the source to point the reporter in the right direction so it may be possible to find the information elsewhere. Such a situation was described in the movie "All the President's Men," the story about *Washington Post* reporters Bob Woodward and Carl Bernstein and their efforts to uncover the Watergate scandal that brought down the Nixon presidency. In that movie, Woodward meets his confidential source in a parking garage in the middle of the night.

Bob Woodward

The source agrees to keep Woodward on the right track in his investigation, but will not directly give him information.

The practice is similar to the old game of *Hot and Cold* where someone hides something and then lets the other player know how close he's getting to it by *hinting* that he's getting "hot" or "cold" the closer or farther away he gets from the item. Similarly, the source may be persuaded to provide the same kind of assistance without actually revealing any information. Thus, the reporter is more likely to find the information on his own or from another source willing to go on the record. The problem is that it may take weeks or months to get the information using this technique. Sometimes one may not get it at all.

Nevertheless, until state legislatures and the Congress provide an absolute shield law or the courts recognize that reporters have the same privilege as patients and clients have with their doctors and lawyers, journalists will need to exercise care when dealing with confidential sources.

CHAPTER 10

Free Press/Fair Trial

In all criminal prosecutions, the accused shall enjoy the right to a speedy and public trial, by an impartial jury of the state and district wherein the crime shall have been committed, which district shall have been previously ascertained by law, and to be informed of the nature and cause of the accusation; to be confronted with the witnesses against him; to have compulsory process for obtaining witnesses in his favor, and to have the assistance of counsel for his defense.

—*Sixth Amendment to the U.S. Constitution*

When Constitutional Rights Collide

What happens when the right to a fair trial—guaranteed by the Sixth Amendment—and the right to a free press—guaranteed by the First Amendment—conflict? Both fundamental liberties are central to our ideal of a free society. Therefore, the courts are committed to ensuring both are protected—even when those rights are at odds with one another. Yet, reconciling them is often easier said than done.

The problem occurs most frequently when the news media exhibits its hunger for the lurid and sensational. Trials involving the rich and famous or those defendants accused of grisly crimes usually erupt in media feeding frenzies. This fascination often overshadows the Press's nobler goal of reporting on trials deliberately and impartially. The Press also forgets its more important watchdog role of monitoring the courts and the judicial process. The result instead is a quest to be first with the most graphic and sordid information, sometimes undermining a defendant's ability to get a fair trial.

This interest in the inflammatory interferes with fairness in several ways. It makes finding and seating an impartial jury difficult since many in the jury pool may have already made up their minds about the guilt or innocence of the accused from press reports. Stories of past criminal records, alleged confessions, inconclusive lie detector tests, and other unsubstantiated and often inadmissible information stir up emotions and give potentially false impressions. They urge people to convict or acquit on the basis of feelings instead of facts.

Such news coverage turns the Court into a circus, demeaning the administration of justice. People begin to see the court process more as entertainment than an important and serious function of society. In addition, it leads the public to misunderstand the frequency and nature of crime.

This media zeal is not new, but the intensity and reach of the media has increased, often making it more difficult today for the Court to guarantee a fair trial. As a result, the Court, as in other matters, has sought ways to deal with the problem.

An early example of a decision that was overturned because of prejudicial pretrial publicity is *Irvin v. Dowd*, 366 U.S. 717 (1961). The U.S. Supreme Court said intense media coverage had interfered with the defendant's rights when it reversed the murder conviction of Leslie Irvin, who had been convicted of killing six people in or near Evansville, Indiana, in the early 1950s. The county prosecutor had issued press releases calling the defendant "Mad Dog" Irvin, and extensive media coverage included reports of a confession that Irvin later denied as well as stories about his criminal past that would not have been admissible in court.

The defense had asked for and received a change of venue. But moving the trial to a nearby county where the coverage was just as intense did little to mitigate the media damage. Before hearing any of the evidence, 8 of the 12 jurors said they thought he was guilty, though they added that they could still be fair. Irvin was swiftly convicted.

As a result of the Court's reversal, he was retried, convicted again, and sentenced to life in prison.

Sheppard v. Maxwell

In what has come to be viewed as the landmark decision regarding prejudicial media publicity, the U.S. Supreme Court went even further in *Sheppard v. Maxwell*, 384 U.S. 333 (1966), handing down a number of suggestions judges could follow to control publicity and protect defendants.

The case involved Cleveland, Ohio, osteopath Dr. Sam Sheppard whose conviction for murdering his pregnant wife in their home in 1954 would later prompt the fictionalized television series and movie, *The Fugitive*.

Portrayed by the Press as "the crime of the century," Sheppard said he was asleep downstairs on the sofa when he heard his wife scream upstairs. As he ran to check on her, he said he was hit from behind by a "bushy-haired" intruder and knocked unconscious. He later testified that he awoke to find his wife dead.

Despite the fact that no hard evidence linked him to the crime, his account of the matter was generally vague, confusing and suspicious. Soon afterward local news media demanded that he be tried for the crime and convicted. He was subsequently charged with second-degree murder.

The ensuing media coverage grew intense. Reporters swarmed the coroner's inquest, reported things that were inadmissible at trial, and broadcast live coverage of the proceedings, generally taking over the courtroom.

In the end, Sheppard was convicted and sentenced to life in prison. Ten years later the Supreme Court overturned his conviction, noting that the intense and prejudicial coverage had denied him a fair trial. He was retried for the crime in 1966 and found not guilty.

In its 8–1 decision, the Supreme Court said judges must protect a defendant's right to a fair trial by controlling the trial process as well as those who participate in it. It said the Press had an important role to play in covering the courts, but that such a role did not include a right to jeopardize court proceedings.

To ensure defendants were protected from the effects of sensational media publicity, the Court offered judges several suggestions as a result of the *Sheppard* case, adding if they did not take better control of things, more criminal decisions might be overturned in the future. Instead, the Court said if faced with intense and extensive media coverage, judges could:

1. Allow the publicity to subside by delaying or continuing the trial, if necessary.
2. Relocate the trial by ordering a change of venue to where the publicity will be less intense.
3. Allow for extensive questioning of prospective jurors during *voir dire*.
4. Isolate or sequester the jury during the trial to keep them away from the Press and public.
5. Issue restrictive orders, otherwise known as "gag" orders, to trial participants to keep them from talking about the case to the Press during the trial.
6. Protect witnesses from the Press.
7. Admonish the jury by instructing them to set aside any pre-conceived ideas of guilt or innocence and to not talk to the Press.
8. Limit Press attendance, if possible, by establishing press pools and requiring a few reporters to report for everyone else.
9. Order a new trial, if all else fails.

Seating an Impartial Jury

Many of the suggestions were directed at ensuring that a fair, impartial jury could be seated. The assumption was and is that extensive and intense pretrial publicity makes it more unlikely to do that. Yet social scientists have not firmly established that such publicity automatically damages a defendant's ability to get a fair trial. In short, it depends on the circumstances of each case.

Therefore, a judge must first evaluate the trial situation. The Supreme Court fashioned a test to help judges do just that in *Skilling v. United States*, 130 S. Ct. 2896 (2010). There, the Supreme Court said pretrial publicity had not interfered with the jury's decision to convict Jeffrey K. Skilling, the former head of Enron, for fraud after the company failed and thousands of people lost their jobs. In deciding to reject Skilling's appeal, the Court said judges must look at five factors to determine if there is potential juror bias. These elements have become known as the *Skilling Test.* The Court said judges should:

1. Look at how much media interference exists.
2. Look at the size of the community where the crime occurred.
3. Look at the tone of the publicity.
4. Look at how much time has passed since the crime occurred.
5. Look at how the crime has affected the community.

The Court has never required there be a total absence of publicity, which would make seating a jury next to impossible. Former Supreme Court Justice Thurgood Marshall declared in *Murphy v. Florida*, 421 U.S. 784 (1975), that the Constitution requires defendants have a "panel of impartial, indifferent jurors." However, he added, "They need not . . . be totally ignorant of the facts and issues involved."

The goal, rather, is to find individuals who can set aside their knowledge and opinions of a case and render a verdict on the basis of just the evidence presented in court. Thus, the Court looks to alleviate the surrounding publicity to the point where a juror's claim to impartiality is believable.

To meet this goal, judges routinely rely on those remedies suggested by the Supreme Court in the *Sheppard* case to mitigate the impact of publicity on a trial. Voir dire, continuance, change of venue or veniremen, admonition, and sequestration all reduce the potential damage of publicity surrounding any case and are used routinely.

• *Voir Dire*

The initial step in selecting an impartial jury is referred to as *voir dire*, a French phrase meaning to "speak the truth." The process begins when the Court gathers potential jurors at random from the county in which the trial is held. The court clerk usually selects them from a list of registered voters or a list of licensed drivers. Citizens selected receive a *summons* in the mail, ordering them to appear at the courthouse on a certain date at a certain time. (Failure to appear could result in a citation for contempt of court.)

On the specified date, those summoned generally gather in a large room where they wait for their names to be called for service. Those called for a specific trial follow a bailiff to the courtroom where a judge is in need of a jury. If their name is again called, they take a seat in the jury box to answer questions posed either by the judge or, in most cases, by the attorneys. The questions are designed to determine the prospective juror's fitness to serve. The lawyers take turns asking questions.

Relevant questions may concern a prospective juror's background, life experiences, and opinions. The goal is to determine whether the person can listen to the evidence presented at trial and offer an impartial decision based on that evidence. Lawyers will also try to assess any biases that may weigh against them or their clients. For example, if one potential juror has himself been robbed, asking him to sit in judgment of someone accused of robbery may sway his opinion regardless of the facts presented in court.

If a prospective juror is thought to be unfit for duty, an attorney can ask the court to excuse the person. This is called challenging the juror. Lawyers can offer *challenges for cause* or they can offer *peremptory challenges*. If the lawyer asks a judge to dismiss a juror for cause, he must offer a good reason to have the juror removed. Examples might include showing that a juror holds a prejudice or that he is somehow related

to one of the parties on trial. There is no limit on the number of challenges a lawyer may make for cause.

Peremptory challenges are made without the need to show any cause. Judges may not refuse a peremptory challenge. However, lawyers are limited in the number of peremptory challenges they may make. Depending upon the kind of case, the crime involved, state statutes, or the judge, lawyers may make as few as two or as many as 20. Lawyers make peremptory challenges when the judge will not excuse a potential juror for cause and they have an intuition that the person will vote against them.

Some lawyers hire jury consultants to help them profile jurors. The consultants rely on experience, psychological tools, and other means to find those potential jurors who are sympathetic to their case.

Once both sides agree on who will sit on the jury, the jurors are impaneled and sworn in.

• Change of Venue

In some cases, the publicity may be so intense it becomes necessary to move the trial to another location. This is called a *change of venue*. In a criminal trial, either side may request a change of venue. If the judge grants the request, the entire trial process—including the judge, lawyers, and witnesses—moves to another location, and the jury will be selected from citizens there. Such moves are expensive and sometimes fail to alleviate prejudicial media coverage since the media simply follow the trial to the new location.

State trials can be moved to any other location in the state. Federal trials can be moved to another federal district court, though judges are supposed to keep them as close as possible to the original venue. The defendant must agree to the move.

• Change of Veniremen

Instead of moving the entire trial to another location, sometimes the Court will get a jury from another, distant community where people are less familiar with the case. This process, called a *change of veniremen*, is also expensive, and some lawyers believe the inconvenience to the jurors may make them hostile to the defendant. To pick a jury in another location, judges and lawyers usually must visit the distant community, select a jury and transport it back to the location of the trial. The state must pay for the jurors' food, transportation, and shelter during the trial.

• Continuance

A *continuance* is a postponement of the trial. Since the Sixth Amendment guarantees a defendant the right to a speedy trial, he must waive this right if he and his attorneys believe the delay will lessen the publicity, allow for matters to cool down, and provide him with a better chance of receiving a fair hearing. Such a move creates other problems, however. It sometimes means the defendant will need to spend more time in jail awaiting trial. In addition, it may make it more difficult to recall witnesses. However, by allowing the community time to forget some of the sensational coverage, the chance of finding a more impartial jury increases.

• Jury Admonition

Instructing or warning the jury not to talk to others or read or listen to prejudicial publicity about the case while it is in progress is called *jury admonition*. Thus, jurors may not follow news accounts of the trial. Judges routinely tell jurors also not to talk about the case among themselves or form any opinion about the guilt or innocence of the defendant until all the evidence has been presented. Admonition also routinely involves instruction about the law and that jurors only base their verdict on the facts presented in court and not on sympathy or speculation.

The advent of social media has made this tool less effective in some cases. Jurors have been caught using Google to research questions and Twitter to communicate with outside sources. Such action may result in disciplinary measures by the judge.

• Sequestration

In cases where prejudicial publicity is most extreme, judges may isolate— or *sequester*—a jury during the trial. Often, this means housing them in a nearby hotel and limiting their contact with the outside world. Jurors resent this procedure because it often means limited contact with their families and harm to their businesses. But sometimes it's necessary, not only because of intense media publicity but also to protect the jurors from outside threats to their safety.

Sequestration means the jurors are in close contact with each other during the entire trial. They eat together, socialize with one another, and travel to and from the courthouse together. Court personnel screen their phone calls and emails, if the judge allows such communication at all. Sequestration is used only if the judge believes nothing else will work to prevent publicity from contaminating the jury process. It is a costly, disruptive move, and as with changing veniremen, may provoke juror prejudice against the defendant.

Restrictive Orders

Ultimately, it is up to the judge to make sure a defendant gets a fair trial, regardless of how the Press covers it. The Supreme Court in ruling on the *Sheppard* case made it clear it would hold the judge responsible in every case to make sure prejudicial publicity did not interfere with the judicial process. The Court also suggested that to protect the trial process judges could use their authority to prevent trial participants from discussing prejudicial information outside of court.

As a result, judges have gone beyond the methods already mentioned and begun issuing *restrictive orders*. Sometimes referred to as *restraining orders*, they are designed to control the behavior of the trial participants and in some cases the media. They attempt to specifically limit who can talk about the case, as well as what they can say and when and to whom they can say it.

The theory is that if prejudicial information is prevented from getting to the Press, it can't be published or broadcast. That, in turn, will, lessen the effects of prejudicial publicity on the trial.

Generally, restrictive orders aimed at trial participants are less troublesome than those aimed at the media. The Supreme Court ruled in *Mu'Min v. Virginia*, 501 U.S. 1269 (1991), that restrictions on what attorneys can say during the trial don't conflict with the First Amendment's nearly universal ban on censorship. The Court reasoned that lawyers and possibly other trial participants are part of a unique government process that could be harmed by the revelation of sensitive information. The Court said judges therefore have the authority to limit participants' outside comments and actions if those comments pose a "substantial likelihood" of interfering with a fair trial.

Consequently, orders directed at trial participants are usually held to be constitutional since the Court, in essence, is saying judges have a right to control matters *directly* related to the court process. If judges have first considered alternatives to restrictive orders, the restrictions they issued are narrowly tailored, and they have identified evidence of a substantial likelihood that intense media coverage will jeopardize a fair trial, the Supreme Court will uphold the orders. Those orders generally end, however, when the trial process is over. Trial participants include police, witnesses, lawyers, court personnel, jurors, and anyone else who might have a *direct* bearing on the trial verdict.

Often referred to by the Press as "gag orders," these restrictions nevertheless represent a form of prior restraint or censorship that raise serious First Amendment questions when they are aimed at the Press. The Supreme Court, too, has recognized such orders as problematic because they directly infringe on speech not *directly* concerned with the court process and interfere with free press rights.

Unlike those orders restricting trial participants, gag orders aimed at the media are usually designed to limit certain details of a case, such as a defendant's confession or criminal record.

The Court addressed the matter of gag orders aimed at the Press in *Nebraska Press Association v. Stuart*, 427 U.S. 539 (1976), ruling that they were extraordinary remedies and presumptively unconstitutional. As with the *Sheppard* case, this one involved another sensational murder trial.

Erwin Charles Simants, a 30-year-old unemployed handyman, borrowed his brother-in-law's rifle, entered the house of a neighbor, and killed six members of the James Henry Kellie family. He later turned himself in to police and confessed to the crime. Simants was said to have an IQ of 75, however, and there were concerns about whether he understood his rights.

As national media descended on the town, a judge ordered the Press not to publish the confession and other inflammatory information. The Nebraska Press Association appealed the order to District Court Judge Hugh Stuart who upheld the ban, which was largely upheld again by the Nebraska Supreme Court. The order banned the Press from even mentioning the confession.

The Press Association again appealed the order to the U.S. Supreme Court, which ruled unanimously that it violated the First Amendment. Wrote Chief Justice Warren Burger: "If it can be said that a threat of criminal or civil sanctions after publication 'chills' speech, prior restraint 'freezes' it at least for the time."

The Nebraska Press Association Test

Nevertheless, the Court said in "extraordinary circumstances" gag orders against the media might be allowed in future cases. In what has become known as the *Nebraska Press Association Test*, the Court fashioned a three-part checklist the judge must follow before issuing restrictive orders against the media. The judge must find:

1. That intense and pervasive publicity surrounds the case.
2. That no other alternative measure is likely to mitigate the effects of the pretrial publicity.
3. That the restrictive order aimed at the Press will in fact effectively prevent prejudicial material from reaching potential jurors.

Before issuing such an order, judges must show with compelling evidence that the gag order addresses information that presents a clear and present danger to a fair trial. The order must be narrowly tailored to limit only that information that is necessary to accomplish the court's goal. Such gag orders are to be used only as a last resort. Even so, the great majority of such orders are still found to be unconstitutional and overturned on appeal.

Closed Courtrooms

Copyright © of Mark Zimmerman. Reprinted by permission.

Faced with the prospect of having their restrictive orders declared unconstitutional, judges began trying another tactic in the late 1970s. They began to close judicial proceedings and documents to prevent adverse publicity, a move which was not recommended by the Court as a universal solution to the problem and which has created additional free press/fair trial problems.

Preliminary hearings became an early target of judges concerned about prejudicial publicity. A preliminary hearing determines if there is enough evidence against the defendant to proceed to trial. It serves as a check against police and prosecutors and is designed to make sure people are not unnecessarily charged with a crime.

In such hearings, the prosecutor presents evidence to the judge. If enough evidence exists, the judge orders the trial, regardless of the strength of the defense's case. Since typically only the prosecution presents evidence, the hearing is likely to appear to be one-sided, and although defense attorneys may cross examine witnesses, those news reporters present will usually hear only information that is damaging to the defendant. The result is often a lopsided story that prospective jurors may read before trial, affecting their impression of the case. By closing such hearings, judges hoped to eliminate pretrial publicity that might taint the jury pool.

Pretrial hearings to suppress evidence were also targeted. Here, lawyers would present motions to exclude evidence from trial, often because police obtained it during an unlawful search or seizure. The Court considered these likewise problematic since even though a judge might rule the evidence inadmissible at trial, a story about it on the evening news would again perhaps sway potential jurors' perceptions of the defendant.

For these reasons, lawyers and judges often are in favor of closed hearings. They also note that open hearings damage reputations of defendants not bound over for trial for lack of evidence. On the other hand, journalists argue that since the vast majority of cases are settled out of court through a process of plea-bargaining, the public is denied a chance to monitor the justice system.

The Press challenged these court actions, noting that throughout American history, courtrooms have generally been open to the public. Nevertheless, the U.S. Supreme Court in *Gannett v. DePasquale*, 443 U.S. 368 (1979), upheld a judge's order preventing a reporter from a pretrial evidentiary hearing. In that case, two young men were charged with the killing of a former New York policeman. They confessed and were later indicted by a grand jury. Due to intense publicity both the defense and prosecution agreed to close the pretrial hearing. As a result, Judge Daniel De Pasquale barred the Press and the Gannett newspapers appealed.

The high court affirmed the judge's decision in a 5–4 ruling. Justice Potter Stewart, writing for the majority, conceded that "there is a strong societal interest in public trials" and that "there is no question that the Sixth Amendment permits and even presumes open trial as a norm." But he said under the Sixth Amendment the right to a public trial belongs to the defendant, and that it was a right the defendant may waive.

Justices Marshall, Brennan, Blackmun, and White dissented, noting that, "secret hearings . . . are suspect by nature."

As a result of the decision, courts began to close hearings—and now trials as well—more frequently. At least 100 more would be closed throughout the nation within the year. In response, several justices publicly condemned the practice. And shortly thereafter, the Supreme Court agreed to review a case involving a closed trial.

In *Richmond Newspapers v. Virginia*, 448 U.S. 555 (1980), the Supreme Court voted 7–1 (Justice Lewis Powell did not participate.) to overrule a judge's decision to clear the courtroom of media and spectators prior to the fourth trial of a man accused of murder. The three previous trials had either ended because of technicalities or mistrials. The man was ultimately acquitted.

In what was considered a major victory for the Press, the Court recognized for the first time that the First Amendment guarantee of a free press includes an inherent right of access to information. Noted Chief Justice Warren Burger:

> *We hold that the right to attend criminal trials is implicit in the guarantees of the First Amendment; without the freedom to attend such trials, which people have exercised for centuries, important aspects of freedom of speech and of the press could be eviscerated.*

Burger said that although such a right was not directly stated in the Constitution, neither were several other rights that had been recognized by the Court, including the rights of association and privacy.

The Richmond ruling did not overturn the earlier Gannett decision, which still left courts able to close hearings, nor did it expressly say courts could never close trials, though it could only be done under extraordinary circumstances. Said Burger:

> *"Absent an overriding interest articulated in the (judge's) findings, the trial of a criminal case must be open to the public."*

The Court said open trials advance core First Amendment values of protecting freedom of communication relating to how the government functions, and that it enables citizens to evaluate government performance and maintain faith in the judicial system.

The Court has also said the decision to close a trial must be made on a case-by-case basis and that a trial may be closed under two conditions: 1. if the state can show a compelling government interest and 2. if the closure is narrowly tailored to serve that interest. Thus, a strict scrutiny standard applies.

In the case of *Press-Enterprise Co. v. Superior Court*, 464 U.S. 501 (1984), the Supreme Court extended the rule requiring openness to include the jury selection process. The Court unanimously overturned a California judge's decision that closed nearly six weeks of *voir dire* prior to a murder trial. The Riverside Press-Enterprise appealed the decision. The judge had also refused to make a transcript of the proceeding public. The defendant was convicted of raping and killing a 13-year-old girl. Chief Justice Warren Burger again noted that jury selection, like other parts of the trial process, was traditionally open and should remain so except in extraordinary situations.

Two years later, the Court added preliminary hearings and other pretrial proceedings to the open list unless again there was a substantial probability that the defendant's right to a fair trial would be prejudiced. In *Press-Enterprise Co. II v. Superior Court*, 478 U.S. 1 (1986), the Court overturned a judge's order to close a 41-day preliminary hearing regarding a male nurse accused of killing hospital patients.

The Court held, 7–2, that the proceedings should be open to the public unless there was a substantial probability that publicity would jeopardize the defendant's right to a fair trial and that other measures besides closure would not adequately protect the defendant's rights.

The Press-Enterprise Test

As a result of these two cases, the Court said two factors—experience and logic—should be used to determine if a court proceeding is presumptively open. The Court said if such a proceeding has been historically open and if openness contributes to the court process, the proceeding is presumptively open. This presumption can be overcome by applying a test the Court created from the cases and referred to today as the *Press-Enterprise Test*. The Court said judges seeking to close a court proceeding must:

1. <u>First determine, using the experience and logic test, if the proceeding is presumptively open.</u>

If the proceeding is presumptively open, the judge must:

2. <u>Demand those seeking to close the proceeding articulate an overriding interest that may be harmed if the proceeding remains open. For example, the defendant will not receive a fair trial if the hearing remains open.</u>
3. <u>Require those seeking closure to prove there is a "substantial probability" that the interest will be harmed if the proceeding is allowed to remain open. In other words, the jury will be prejudiced.</u>
4. <u>Determine if there are reasonable alternatives to closing the proceeding. Closing the proceeding should be a last resort. The Court must ask if voir dire or some other method might work. If there are no alternatives, the judge must:</u>
   a. <u>Make sure there is minimum interference with the Press and public by narrowly tailoring the closure. The Court, for example, must close only that part of the proceeding that will interfere with the defendant's rights.</u>
   b. <u>Prepare a record of the evidence to justify the closure for the appellate court. The Court should detail why alternatives to closing the proceeding will not work.</u>

The Supreme Court has not yet ruled a constitutional right exists to open civil trials to the press and public, but lower courts have ruled that they are.

Not all trials are presumptively open to the media and the public, however. Juvenile hearings and victim and witness protection hearings, for example, are usually not open, though they are not presumptively closed either. The Court often attempts to shield juvenile victims from further trauma and stigma and give juvenile offenders a better chance at rehabilitation by keeping their names out of the news. Again, whether a case is open may be decided on a case-by-case basis. Nevertheless, news reporters who legally obtain information outside the court process about juvenile cases generally may publish it without punishment.

If juveniles commit serious felonies, they are often tried as adults, in which case, the trial would be open.

Likewise, victims of sexual assault are often shielded when they give testimony during trial. The Court closes only that part of the trial that is necessary to protect the victims from further trauma. The goal, too, is to encourage women who have been raped to come forward so offenders can be prosecuted.

The Federal Judicial Center's guide, *Sealing Court Records and Proceedings*, notes a range of proceedings that are presumptively open. The guide is accessible at www.fjc.gov. Among those hearings that are presumptively open are pretrial detention hearings, bail hearings, plea hearings, attorney disciplinary hearings, sentencing hearings, and *voir dire* proceedings. Grand jury proceedings are always secret.

Challenging Closure

What is a member of the media to do if a judge decides to close a presumptively open proceeding? Given the Court's rulings on the matter, anyone in the public or media may challenge the decision in open court. This may take a bit of courage. Those who object must stand up immediately when the motion is made to close the proceeding, address the judge as "Your Honor," and ask to be recognized by the Court. Once the judge has done so, they should state they object to the closing of the courtroom and ask the decision be delayed until they can get an attorney to file a formal objection to the closure.

Those who work for a media outlet should discuss with an editor or supervisor the possibility of raising an objection before the need arises. Otherwise, if the reporter objects and the editor later refuses to call the attorney, the reporter may be on his own to hire a lawyer to make the objection.

If the editor agrees the news organization will back the reporter and call a lawyer if needed, the reporter should inform the judge that the reporter's news organization objects to the closing. This shows that the reporter has more clout and is serious about preventing the closure. It also tells the judge a powerful news organization is behind the motion. If the reporter knows the name of the company lawyer, he should identify him. Again, this provides more credibility. Most importantly, the reporter should ask that the objection be made part of the court record. This is important later for matters of appeal.

After making the objection, the reporter should ask the judge for a brief recess to call the lawyer. If the judge refuses the request and orders the reporter to leave, the reporter should promptly leave the court and not argue. Those who refuse the order will be found in contempt.

After leaving the courtroom, the reporter should write a brief note to the judge explaining that the news organization objects to the closing and the reporter will contact his editor or lawyer immediately. Then the reporter needs to give the note to a court bailiff or officer with instructions to give it to the judge. The reporter needs to contact the editor.

The good news is that such motions, even by reporters or members of the general public, are serious, and an appellate court expects the judge to take them seriously. *The First Amendment Handbook* by the Reporters Committee for Freedom or the Press offers tips for journalists and others facing a motion for closure.

Accessing Court Records

Court documents have been open to the Press and public since colonial times. Common law decisions and many state constitutions provide a long history of required access. After the Supreme Court's decision in the *Richmond Newspapers* case and other subsequent cases, a First Amendment right of access to many documents can also be claimed.

However, as with trials and other court proceedings, judges also have been inclined to close off records to prevent prejudicial publicity, help litigants avoid embarrassment, encourage parties to settle matters outside of court, and accomplish other matters. Some sources have noted an increasing trend in the practice. In 2008, the *Tulsa World* reported

Tashatuvango/Shutterstock.com

more than 2,000 Oklahoma court cases were sealed between 2003 and 2007, including those involving divorce and wrongful death settlements, and even name changes.

Such action is just as troublesome to journalists and others who wish to monitor the Court as closed court proceedings. Although the right of access, as in judicial proceedings, is not unlimited, those judges who rule to close off records are likewise supposed to first apply the Press-Enterprise Test in an effort to balance competing interests. Again, First Amendment concerns must be weighed against matters such as a defendant's right to a fair trial, national security threats, privacy interests, trade secrets, and other things.

Courts generally establish rules and policies for those wishing to retrieve and review court documents. However, despite such rules, the Supreme Court has held the media may not be punished for publishing legally obtained and truthful information from court records in most instances.

In *Florida Star v. B.J.F.*, 491 U.S. 524 (1989), the Court said states can only impose penalties on the Press for publishing legally obtained truthful information if they can demonstrate that such a penalty is "narrowly tailored to a state interest of the highest order."

The courts have ruled a wide range of documents are presumptively open, including evidence introduced in court, a court docket sheet or index to court proceedings and documents, documents filed in regard to pretrial proceedings, plea agreements, presentencing and post-sentencing reports, indictments, search warrants, and affidavits, to name a few. Nevertheless, the Court may find in some instances an overriding interest in keeping them closed.

Journalists and others may find it difficult to get juror records. Judges often work to ensure names and addresses of those who serve are kept confidential even though in most trials such information is regarded as public record. Judges have been known to refuse to release the information even after the trial is over. The rationale is to protect jurors from media harassment and protect the deliberative process. Nevertheless, barring the Press from juror information indefinitely is in most cases unconstitutional. Federal judges refer to *The Handbook for Jurors* by the U.S. Judicial Conference to determine jury access. Generally, it is up to each juror to decide if they want to talk to the media.

Other documents that may be routinely closed include out-of-court settlements (such agreements are often considered private matters), protective court orders and national security matters.

Electronic Records

With the advent of the Internet and other social media, more courts have designed and implemented electronic record storage and retrieval systems. The National Center for State Courts and the Justice Management Institute advocated the posting of records online and suggested they be open to the public. Meanwhile, the Conference of Chief Justices and the Conference of State Court Administrators launched an effort to establish guidelines for public access.

In the federal court system, electronic access is provided through the Public Access to Court Electronic Records at www.pacer.gov. Meanwhile, online access at the state level is uneven. Some provide statewide access; others offer it on a county by county basis. Some limit who can use the online system and what documents can be obtained electronically. Some charge fees for some people and not others. Those who use the service a lot, like journalists and lawyers, often must pay thousands of dollars year. Even occasional users may find the fees exorbitant. Some systems aggregate information, allowing journalists and others to study trends; again, other systems do not.

Recording, Photographing and Televising Court Proceedings

More than 30 years ago, the Supreme Court ruled that just because there was a presumptive right of access to the courtroom did not mean that journalists could bring their cameras with them. In *Chandler v. Florida*, 449 U.S. 560 (1980), the Court left that up to the states.

In a case in which two police officers were convicted of burglary, the Court said Florida's rules allowing television coverage of the trial without the defendants' consent did not prevent them from receiving a fair trial. In their 8–0 decision, the Court refused to overturn Florida rules allowing such coverage and said other states were free to make their own rules regarding the matter.

The court did note that in certain cases a defendant might be able to show the presence of cameras interfered with his right to a fair trial, but that just because cameras were present did not inherently mean a case was prejudiced. Said Chief Justice Warren Burger:

> *An absolute constitutional ban on broadcast coverage of trials cannot be justified simply because there is a danger that, in some cases, prejudicial broadcast accounts of pretrial and trial events may impair the ability of jurors to decide the issue of guilt or innocence uninfluenced by extraneous matter.*

Burger added that the two defendants had not shown the cameras had jeopardized their trial.

Despite the ruling, many judges have long believed that print media coverage of trials sufficiently protected both the Press and public's need to monitor the courts. Cameras, therefore, were not needed. This belief, nevertheless, has not stopped the broadcast media from pushing for more access.

Today, the presiding judge generally determines if cameras are to be allowed. Court rules further determine the conditions under which they may be used. Often, this concerns both the number and placement of the cameras. In some situations all the trial participants must agree before cameras are allowed. The judge also can order the camera turned off at certain points in the trial to prevent presentation of some evidence from being photographed, such as crime scene photos. By early 2000, all 50 states allowed television or still photography coverage of some judicial proceedings.

Federal courts have yet to allow cameras in the courtroom. Federal Rule of Criminal Procedure 53 bans cameras from criminal trials. Televised civil proceedings are banned by federal policy.

Judges generally are suspicious that cameras in the courtroom affect witness testimony, discourage other witnesses from testifying and turn lawyers and other court personnel into want-to-be actors. Judges also believe that when the media is allowed to bring cameras into the courtroom, reporters are more likely to sensationalize the proceeding instead of reporting objectively, often taking things out of context.

The belief is not without historical evidence. Cameras were generally banned from courts following the 1930s trial of Bruno Hauptmann, who was convicted of kidnapping and killing the baby of famed aviator Charles Lindbergh and his wife. Cameras during the trial had turned the courtroom chaotic.

The U.S. Supreme Court is adamant about keeping cameras of any kind out of its proceedings.

Journalists should review the laws of the state where they work to determine whether cameras are allowed. A good source is the Radio-Television News Directors Association website, www.rtnda.org.

New Technologies in the Courtroom

The courts generally have been slow to embrace "new" media. Many courts are still trying to determine the boundaries of social media use. Some have banned texting and tweeting altogether during court proceedings, calling such activities a disruption to the somber nature of the judicial process. Others permit such use if the person tweeting or texting doesn't disrupt proceedings.

More troublesome is the use of such media by jurors. In some cases, juror use of new media has led to mistrials. Jury instructions generally mandate that jurors not use cell phones, computers, or other technology in court or during deliberations. Nor may they use them to research or discuss the case with others outside of court.

Some courts have allowed others to use cell phones inside the courtroom, again on the condition that they not disrupt proceedings. Laptop computer use varies from court to court, though more laptops are being employed, especially by lawyers, as a way to call up cases and other legal information quickly. Courts also differ on when to allow journalists to post real-time news reports during trial.

Although the use of social media has become standard operating procedure for those in the news media, reporters and bloggers would be wise to check with judges and other court personnel before using them in the courtroom.

Bench-Bar-Press Guidelines

After the *Sheppard* case, many state press organizations, bar associations and judicial groups crafted cooperative guidelines to help both lawyers and journalists work together. Many of these agreements help lawyers better understand the goals and practices of journalists and journalists better understand court policies and procedures. The ultimate goal of such agreements is to help journalists provide better and less sensational coverage of criminal hearings and trials.

The guidelines also often help law enforcement officers understand what information about a criminal suspect or crime may be provided to the media without later jeopardizing a trial. They also usually offer journalists a list of what kind of information—such as that detailed in this chapter—can harm a defendant's chance at a fair trial if released.

This effort to reach a common understanding is not legally binding. In fact, the Supreme Court in *Nebraska Press Association v. Stuart* noted that news decisions are the domain of editors, not judges. Although many news organizations attempt to at least consider such guidelines, they are reluctant to endorse them outright in fear that later judges will use the guidelines to punish those members of the media who don't follow them.

Eliminating Prejudicial Reporting

What can the Press do to lessen the effects of pretrial publicity? The obvious answer is to refrain from focusing on the sensational. More specifically, reporters should avoid certain kinds of stories, including:

1. Reports of confessions or suggestions that there might be a confession. Sometimes people confess to crimes they did not commit or may retract their confession.
2. Reports about the results of lie detector tests or other tests or the defendant's refusal to take such tests. Many tests cannot be admitted as evidence at trial. Other tests, such as those concerning DNA, are not always conclusive.
3. Reports of a defendant's past criminal record. Just because someone may have committed an earlier crime does not mean he is guilty of the present charge.
4. Reports that impugn the credibility of witnesses or other court participants.
5. Reports concerning the defendant's character or acquaintances. Just because someone is unkind or associates with other nefarious characters, doesn't mean they committed the crime.
6. Reports that suggest a person is guilty before a verdict is given.

Also, paying closer attention to media ethics probably would alleviate many of the problems. In the end, journalists should ask themselves if reporting a particular piece of information would enlighten the public about an important matter or just serve to embarrass or harm people. A need to know is more justifiable than a right to know.

CHAPTER 11

Obscenity

Defining Sexual Expression

Former U.S. Supreme Court Justice Potter Stewart once famously said during a moment of frustration that he would not even attempt to define hard-core pornography, noting that he probably could not intelligibly do so. But he went on to add "I know it when I see it."

His statement has come to signify how difficult it is to categorize a form of expression that defies easy legal interpretation yet has generated legions of moral crusaders determined to stamp it out—regardless of how one defines it.

Such efforts to eliminate all things sexual are difficult, at best. The fact remains that sexual expression is everywhere in our society. We see it on TV, in the movies, and on the Internet. Print ads and commercials use sex to sell us everything from burgers to beer. Our attitudes about fashion and our views on masculinity and femininity are shaped by the popular perception of what is sexy. Like it or not, sex and the communication of sexual things is part of the Western culture.

Sexual expression, of course, is not new. It has existed in art and literature for thousands of years. Michelangelo's famous statue "David" in Florence, Italy, depicts the biblical hero fully naked, and the "Venus de Milo" in the Louvre Museum in Paris, France, is presented bare breasted. The topic is found in James Joyce's epic novel *Ulysses* as well as many other great literary works. It's even discussed in the biblical text, *Song of Solomon*. Yet by today's standards, few would consider these

lornet/Shutterstock.com

expressions obscene. And nudity by itself is generally not enough to invoke the wrath of the populace.

It's the hard-core depiction of raw, sexually explicit sex that prompts society and the courts to repel. And that's where the Court spends most of its time in dealing with such matters.

In today's legal lexicon, three terms are used to define different aspects of sexual communication involving adults. It is helpful to review each of them briefly before launching a discussion of sex and the law. They include *obscenity, pornography, and indecency*.

Obscenity represents a narrow class of material often referred to as *hard-core pornography* that the U.S. Supreme Court has ruled is unprotected speech under the First Amendment. In short, it is illegal. The Court follows a set of guidelines called the *Miller Test* that it fashioned from an obscenity case to determine if sexual expression is outside the law.

Pornography is a vague, legally imprecise term that usually refers to protected sexual material. For example, *Playboy* magazine was widely considered pornographic, when it ran nude photos, but not obscene. Such material is often referred to as *soft-core pornography*.

Indecency is another legal term often referred to as *adult material* that is legal but nevertheless can be banned on broadcast radio and television to protect children. It includes both words and pictures.

Today, federal law prohibits both the importation and distribution of *obscene* works and bans minors from appearing in any sexually explicit media, whether it's obscene or merely pornographic. The federal Racketeer Influenced and Corrupt Organizations Act (RICO), normally used to combat organized crime, also allows the government to seize the assets of businesses that deal in obscenity. In addition, all 50 states have laws that try to control obscenity. Overall, government officials have gone to creative lengths to control what many claim to be a growing societal problem, using everything from postal regulations to zoning ordinances to nuisance laws to fight objectionable sexual expression.

The Problem with Obscenity

Obscenity in the United States refers only to sex. The definition does not include violence, despite growing concerns over violence in the movies, on television and especially in video games. Generally, Americans are far more comfortable seeing violence than sex.

Although America's unease with sex is not unique, it is perhaps more pronounced than in Europe. There, displays of violence in the media are reviled, but sexual expression is more tolerated.

Generally, cultures with a strong religious heritage make more of an attempt to control sexual expression or prohibit public displays of intimacy altogether. This concern over sex in America, too, can be traced to a strong religious ethic that often views sex as sinful, especially outside of marriage. This religious view holds that sex is an act of intimacy designed only to promote the marital relationship and provide children.

Graphic and course displays of sex outside of marriage are believed by many to be demeaning and harmful psychologically, especially to children. Such displays, they argue, treat people as nothing more than objects and, thus, devalue them and society.

Nevertheless, sexual expression has increased in recent years due to the Internet, cable television, and a view that such material causes little or no harm to adults. Scarce government funding also makes prosecution of obscenity cases less of a priority.

Early Regulation of Sexual Expression

America's unease with sex is not new. Efforts to stamp out immoral influences have occurred at various periods in American history, especially during the Victorian Period of the late 1800s when fashions dictated that women be covered from head to toe. Obscenity laws in America, however, extend back as early as 1712 when Massachusetts made it a crime to publish "any filthy, obscene, or profane song, pamphlet, libel or mock sermon." The common law also addressed the issue, focusing on the corruption of youth and disruption of order.

In England in 1857, Parliament passed the Lord Campbell Act that established an obscenity standard that was adopted in America. In applying the law to the obscenity case of *Regina v. Hicklin*, L.R. 3 Q.B. 360 (1868), the English Court noted that "the test of obscenity is this, whether the tendency of the matter charged as obscenity is to deprave and corrupt those whose minds are open to such immoral influences and into whose hands a publication of this sort may fall."

DragonPhotos/Shutterstock.com

Since it was possible for such material to fall into the hands of children, the *Hicklin Rule* meant adults only could be exposed to that which would be acceptable to children. Even if part of the work was unfit for children, the entire work was to be considered obscene. The rule remained the obscenity standard in the United States until the 1930s. As a result, the courts held some of the most revered classical literature to be obscene.

During the time the *Hicklin Rule* was in effect, Congress passed additional legislation regarding obscenity. In 1873, Anthony Comstock managed to persuade Congress to pass what became known as the *Comstock Act*. The law went even further than one passed in 1865 that made it a crime to mail obscene materials. This time Congress authorized the U.S. Post Office to confiscate from the mails any "obscene, lewd, lascivious, or filthy book, pamphlet, picture, paper, letter, writing, print, or other publication of an indecent character."

The law did not make an attempt to define what was obscene. That decision was left to Anthony Comstock, who also was appointed as a special postal inspector to enforce the law. As a result of these laws and the moral crusades that prompted them, the Victorian Age came to be known as "prudish."

(The Comstock Act is still in effect today, though the courts have limited what can be considered obscene. In addition, Congress has passed legislation outlawing the distribution of obscenity over the Internet.)

The *Hicklin Rule* was all but abolished in 1934 when an appellate court held in *One Book Entitled "Ulysses" v U.S.*, 72 F.2d 705, that James Joyce's classic novel *Ulysses* was not obscene. The Court affirmed a trial judge's decision that the work should be judged as a whole and on its effects on a person with average sexual instincts instead of how it might affect children or the most corruptible members of society.

Following the *"Ulysses"* court's lead, the Court finally ruled in a landmark case in 1957 that the First Amendment does not protect obscenity at all. In *Roth v. U.S.*, 354 U.S. 476, Samuel Roth was convicted of mailing materials that federal prosecutors deemed obscene. The Court upheld his conviction.

The case is significant because Justice William Brennan largely adopted the rule that had emerged from the 1934 *"Ulysses"* decision. Brennan said henceforth a work should be considered obscene and against the law if the Court found that an average person, applying contemporary community standards, would find the dominant theme of the material taken as a whole appealed to prurient interests.

No longer would nudity or isolated references to sex, taken alone, be considered obscene.

The Court made it even more difficult for government officials to prosecute obscenity cases when it ruled in *Memoirs v. Massachusetts*, 383 U.S. 413 (1966), that a 200-year-old classic erotic novel often referred to as *Fanny Hill* was not obscene. In making the ruling, Justice Brennan suggested adding two other elements to the *Roth Test*. First, the work had to be "patently offensive," that is, it had to depict ultimate sexual acts, and second, it had to be "utterly without redeeming social value."

That a work was without any redeeming social value was difficult to prove, and it made obscenity prosecutions after the decision difficult.

The Miller Test

As the liberal Warren Court era came to an end in the late 1960s and President Richard Nixon began to appoint more conservative justices to the Court, the definition of obscenity was revised again. In the landmark decision of *Miller v. California*, 413 U.S. 15 (1973), the Court abandoned the idea that a work had to be without any redeeming social importance before it could be declared obscene. The Court also discarded the idea that there was one national view of what was obscene, allowing each state to determine obscenity according to local values.

As a result, it became easier to prosecute obscenity cases than it had been under the Warren Court. In making the changes, the Court also fashioned a new test to determine just what was obscene. The test became known as the *Miller Test*, and it still determines obscenity today.

The 5–4 *Miller* decision came after Marvin Miller was convicted of violating California law when he sent unsolicited brochures containing pictures of men and women having sex to a restaurant as part of a campaign to sell adult material. Those who received the mail complained to police and Miller was prosecuted. After he was convicted, he appealed the decision to the U.S. Supreme Court.

In upholding the conviction, the Court, in crafting the *Miller Test*, said material was obscene if:

1. <u>An average person, applying contemporary local community standards, finds that the work, taken as a whole, appeals to prurient interests</u>.
2. <u>The work depicts or describes, in a patently offensive way, sexual conduct that the applicable state law defines and says is prohibited, and</u>
3. <u>The work, taken as a whole, lacks serious literary, artistic, political or scientific value.</u>

The Court said each element of the test had to be met before the work in question was to be declared obscene. If just one element was missing, the work was not obscene and the First Amendment protected it.

To better understand the test, it is important to more fully review each of the elements.

The **first element** of the test requires that the work be judged from the standpoint of an average person. Therefore, the Court has said one shall not look at the work from the standpoint of someone who is overly sensitive, such as a child, or someone who is overly callous. It must be judged as if the trier of fact in the case is looking through the eyes of all the adults in a community. (The trier of fact may either be the judge or the jury. In most cases, it is the jury.)

Whoever is reviewing the elements must then—looking through the eyes of an average person—apply the current cultural standards of the community in judging the work. In other words, what are the sensibilities of the average person in the community? What would they tolerate? Community standards generally mean state standards. The perspective is important since people in Oklahoma may view sexual matters differently than people in California.

The distinction also has other legal significance in that those prosecuting an obscenity case, such as postal officials, may choose to file their complaint wherever the alleged obscene material passed. The case, for example, could be filed in the community from which the material was sent or in the community where it was delivered—or in any community en route. This process is called *forum shopping,* and it gives prosecutors a chance to file the case wherever they believe they stand the best chance of gaining a conviction.

Next, the work must be judged as a whole. Lifting passages or particular scenes from the entire work and declaring the whole thing obscene is not permitted.

The final portion of the first element requires that the average person—applying those community standards—must find the entire work appeals to prurient interests. The Court has defined prurient interests as those that appeal to a shameful or morbid interest in sex, nudity, or excretion.

The **second element** requires that the trier of fact find the work patently offensive. The Court has said only hard-core pornography meets this standard. The Court has defined patent offensiveness as material including "representations or descriptions of ultimate sexual acts, normal or perverted, actual or simulated" and "representations or descriptions of masturbation, excretory functions, and lewd exhibition of genitals." To meet the test, state law must define what is obscene. States generally contain the Court's descriptions of patent offensiveness in their definitions of what is outlawed.

The **third and final element** of the test represents a kind of check on overly prudish judges and juries intent on convicting someone without first considering whether the work has some merit. Generally, the jury considers the first two elements of the test and the judge, who is supposed to embody reasonableness and be less influenced by community sensibilities, plays a more prominent role in deciding the last element.

Unlike the *Roth Test*, which required a work to be "utterly without redeeming social value," the *Miller Test* offered prosecutors a better chance of securing a conviction, since it limited the criteria on which a work could be found to have merit.

Yet, to protect the defendant from an overly conservative community, the Court said in *Pope v. Illinois*, 481 U.S. 497 (1987), that national standards, not local ones, should be used in deciding whether a work has serious value. The Court also said in that case the work should be viewed through the eyes of a reasonable person, suggesting an objective rather than subjective approach to analyzing the work. As a result, judges and juries may consider expert witness testimony from both the defense and the prosecution to help them determine whether the work has serious value.

Although laws exist to prevent the manufacture, sale, distribution and exhibition of obscene material, the Supreme Court has said the First Amendment protects all but child pornography once it is inside one's home. In *Stanley v. Georgia*, 394 U.S. 557 (1969), the Court overturned an obscenity conviction that occurred after police came across what they believed to be obscene films while searching Robert Eli Stanley's home for bookmaking materials. Said Justice Thurgood Marshall:

> *Whatever may be the justification for other statutes regulating obscenity, we do not think they reach into the privacy of one's home. If the First Amendment means anything, it means that a state has no business telling a man, sitting in his own house, what books he may read or what films he may watch.*

The more conservative Nixon Court, however, later upheld a federal ban on mailing obscenity even to consenting adults.

Variable Obscenity

While soft-core pornography is legal for adults, many states have adopted variable obscenity statutes in an effort to further protect children from sexual matters. These laws permit the sale of such material to adults while banning it from anyone under age 18. The Court has held such statutes are permissible so long as they don't interfere with an adult's right to buy the constitutionally protected material. Thus, *Playboy* could be sold to an adult, but not to a minor.

The Court ruled such double standards were permissible in *Ginsberg v. New York*, 390 U.S. 51 (1968), when it said the First Amendment did not protect the owner of a Long Island restaurant who sold "girlie" magazines to a 16-year-old boy. Justice William Brennan said New York had an important state interest in protecting children.

The Court later noted that such laws had to be narrowly construed. A ban on nudity would not be permitted. Only material that was significantly erotic to juveniles could be banned.

Child Pornography

The normal definitions for obscenity and pornography do not apply when it comes to children. Producing, distributing, selling, or even possessing sexually explicit content involving children is against the law. And where the government may sometimes be lax in its prosecution of adult obscenity cases, it aggressively pursues those that involve children.

Under federal law, child pornography is defined as "any visual depiction . . . involving the use of a minor engaging in sexually explicit conduct . . . or such visual depiction has been created . . . to appear that an identifiable minor is engaging in sexually explicit conduct." Such conduct can include actual or simulated sexual intercourse, masturbation or lewd exhibition of the genitals or pubic area.

States and the District of Columbia also have child pornography laws.

Government officials justify such laws because of the emotional and physical harm done to minors in the creation of such material and because it promotes the exploitation of children by adults, encourages pedophilia, and serves as a permanent record of that exploitation that can haunt children the rest of their lives.

Officials need not follow the Miller Test in the prosecution of cases involving child pornography. The U.S. Supreme Court in *New York v. Ferber*, 458 U.S. 747 (1982), made an exception to the Miller Test when it upheld the conviction of a person who sold pornographic films of young boys to an undercover police officer. The Court noted that the law was necessary to protect children.

Consequently, unlike in the Miller Test, it is not necessary for prosecutors or the Courts to consider such things as community standards and artistic value. All they must do is prove the defendant possessed or made a photograph or film of a minor engaged in sexually explicit conduct. If a film producer wants to create a scene for literary or artistic reasons, the Court said a younger-looking adult could be used.

The Court went a step further in *Ashcroft v. Free Speech Coalition*, 535 U.S. 234 (2002), when it said computer-generated images that only appear to show someone under age engaged in sex were permitted, noting that real children were not being used in the sex trade. However, the Second Circuit Court of Appeals ruled in *U.S. v. Hotaling*, 634 F.3d 725 (2011), that digitally altering a photograph or film to put a real minor's face onto the body of an adult in a sexual position is still considered child pornography.

In *U.S. v. Williams*, 553 U.S. 285 (2008), the Court upheld the *PROTECT* (Prosecutorial Remedies and Other Tools to End the Exploitation of Children Today) *Act of 2003* that was designed to eliminate pandering of child pornography. The Act prohibits the advertising, promoting, or soliciting of material that is *believed* to be child pornography involving real minors even if the material does not involve real children. Thus, someone who solicits child pornography from an undercover agent violates the law, as does a person who advertises child pornography—virtual or otherwise—purporting to involve real children.

The Court has also held that victims of child pornography can seek restitution from those who created images of them as well as those who possess the images. The victims can recover damages for physical and psychological harm as well as other costs and losses associated with the crime.

"Sexting"

"Sexting" involves sending sexually explicit images via the Internet or cellphones. Prosecutors classify it as child pornography if it involves minors and more than mere nudity is involved. Officials have noted that the incidence of sending sexually explicit photos as text messages is increasing among minors themselves who take erotic pictures, often of their own or a friend's body in various stages of undress, and send them to others or post them online. If prosecuted as child pornography those convicted can receive stiff jail terms. As a result, some state legislatures have passed laws that carry lighter sentences for teens who have been convicted of making and possessing such material.

Axel Bueckert/Shutterstock.com

Other Ways to Regulate Obscenity

The following are some of the different ways the government has interrupted the flow of obscenity and discouraged pornography.

• Postal Regulations

Although it is illegal for the government to tamper with first-class mail, sending obscenity through the mail, as noted earlier, is against the law under the Comstock Act. The Postal Service also checks the Internet.

In addition, Congress passed the *Pandering Advertisement Act* in 1968 to allow postal patrons who receive sexually offensive mail to require

B Brown/Shutterstock.com

the Post Office to demand that those who mailed the material take the patrons' names off their mailing lists. The Supreme Court upheld the law in *Rowan v. Post Office*, 397 U.S. 728 (1970). Said Chief Justice Warren Burger: "It seems to us that a mailer's right to communicate must stop at the mailbox of an unreceptive addressee."

Congress added a provision in 1971 allowing postal customers to demand their names be removed from mailing lists even before they receive objectionable sexual material.

• Film Censorship and Ratings Systems

As soon as the movie industry emerged, citizens' groups worked hard to censor films they considered an affront to public morality. As a result, cities and states organized film censorship boards and banned those films they found offensive. This application of prior restraint, which would have been illegal had it been used against any other medium, was common from the 1920s until the 1960s.

Early Court decisions viewed movies as a business and not a medium of expression to be protected by the First Amendment. In *Mutual Film Corp. v. Industrial Comm'n of Ohio*, 236 U.S. 230 (1915), Justice Joseph McKenna, in a unanimous decision, said movies did not communicate ideas or public opinion and had a capacity for evil. The decision was due in part to the fact that early movies were not well made and thus dismissed as frivolous entertainment.

The idea held until 1952, when the Court in *Burstyn v. Wilson*, 343 U.S. 495, overturned a ban by New York authorities of the film *The Miracle* that depicted a girl who gives birth to a child she thinks is Jesus. Religious leaders had protested the movie. The Court, nevertheless, granted the movie First Amendment protection and said for the first time in the ruling that films were "a significant medium for the communication of ideas."

Despite the decision, censorship of movies continued, partly because the Court offered no guidelines for reviewing films. It wasn't until *Freedman v. Maryland*, 380 U.S. 51 (1965), that the Court required procedural rules to protect First Amendment concerns. The Court in that case, appealed by a film exhibitor who said Maryland's movie review law was too slow, said licensing systems should operate more quickly and require the censor, not the exhibitor, to prove that the work was against the law. The Court also said only a court could grant any final censorship order.

The Court scrutiny of censorship boards led to their gradual decline. Today, no government censorship boards exist.

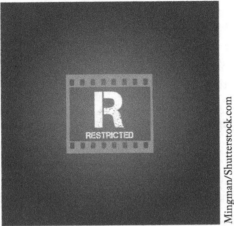

Their extinction is also due in part to the Motion Picture Association of America's adoption of a rating system in 1968 that alerted moviegoers to the content of a film before they entered a theater to view it. By offering a G, PG, PG-13, R, or NC-17 rating, the film industry today protects the public from potentially offensive content while helping to eliminate outside control by censorship boards.

• Internet Filters

Attempts to censor the Internet began when Congress passed the *Communications Decency Act of 1996.* The law was an effort to outlaw indecent and patently offensive material, in addition to obscenity, from any part of the Internet that could be accessed by minors. The act, however, met with a flurry of lawsuits amidst a worldwide protest of government censorship.

The Court ruled in *Reno v. ACLU,* 521 U.S. 844 (1997), that the law was overly broad and vague and, therefore, largely unconstitutional. The Court said, as written, the law could have been used to criminalize even the discussion of abortion and breast cancer. In making the ruling, the Court went a step further and said the Internet should be afforded the highest level of First Amendment protection.

The decision is significant because the Court said the government could not ban material that was not obscene from the Internet. Had the Court upheld the law, it would have allowed the Internet to be legally regulated like on-air broadcast media. The Court, rather, determined the Internet should be afforded the same protection as books and newspapers. The Court did, however, uphold the Act's ban on sending obscene material over the Internet.

In addition, the Court concluded there are other ways to protect children from adult material on the Internet, including the use of software filters on computers.

Congress took the cue and passed the *Children's Internet Protection Act* in 2000. The law required the Federal Communications Commission to adopt rules that would mandate that libraries and schools install Internet filtering software to prevent children from viewing such material in those public government facilities. Those institutions that did not comply would not receive federal money for online access.

The Court subsequently upheld the law as constitutional in *U.S. v. American Library Association*, 539 U.S. 194 (2003), noting it was a valid exercise of Congress' spending power. The Court also said there was nothing to prevent librarians from allowing adults to bypass the filter or provide separate computers that don't have the filters.

• Withholding Government Grants

In *NEA v. Finley*, 524 U.S. 569 (1998), the Supreme Court, upholding the right of Congress to demand that the National Endowment for the Arts follow certain standards in awarding grants, held that those who make such awards to artists can look to "standards of decency and respect for the diverse beliefs and values of the American people." Such action, the Court said, does not violate the First Amendment.

Again, the Court said Congress is within its power to decide how to spend government money. The ruling is largely insignificant since the NEA no longer gives much money to individual artists. Most money is given to arts organizations that utilize community experts and their own screening criteria.

• Nuisance Laws

In an effort to eliminate adult-oriented businesses, some local governments have attempted to use laws declaring them a public nuisance. In

Vance v. Universal Amusement, 445 U.S. 308 (1980), however, the Court said such laws could run afoul of the Constitution.

In the *Vance* case, the Court found a Texas nuisance law that allowed police to close down an adult movie theater because the owner had shown obscene films in the past lacked constitutional safeguards. The law did not require the government prove the theater was exhibiting obscene material at the time of its closure.

• Zoning Ordinances

In an effort to control adult-oriented businesses, many communities have resorted to segregating them in certain areas of a city through the use of zoning laws. The Supreme Court has said this is permissible so long as the attempt is not done to eliminate them altogether or significantly reduce their number from a community.

In *Young v. American Mini-Theatres*, 427 U.S. 50 (1976), the Court upheld a Detroit law that limited the number of adult-oriented businesses in any given neighborhood. The Court said the city had not attempted to ban them, but instead used an intermediate scrutiny standard to control the time, place, and manner of where they were located.

However, the Court made it clear in *Schad v. Mt. Ephraim*, 452 U.S. 61 (1981), that a community could not ban the existence of adult-oriented businesses altogether unless they violated obscenity laws. The Court said a community's ban on nude dancing and other live entertainment was in violation of the First Amendment.

Generally, cities have either attempted to cluster the businesses into a certain area of town or limit them to some distant and remote industrial area away from churches and schools. Such was the case in *Renton v. Playtime Theatres, Inc.*, 475 U.S. 41 (1986), when the Court upheld an ordinance that prohibited such business from locating within one thousand feet of schools, parks, churches, and residential areas.

The Court has said such moves are permissible if they are done to reduce the *secondary effects* of an adult-oriented business. Such effects include increased crime, decreased property values and the spread of sexually transmitted diseases.

However, a city using such tactics must prove that its zoning law is aimed at reducing such problems and is not directed at eliminating the expressive speech inside the businesses. Again, the Court in such cases is requiring the community to use an intermediate scrutiny standard by showing the law serves a substantial government interest, does not ban all adult-businesses or significantly reduce their numbers and allows for alternate means of such communication. Communities generally can meet the standard by relying on testimony from experts who study secondary effects.

Another tactic communities use to discourage adult-oriented businesses is to pass laws that limit expressive conduct in the businesses. For example, cities may require "nude" dancers to wear G-strings and pasties. The Supreme Court in *City of Erie v. Pap's A.M.*, 529 U.S. 277 (2000), said such regulations requiring minimal attire has a minimal affect on the message.

Communities are also permitted to pass reasonable laws that are supposed to prevent sexual contact between customers and dancers, such as lap dances. Intermediate scrutiny standards are again required.

Broadcast Indecency

Indecency, as noted above, is in a category of its own when it comes to sexual material. If obscenity is outside the law and pornography, other than that dealing with children, is permissible, indecency falls somewhere in between.

It can be described as patently offensive, non-obscene, expression that deals largely with excretory descriptions and filthy words. The Court has said it may be considered indecent even if it has serious social value. The Federal Communication Commission, which regulates broadcasting, has defined it as "language or material that, in context, depicts or describes in terms patently offensive as measured by contemporary community standards for the broadcast medium, sexual or excretory activities or organs." Depending upon when and where it is communicated, it may be legal or illegal.

For example, such material is protected in newspapers, books, magazines, movies, audio recordings and on the Internet, as well as in the majority of cable programs. The Court reasoned because people are paying for it, they are less likely to find such content objectionable. If they find the material offensive they can turn away. The Court also believed adults could more easily screen such material from children.

But the *Communications Act of 1934* makes it illegal to send indecent material via on-air radio and television broadcasts during the day and early evening. The reason is that such material, if broadcast over the airwaves at that time, often comes upon people unexpectedly and without invitation. It is more pervasive and more likely to reach children. If children are present there is no time to shield them from the material. However, the FCC does permit a government-recognized *safe harbor* period that allows indecent material to be broadcast from 10 p.m. to 6 a.m. when children are expected to be asleep. Those broadcasters who violate the law can receive stiff fines.

Although the law had been in effect for decades, the FCC first acted against on-air indecency in 1975. The action was in response to a father's complaint that his son had been exposed to a New York radio station's broadcast of comedian George Carlin's "Seven Filthy Words" monologue. The FCC had deemed the words indecent and prohibited them from being broadcast over the air. Carlin repeated the words several times during the 2 p.m. broadcast. As a result, the FCC fined the Pacifica Foundation, which operated the station.

Thomas Pajot/Shutterstock.com

In *FCC v. Pacifica Found.*, 438 U.S. 726 (1978), the Supreme Court defined indecent broadcast speech as that which is in "nonconformance with accepted standards of morality." The Court noted broadcasters have limited First Amendment protection because of broadcast spectrum scarcity. The Court said the FCC had the power to regulate the spectrum to prevent chaos within the broadcast industry. Further, the Court found the FCC could not censor material under the First Amendment unless it could show a compelling state interest and used the least restrictive regulatory method to do so. In *Pacifica*, the Court determined the compelling state interest was to protect children.

The *Pacifica* ruling established the rationale for restricting indecent speech in broadcast but not in other media. The FCC later modified its rules, defining even fleeting on-air expletives and images as indecent.

However, in *FCC v. Fox Television Stations*, Inc., 132 S. Ct. 2307, 2320 (2013), the Supreme Court refused to overturn a Third Circuit court of Appeals decision that said the FCC could not fine Fox Television for broadcasting a fleeting image of Janet Jackson's breast during a wardrobe malfunction at the 2004 Super Bowl halftime show since the FCC had changed the rules after the incident. Applying the law retroactively would not be fair.

The FCC has since begun reconsidering its regulations regarding indecency.

Cable Indecency

The Court is more concerned with indecency when it is broadcast over the air than when it comes into someone's home via cable or satellite. The Court reasons that by paying for it, the consumer is inviting the material into their home. The same rationale of the safe harbor rule, therefore, does not apply to cable or satellite media. The Court figures parents can limit access of such material to their children by not subscribing to it.

Congress did address indecency over cable television when it passed the *1984 Cable Act* and required those who operate cable systems to provide lockboxes to customers so they could block certain channels. In the *Telecommunications Act of 1996*, Congress also permitted cable operators the right to refuse to transmit any public access program over a public, educational, or government (PEG) access channel that contained obscenity, indecency, or nudity. This latter provision has not been challenged in Court, though other provisions in the act have been held to be unconstitutional.

Violence

The First Amendment protects violent expression. Despite a growing clamor from some scholars, child advocates, parents and politicians to require restrictions on violent content in the media, the Court has held firm that such work is protected.

In the mid-1990s, Congress considered the impact of violent content and required television manufacturers to include an electronic chip in their TV sets that would enable parents to block certain programming.

Meanwhile, the television and motion picture industry created its own TV Parental Guidelines, a rating system that all broadcasters and networks have voluntarily followed. The system is similar to the one used by the Motion Picture Association of America.

More recently, violent content in video games has generated greater concern since much of it is directed at minors. Some advocates of legislation limiting access to media containing violent material say it can lead to aggressive attitudes and behavior among children.

Nevertheless, in *Brown v. Entertainment Merchants Association*, 564 U.S. 786 (2011), the Court overturned a California law that prevented minors from buying or renting violent video games. The Court said such material communicated ideas and was therefore protected under the law. The Court noted that little and conflicting evidence existed to prove playing such games harmed children.

Despite attempts to put violence outside the law, the definition of obscenity in the United States still only concerns sex.

CHAPTER 12

Intellectual Property

Protecting Creations of the Mind

Intellectual property—which concerns copyright, patent, and trademark—is an area of law that protects creations of the mind—those products or unique expressions that result from an idea. Although it is often viewed as intangible property—something one can't touch—it nevertheless provides us with much of what we own and experience.

For example, you may possess a music video. That is your personal property. You may sell it, give it away, or destroy it. But you only own the physical item; you do not own the music that's recorded on it—the unique order of notes and lyrics. Those belong to whoever wrote them, or to be more legally precise, to the copyright holder.

Thus, the words in the books you read and the movies on the DVDs you watch are all examples of intellectual property. So, too, are the inventions you use and the trademarks you see on the products you buy. They are all someone else's creations.

The purpose of intellectual property law is to promote creativity and invention by protecting the creator's right to profit from his labor. Without such law, there would be little incentive to make new things. It is important to media law because copyright protects unique expression.

Intellectual property protection became necessary soon after the invention of the printing press in the 15th century. Before then, manuscripts had to be printed by hand, a laborious task that made stealing someone else's work hardly worth the effort. But the new printing press enabled printers to make multiple copies of a manuscript and make

Henry VIII

a profit. Thus, it became easier to steal another's work.

To address the problem, English King Henry VIII granted the first royal printing privilege in 1518. This new licensing scheme gave the king direct control over who could print any book, tract, or other writing.

The early goal was not to protect authors, however. They usually just sold their work to the printers and then went off to write something else. The king had an ulterior motive. His goal, rather, was to silence critics of the Crown. Consequently, those who printed without official permission could end up in jail, or worse.

The first real law to protect *authors* appeared in England in 1710. The *Statute of Anne* protected writers if their works were registered with the government. The protection lasted 14 years, but could be renewed for another 14 years. After that, it went into public domain, and anyone could use it without the author's permission.

America largely borrowed from the English law. Twelve of the original 13 states had copyright laws even before the Constitution was ratified. Later, the Founding Fathers, realizing the importance of such protection for creators and inventors, and especially for a new nation trying to expand, included laws protecting intellectual property in the U.S. Constitution. In Article I, Section 8, they made both patents and copyright a matter of federal law, noting:

> *The Congress shall have the power to promote the progress of science and the useful arts, by securing for limited times to authors and inventors the exclusive right to their respective writings and discoveries.*

The Copyright Act of 1790

After the Constitution was ratified, Congress passed the *Copyright Act of 1790*. As with the English law, copyright protection lasted 14 years with the possibility of renewal for another 14 years.

Later, the U.S. Supreme Court ruled federal law superseded both the common copyright law as well as any state statutes when it came to copyright cases. Today, copyright is largely a matter of federal law.

Congress has amended the law several times since it passed the first federal statute. In the 19th century, it added protection for maps, charts, prints, and musical compositions. Later, Congress granted protection for photographs and paintings. It also established the Library of Congress and gave that institution the power to register all copyrights.

Meanwhile, much of the rest of the world began to see the need for more widespread copyright protection. In 1886, several countries signed the *Berne Convention for the Protection of Literary and Artistic Works* to make the protection of copyright uniform internationally. The law basically requires those members who sign the agreement to recognize the copyrights of authors, musicians, and other creators from other countries. The United States, however, refused to sign. American publishers were opposed to the treaty since they often republished European works without paying the copyright holder.

Despite the lack of U.S. participation, other changes to American copyright law were moving forward, including the expansion of protection in the United States, which was increased to 28 years with an option to renew the copyright for another 28 years.

As technology changed radically in the early part of the 20th century, Congress finally saw the need for a major overhaul of the copyright law, and in 1976 it passed the Copyright Revision Act, which became effective on January 1, 1978. In addition to other things, the law pre-empted nearly all state laws protecting intellectual property and brought American law more in line with international copyright law.

As America began to produce more creative works, publishers, software designers, moviemakers and others finally found they needed international protection. They lobbied the government to abandon its earlier position, and Congress passed the *Berne Convention Implementation Act of 1988*, which allowed the United States to at last join the Berne Convention in 1989.

Copyright Today

Copyright law today protects a wide range of creations, including literary works, musical and dramatic creations, choreography, pantomimes, sculptures, graphic works, photographs, paintings, computer software, architectural designs, maps, motion pictures, radio and television productions and any other creation that's fixed in a tangible medium of expression.

The law gives creators the exclusive right to reproduce the work, distribute the work, publicly perform or display the work, and create derivative works from the original. Anyone else who wishes to use the work must first get permission from the copyright holder.

However, the *first-sale doctrine*, contained in the Copyright Act, requires only that the creator receive profit from the first sale of each individual, physical work. This allows the owner of a book, DVD, or other copyrighted work to sell or dispose of the work once he has purchased it. The doctrine was meant to strike a balance between the creator's right to profit from his work and the public's right of access. Thus, used books may be given to libraries without payment to the copyright holder.

snake3d/Shutterstock.com

The first-sale doctrine has its limits. Concerned that people would rent music CDs and make copies of them, Congress has since required those who rent such items to get the copyright holder's permission. Congress also prevented the renting or sharing of computer software. Software creators license their work, which eliminates the first-sale right to transfer the work since the user doesn't technically own it.

The U.S. copyright law, adopted from the Berne Convention, also grants creators *moral rights*. This prevents another from distorting or modifying a work that would harm the creator's reputation. Under the U.S. law, creators also can prevent their name from being removed from their work or having their name attached to a work they did not create. The law applies to drawings, prints, sculptures, paintings and certain creative photographs. It does not apply to motion pictures, broadcasts or writings.

Unlike libel and invasion of privacy laws, which protect personal rights, and generally can't be passed on to others, intellectual property is just that—property. Therefore, the law also allows it to be transferred to others or passed on to heirs after death.

News and other factual information cannot be copyrighted. Copyright, rather, protects *unique expression*. Thus, no one can lay claim to a particular news event and declare that only they have the right to cover it. Facts belong to everyone. Instead, copyright protects the unique description or presentation of news or other facts.

In *Feist Publications v. Rural Telephone Service Co.*, 499 U.S. 340 (1997), the Court held that telephone directory information is not copyrightable because a mere list of facts is neither original nor creative.

It is not possible to copyright an idea, though as with processes and inventions and utilitarian items such as lamps, the manifestation of an idea may be patented. For example, the unique design of a patented item may be copyrighted, such as the design of a Tiffany lamp. So too, words and short phrases may not be copyrighted, though they may fall under trademark protection in some situations.

The U.S. government creations are not copyrightable, either. And court rulings allow for other exceptions. Individuals, for example, may record television broadcasts at home for personal use. In *Sony Corp. of America v. Universal City Studios*, 464 U.S. 417 (1984), the Supreme Court held 5-4 that the use of VCRs to tape programs in their homes for personal use was not a violation of the Copyright Act. The court referred to this as "time shifting." The ruling would not, however, allow someone to copy a rented movie for personal use.

Extemporaneous work—such as improvisational sketches, speeches, and other such performances—are not subject to federal copyright law, though common law copyright still protects them. Thus, it would be a common law violation to record such performances without the creator's permission.

Only original works may be copyrighted. But novelty or quality is not a requirement. The work only needs to be recognizable as that of the creator.

In some cases that can be difficult to determine. In *Star Athletica, L.L.C. v. Varsity Brands, Inc., et al*, 580 U.S. ___., 136 S.Ct. 1823 (2016), the U.S. Supreme Court held that features incorporated into the design of a useful article can themselves be copyrighted. The case involved the design elements on a cheerleading uniform.

In the 6-2 decision, the Court said that copyright protection extends to "pictorial, graphic, or sculptural features" of the "design of a useful article" only if they "can be identified separately from, and are capable of existing independently of, the utilitarian aspects of the article."

The Court said in this case the "surface decorations on the cheerleading uniforms are separable and therefore eligible for copyright protection," noting that they could qualify as two-dimensional works of art had they been applied in another medium.

Although the United States is a member of the Berne Convention, the U.S. Copyright law by itself does not generally reach outside of the U.S. boundaries. The exception may be when someone violates the law within the United States and then distributes the pirated copies outside the country. Some lower federal courts have adopted a *predicate-acts doctrine* that allows copyright holders to sue for damages that occurred as a result of foreign violations linked to the domestic infringement.

Copyright protection automatically occurs from the moment of creation. However, to prove something is protected it is advisable that the creator register the work with the U.S. Copyright Office in Washington, D.C. and place the copyright symbol © in a conspicuous place on the work. The notice should also include the word "Copyright" as well as the year it was copyrighted and the author's name, e.g., "Copyright © 2015 by (author's name)."

The registration should occur as soon as the work is created. The law provides a 90-day window. Registration forms are available at the U.S. Copyright Office website, www.copyright.gov. Fees for registration range from \$35 to \$65, depending upon whether registration is done online or with a paper application. In addition, the registering party usually also must send two copies of the work to the Library of Congress. (This must be done even if one is not registering the work.) Registration must be completed before one can file suit against a copyright infringer.

A less dependable way to protect one's work, but a technique that may prove persuasive in court absent a valid copyright registration, is to have the creator mail a copy of the work to himself via sealed, registered mail before sending the work to an editor or anyone else. The official postmark stamps covering the seals of the unopened envelope provide the owner with persuasive evidence that the contents belong to him as of the date of the postmark.

Copyright and the Internet

Copyright law applies to computers and the Internet as well as to books, newspapers, movies, music and any other means of expression. Yet technological developments have made unauthorized copying of other's works easier. Many, in fact, have come to believe that if something is on the Internet, it is free for the taking. The law says otherwise.

Concerns over widespread copying as well as contributory infringement, made easier in the computer age, led Congress to adopt the *Digital Millennium Copyright Act* in 1998. Although the Copyright Act of 1976 already provides protection for digital works, the DMCA law goes even further in prohibiting the manufacture, sale or importation of devices that would make it possible to get around encryption codes protecting copyrighted material. The act, therefore, makes it illegal to disable anti-copying devices in a DVD player or other devices.

The law also addressed Internet Service Providers' concerns over subscribers who post copyrighted material on ISP websites without their knowledge. The law shields the providers from a copyright infringement claim if they remove protected information once notified by the copyright holder. Nevertheless, those providers who knowingly disseminate copyrighted material without permission are not protected by the act.

Perhaps, the biggest problem regarding unauthorized on-line use concerns music file sharing. The courts have sided with music industry officials and ruled that downloading music without paying for it is illegal, but preventing such activity has proved difficult.

The introduction of such devices as iPhone and services such as iTunes by Apple Computers, or other devices and services by other computer companies, has helped reduce the problem. Such innovation allowed for the legal downloading of music, and prompted music companies to make deals with Apple and other computer manufacturers. In exchange for a small fee for the use of each song, the record company would allow access to the music.

The DMCA also requires that digital programmers and broadcasters pay royalties for streaming copyrighted music and other copyrighted material on their websites. Royalties go to music licensing agencies such as the American Society of Composers, Authors, and Publishers (ASCAP) and other such agencies as well as to the record companies who produced the recordings.

Copyright and Music

Music copyright is somewhat more complicated since it can involve several layers of copyright protection. This is because there are several layers of creation, and each layer is usually someone else's work.

Typically, these layers include the composition of music and lyrics, the recording by the musicians and record producer, and the CD or other tangible medium on which the music is recorded.

Artists, broadcasters, storeowners, and others who use a songwriter's composition must pay a fee to the composer or music publisher or whoever else holds the copyright. Since it would be impossible for every writer to contract with every person who wants to use it, composers and publishers rely on music licensing organizations to collect fees for them. These organizations include the American Society of Composers, Authors and Publishers (ASCAP), Broadcast Music, Inc. (BMI), and Society of European Stage Authors (SESAC).

The composers and publishers contract with the organizations, which in turn issue licenses to those who want to play or perform the music. The fees range from a few hundred dollars each year for a local bar with a band to millions each year for a TV network. The amount each composer and publisher receives depends on how often the work is used. Generally, the fees are compiled on the basis of how often they are

Oleksiy Mark/Shutterstock.com

played on radio stations around the country. Radio stations pay flat fees for *blanket licenses*, which account for about 3 percent of the station's net revenue. Bars and other venues have different fee pricing.

The organizations' representatives police nightclubs and other music venues to make sure their clients' music is not being pirated. Those who fail to pay royalties may face lawsuits for infringement.

However, under the *Fairness in Music Licensing Act of 1998*, Congress said some businesses could play music in their stores without first gaining permission of the copyright holder. The law allows small businesses to play music on radio and television sets. It does not apply to live music performed in the store.

ASCAP and the others license only the performance of the music. But the right to perform is different from the right to record. Recording someone else's music and lyrics involves yet another license.

Once a composition has been publicly performed, the law requires the copyright holder to allow anyone else permission to make a sound recording of the song. The copyright holder may not allow one person to record the work and prohibit someone else from doing so. This is called a *compulsory license*. The recording artist must pay a royalty for each copy of the song that is sold. The law applies only to individual songs.

The only other area where compulsory licensing is required is with cable TV. The 1976 Copyright Act requires cable operators to pay royalties for television programming. This extends to cable, satellite delivery systems and Internet broadcasters. The Copyright Royalty Board in the Copyright Office determines the amount of the royalties.

Those who make a sound recording on some fixed medium, such as a CD, also have copyright protection. The recording is not the songwriter's composition. Neither is it the phonorecord on which the music is recorded. It is the original way in which the composition is recorded. It is how the performers, producers and editors put the recording together.

The copyright in such cases may be held by those who created the record, or the recording company may hold ownership if those who performed the work only agreed to contract for their labor. Most musicians who perform someone else's song sign a contract with the recording company for a share of the record's sales. However, it is against the law for members of an audience to make recordings of a musician's live performance of a work, even if he doesn't hold the copyright to the song.

Those who own the copyright to sound recordings can prohibit others from copying the work, making a derivative work or distributing the work without permission. Others, of course, may still make their own recording of the composition.

The CD or other object on which the recording is made is also protected by copyright. Broadcast stations and others who want to copy recordings must get a *master use license* from the recording company that holds the copyright.

And, finally, if the recording is used in a TV broadcast, film or video as background music, a *synchronization license* is required. The license allows the broadcaster or filmmaker to synchronize the music with images on the screen. Synchronization licenses must be obtained from the composer and music publisher.

Duration of Copyright

Under the new copyright law, work created after January 1, 1978, is protected for the life of the creator, plus 70 years. This gives the creator and his heirs the right to profit from his work. After that, the work enters the public domain, which means anyone can use it without getting the permission of the copyright holder or paying royalties for its use.

Works-for-hire are creations made for and paid by another. For example, most news reporters who work for a newspaper or TV station receive a salary. They do not own the stories they write; those belong to the newspaper or TV station. Consequently, they may not use them without permission of the media outlet, which holds the copyright. Works-for-hire are protected for 95 years after publication.

Except in the case of works-for-hire, the law allows authors to cancel their transfer of copyright to someone else after 35 to 40 years. Thus, they can get their copyright back.

Freelancers, those who work as independent contractors and peddle their writing to magazines and newspapers for a fee, generally retain the copyright to their work unless they specifically transfer all rights to the publication. Most freelancers, however, sell only First North American Serial Rights, which grant the publication the right to publish the work anywhere in North America first. After publication, the author is free to sell the story to someone else.

Copyright Infringement

Those who break copyright law are considered infringers and can face a variety of legal consequences. A court can order the infringer to stop the unauthorized use, impound any unauthorized copies that have been made, and require the violator to pay actual or statutory damages as well as the plaintiff's attorney's fees. Actual damages include forfeiture of any profits the infringer made. Statutory damages can range from $750 to $30,000 or higher. Infringers can also face criminal charges if the violation was willful and for commercial gain.

To prove infringement, the copyright holder must show that the person had access to the work, that the pirated work is substantially similar to the original creation, and that the copyright holder had filed and received a valid copyright.

Proof of direct infringement is not always necessary. Evidence that the defendant aided or contributed to the infringement may be enough to sustain a case. This is called *contributory infringement*. Also, someone who benefits from an infringement or encourages another to break the law may be liable.

Icon design/Shutterstock.com

Unfair Competition

Another kind of infringement involves unfair competition, often referred to as *misappropriation*. A product of common law, it largely focuses on preventing one news medium from taking advantage of another's work.

The tort primarily evolved from the U.S. Supreme Court decision concerning *International News Service v. Associated Press*, 248 U.S. 215 (1918), in which the Court held that a business cannot use another competitor's work and deceive others into thinking it is their own. The decision came after INS had taken AP stories and distributed them to INS customers, passing the stories off as INS work. Although the stories were not copyrighted, the Court held that the INS action unfairly harmed the AP.

Often referred to as the *hot news doctrine*, the Court said such breaking news stories represent the "quasi property" of the news service that wrote them. The Court noted that the important question in any misappropriation case is whether a significant number of people will be misled as to where the material really originated.

The ruling does not prevent another news reporter or service from covering and writing their own story. It only prevents them from pirating someone else's work.

The *Fair Use* Defense

Under the original copyright law, it was against the law to copy any protected work. As a result, teachers, scientists, and other scholars found it difficult to use important information in the pursuit of knowledge without breaking the law. Since the original purpose of the law was to promote creation and invention in the pursuit of art and science, it was argued that the law should not be construed in such a way as to harm such scholarship.

In 1879, the U.S. Supreme Court agreed, ruling in *Baker v. Selden*, 101 U.S. 99, that the purpose of publishing was to "communicate useful knowledge" and that goal would be frustrated if others could not use small amounts of the work without being punished.

In an effort to balance an author's right to compensation against the public's interest in spreading ideas and information in a democracy, the courts, therefore, came to recognize a legal concept referred to as the *fair use doctrine*. This allows the public to copy limited amounts of a copyrighted work without permission from the author for the purpose of teaching and scholarship.

Thus, quoting brief passages from a work to include in news reports, scholarship, criticism, commentary, teaching, parody or satire, the courts said, allowed for reasonable dissemination of information without interfering with the copyright holder's ability to make a profit. The 1976 Copyright Act recognized the doctrine and established criteria for deciding what constitutes fair use. The act notes that four things should be considered, including:

1. The purpose and character of the use.

Copyrighted material used for education, commentary, and scholarship, as noted above, and which is primarily nonprofit, is likely to be considered fair use. However, material used in commercial work may also qualify for fair use.

For example, use of small amounts of copyrighted material in news articles and broadcasts generally qualifies as fair use. Teachers who make a one-time copy of a short book chapter or a brief article from a newspaper for their own use, likely also will be protected from a claim of infringement. Even so, the material should carry the copyright symbol and not cost the student more than the price of copying. Use of historical information and other facts, however, is not copyrightable and can be used extensively, so long as they are contained in an original expression.

Librarians are protected from liability when patrons violate copyright law provided the librarian did not assist the infringer and a notice prohibiting copyright infringement was posted nearby. The Copyright Act does allow librarians to make single copies of small amounts of copyrighted work for patrons.

Copyrighted material that has been *transformed*, that is, used for another purpose, is likely to be regarded as fair use. Transformation usually means more than eliminating something from the original work, though making significant additions might qualify. Generally, the Court will look to see if the work has been turned into a significantly new creation. For example, the late Andy Warhol used the Campbell's Soup can to create a new art form.

Parodies, which borrow from original works for purposes of humor, usually are considered transformative also. The Supreme Court held in *Campbell v. Acuff-Rose Music Co.*, 510 U.S. 569 (1994), that the rap group 2 Live Crew had created such a transformation with singer-writer Roy Orbison's song, *Oh, Pretty Woman*. Nevertheless, the legality of such parodies must still be considered in light of other fair use factors. Courts will necessarily ask how much of the original work was used in creating them and what was the effect on the market.

Other purposes of fair use may include a small amount of a competitor's material in comparative advertising.

2. The nature of the copyrighted work.

The Court also will look at the original copyrighted work to help it decide if fair use exists.

Works that are no longer available because they are out of print are more apt to fall under fair use protection. The original author is less likely to suffer financial harm.

But the Court would be more protective of works that have not yet been published, since the author should be the first to profit from his work. Beating another writer to the press and publishing portions of their yet unpublished work is considered piracy.

The Supreme Court held in *Harper & Row Publishers v. The National Enterprises*, 471 U.S. 539 (1986), that using a significant portion of former President Gerald Ford's memoirs before his book was published was not fair use. The Court noted that summarizing another work was permissible since facts and ideas cannot be copyrighted, but using verbatim quotes was not. Congress later amended the Copyright Act to allow fair use of unpublished work so long as it meets the four-part test for fair use.

The Court is more likely to rule fair use exists, too, when the borrowed work is informational rather than creative. Since copyright protects the unique expression of facts or ideas, courts tend to afford more protection to creative works.

Lastly, is the work designed for one-time use, like a workbook? Making copies of such a consumable work defeats the author's ability to make a profit. Copying small portions from a nonconsumable work, on the other hand, has less of a detrimental effect.

3. The amount of material used as well as how much of it is used in proportion to the whole copyrighted work.

The Court also will try to determine how much of the work was used. Or more importantly, it will ask what percentage of the entire work has been used. This includes paraphrasing as well as verbatim copying. If the paraphrasing is too close to the original expression, fair use may be denied. The Court will also look to see how important the used portion was to the original work. Copying the thematic essence of another's creative work would diminish that work, as in detailing the primary scene of a play.

4. How use of the copyrighted material will affect demand for the original work.

Finally, the Court will look to see if the potential market for the original work or the value of the work itself has been diminished. Will use of the material hurt the copyright holder's ability to make money from the original creation? The Court will also look to see what effect the copying is likely to have on derivative works, such as the ability of the author to sell a screen adaptation of his novel.

Other Defenses to Infringement

In addition to the most widely used fair use defense, plaintiffs can claim other defenses. For example, those who sue for copyright infringement have three years to file their case under the federal statute of limitations. Prosecutors alleging criminal infringement have five years to file. If the statute of limitations has run or passed, the defendant can argue the plaintiff no longer has a right to pursue his case. The defendant may also be able to argue another defense—that the plaintiff has somehow placed his work in the public domain and thus abandoned his copyright.

Trademarks

The second area of intellectual property law concerns trademarks, trade names, and service marks. A trademark is a word, symbol, name, slogan, logo, or design that identifies a company and its goods and distinguishes them from other companies and products. Trade names identify company names. Service marks identify a company's services (rather than products). All are protected under the law.

The goal of such marks is to prevent customer confusion. They are valuable to businesses and service providers because in addition to distinguishing the goods and services of one business from another, they also note the goods are of a certain quality, indicate the goods or services are from the same source, and serve as a primary means of advertisement. As such, they represent important property interests of the companies that created them. Consequently, the law prevents competitors from using marks that are even similar to each other, unless they are for different products or services and such use causes no confusion.

Examples of trademarks include *Q-tips*, *Jell-O*, the design of the *Coca-Cola* bottle, slogans such as *"Just Do It,"* symbols like the Nike "swoosh," and many other distinctive words and marks.

State and federal law protect trademarks. Consequently those who infringe on trademarks can often be sued in both state and federal court. It is also recognized under the common law.

Under federal law, the *Trademark Act of 1946*, otherwise known as the *Lanham Act*, established a national registration system to protect trademarks. Those seeking trademark protection must submit a registration application with the Patent and Trademark Office in Washington, D.C. after first researching to make sure no one else has registered the mark. Searches can be done at the Patent and Trademark Office Library or through the U.S. Trademark Electronic Search Systems on the Internet. The registration fee ranges from $275 to $375.

(The law, however, protects the person who first uses the mark, not the person who first registers the mark, though the person who claims first use must prove that he indeed used it first.)

The Lanham Act also allows businesses to file an "intent-to-use" application, which permits those seeking a trademark to apply as early as three years in advance before using a product or service mark. In this way, a business can reserve a mark for later use.

Lanham Act registration is not available for businesses that only operate locally, but states maintain their own registration procedures to protect local trademarks. Common law also provides protection to local businesses.

Those wishing to register a trademark should consult a trademark lawyer since the process can be complicated.

Icon design/Shutterstock.com

Trademarks, trade names, and service marks can be used on letterhead, in advertising and on products. The symbol ® indicates the mark has been registered. Marks that have not yet been registered can nevertheless include the symbols SM TMfor service mark and trademark to indicate application for registration has been made.

Duration of Trademark Protection

Once the mark has been registered for an initial term of 10 years, it must be reaffirmed in five years, and renewed at 10-year intervals after that. It may be held indefinitely so long as it's used in commerce.

Trademark protection can be lost, however, if the owner fails to use it consistently or allows others to use it. The mark is considered abandoned if it has not been in use for two years. Escalator, dry ice, nylon, linoleum, zipper, and other generic names were once registered trademarks that lost protection after their owners failed to prevent their use by others.

In an effort to give owners more protection, Congress passed the *Federal Trademark Dilution Act* in 1995 providing trademark owners the right to sue anyone who uses the owners' marks on another product. The law allows the holder of a trademark to seek damages from anyone who lessens the capacity of a mark to identify and distinguish goods and services whether they are competitors or their actions create product confusion. Thus, lawsuits also could be filed for "blurring" or "tarnishing" a trademark. Blurring refers to the use of a famous mark for an unrelated product. Tarnishing creates a negative impression of someone else's trademark.

In 2006, Congress added more teeth to the law when it passed the *Trademark Dilution Revision Act*. Under the new law, the trademark owner who claimed dilution of his mark no longer had to prove the mark was harmed, only that a likelihood of harm existed. Many states also have anti-dilution statutes.

Use of the marks in news reports, commentary, parody, satire, and the like is not a violation of the law. Journalists who use trademarks generically, though, can expect to receive nasty letters from company lawyers demanding that they use them correctly.

Marks of Distinction

Generally, any distinctive mark may be used as a trademark. The more distinctive it is, the more likely it can be registered. Geographic names or descriptive terms, such as "top notch," cannot be registered because they are so widely used. Names of living people, unless their name is already closely associated with the business, will not be allowed. Celebrities can register their names to help market their work.

It should be noted, however, that the government's power to pass judgment on some marks recently has been restricted. The U.S. Supreme Court ruled that a registration mark that disparages persons, institutions or beliefs may not be prohibited by the United States Patent and Trademark Office.

In *Matal, Interim Director, United States Patent and Trademark Office v. Tam*, 582 U.S. _____., 137 S.Ct. 1744 (2017), the Court said the United States Patent and Trademark Office violated the First Amendment's free speech clause when it denied Simon Tam, lead singer of the rock group "The Slants," the right to register the group's name. The Patent and Trademark Office had said the registration was barred under the Lanham Act's disparagement clause barring names that may "disparage ... or bring ... into contempt or disrepute" any "persons, living or dead." Tam sued, noting that he had chosen the moniker in order to "reclaim" the derogatory term that had been used so long to indicate Asian persons.

In an 8-0 ruling, the Court said the disparagement clause in the Lanham Act was facially unconstitutional.

The Court said the clause went too far in restricting speech, giving government the unconstitutional power to require a seal of approval on private speech, thus muffling the expression of viewpoints disfavored by government. The decision represents another ruling by the Court that strikes down laws against hate speech that violate the First Amendment.

Often the best way to ensure registration is by making up a unique word, such as *Exxon*. These are referred to as *fanciful marks*. Because they are so unique, it is easier to get them registered. Marks may also receive protection if they take on secondary meaning in connection with a product or service and come to mean something other than the ordinary dictionary definition, such as the use of the word *Apple* for a line of computers.

Domain names that are used in websites and email addresses can be trademarked as well, but not the suffixes .com, .org and the like. Cybersquatters, who register names in hopes of selling them to trademark owners for a profit, prompted Congress in 1999 to pass the *Anticyber-squatting Consumer Protection Act* in an attempt to prevent the practice. The law provides penalties for anyone who registers a domain with the intent of selling it to a trademark holder. It prevents using a name that is the same or similar as the trademark and that disparages or harms the mark.

Another problem area concerns the protection of *trade dress*. Trade dress involves one business imitating the appearance of another or its products. Thus, can one company sell clothing that is similar to that produced by another without infringing on the latter's trademark?

In *Wal-Mart Stores v. Samara Brothers*, 529 U.S. 205 (2000), the Court held that trademark law does not prevent a company from making clothing that looks similar to another company's clothes. The Court noted that the plaintiff, to sustain such a claim, would need to prove the clothing had secondary meaning. That is, the public would have to so strongly associate the design with the original designer as to cause confusion. Infringement would occur only if and when the buyer was deceived into believing he was purchasing the original brand name item.

The ruling allowed Wal-Mart to sell clothes that resembled more expensive, brand name items.

In the end, trademark infringement occurs whenever one uses the protected mark in such a way as to create confusion about the product or its origin. In determining if trademark infringement has occurred, courts will look first to see if there is consumer confusion. To that end, judges will look at the similarity of the marks and the products or services they represent, as well as how long the marks have been in use and which one was used first and how well it is known.

The Court also will look to see if the protected mark may have been diluted. The Court will look to see if the infringer may have made the protected mark less distinctive in some way. Even a likelihood of dilution is enough under the new law and enough to find for the plaintiff in an infringement case. Judges will also look for possible blurring and tarnishing of the mark.

Those guilty of infringing on someone else's trademark will be ordered to stop using the mark. If the plaintiff can prove that infringement caused harm, the Court may also award monetary damages.

If, however, the defendant can show that the trademark was abandoned, obtained illegally, somehow misrepresented the plaintiff's product or origin, or that the defendant used it first, a claim of infringement may be defeated. It is legal under the concept of fair use to use someone's trademark for informational purposes or in comparative advertising, though it is illegal to alter the mark in such an ad.

Patents

The third major area of intellectual property protected in the Constitution concerns patents. There are three different kinds of patents, including:

1. Inventions. Inventions, such as machines or processes, have utility. The light bulb and telephone are examples.
2. Designs. Designs include the way something is constructed or designed, such as tire treads or the unique grill of an automobile.
3. Plants. New plants that can only be reproduced by some other means than natural processes may be patented. Grafting or somehow altering the basic DNA of the plant is usually necessary.

Patents give the patent holder the exclusive right to make, use or sell the invention, design or plant in the United States for 20 years in exchange for registering the patent and making information about it public. The U.S. government must issue the patent for it to be valid. The term "pat. pending" means the patent has been applied for and is awaiting government approval.

The patent process is legally complex and requires a great deal of research to make sure no other similar item has already been patented. Detailed drawings and other information must accompany the application process. Mass communication law generally does not concern patents.

CHAPTER 13

Advertising and Commercial Speech

The Evolution of Commercial Speech Protection

As we have discovered, not all speech is created equal. Political speech, which concerns the discussion of important public issues and goes to the heart of the democratic process, receives the most protection. Obscenity, on the other hand, receives no constitutional protection at all.

Commercial speech, which includes advertising and communication devoted to making money, falls somewhere in between. Deemed less important than speech about political and public matters, the Supreme Court nevertheless has ruled it is important enough to receive some protection under the U.S. Constitution since it communicates important information about products and services to the public.

In fact, the importance of commercial speech today cannot be overstated. It is the most widely used form of expression in our capitalistic society. We are bombarded with advertisements and commercials wherever we turn. Furthermore, the United States represents the largest advertising market in the world. Almost $166 billion was spent on advertising in the United States alone in 2012, and in 2020 that number is expected to reach just under $243 billion, according to Statista, the online statistics portal.

The importance of advertising, however, has not been always appreciated. It's somewhat tasteless beginnings relegated it to second-class status in the hierarchy of protected speech. Hucksterism and unethical and illegal sales tactics made it unworthy of full protection under the law.

Furthermore, advertising was not considered important early in our history and largely ignored by the courts and government officials. The prevailing attitude was that most of it was puffery and opinion and its effects on society were minimal. The doctrine of *caveat emptor* (let the buyer beware) was considered the guiding principle of virtually all business transactions. As a result, up until the late part of the 19th century, commercial speech received little notice.

Everett Collection/Shutterstock.com

Consequently, those who were hurt by false claims had nowhere to turn. The common law offered little relief, and without government regulation, consumers had no recourse other than to suffer the consequences of deceit. As the economy expanded, the problem grew worse.

Government Regulation of Advertising

In response to the growing problem, however, both state and federal government finally took action during the early part of the 20th century.

• Printer's Ink Statutes

Some states passed laws that made advertising fraud a crime. Known as *Printer's Ink Statutes*, which were first proposed in 1911 in the *Printer's Ink* magazine, the laws gave state and local prosecutors the power to pursue criminal charges against fraudulent advertisers within their states. These laws are still in effect today.

In addition, most states since have passed laws against unfair and deceptive acts and practices. These laws give consumers and competitors the ability to sue for civil damages caused by unfair and deceptive business and advertising practices.

• The Federal Trade Commission Act

Following the state action, the federal government also got involved in 1914, establishing the *Federal Trade Commission*, which was designed to stop unfair business practices between competitors. Although the law did little to protect consumers, it did give government some power over advertising.

Later, and particularly after World War I during a time of tremendous growth, advertising became more important and influential. More products filled the marketplace, and personal, disposable income increased.

Together, this meant people could be more selective in their purchases, which meant the need for information distinguishing products grew in importance. Advertising's power increased as it began to drive the economy.

Alina Galieva/Shutterstock.com

In response, the FTC soon launched a full-out crusade against false advertising, and by the 1920s, most of the agency's actions were about trying to stop the practice, contending that such ads were unfair to competitors.

In 1942, the Supreme Court handed down a ruling that seemed to support the government's contention that it could suppress commercial speech whenever it liked. The decision would define the Court's view on the issue for more than three decades.

The case that set the early precedent was *Valentine v. Chrestensen*, 316 U.S. 52 (1942). In it, the Court held that F.J. Chrestensen violated a New York City antilitter ordinance when he distributed handbills to promote a new tourist attraction. Chrestensen had acquired a surplus submarine and attempted to dock it at a pier in New York City. When city officials wouldn't let him pass out leaflets promoting the new business, he printed a protest on the flip side and handed them out anyway, arguing that the city was infringing on his political speech by refusing to allow him to distribute his protest.

The high Court didn't buy his argument, calling it a ruse to get around the law. In response, the Court went even further and ruled that purely commercial speech had no First Amendment protection.

Yet, the Supreme Court later began to change its mind about the issue between 1975 and 1980 in a series of Court rulings that afforded commercial speech at least some First Amendment protection.

The first came in *Bigelow v Virginia*, 421 U.S. 809 (1975). In that case, Jeffrey Bigelow was prosecuted for violating Virginia's anti-abortion laws by publishing an ad in *The Virginia Weekly* for abortion services in New York in 1971. At the time abortions were legal in New York, but abortions and advertisements supporting them in Virginia were not. (The *Roe v. Wade* decision legalizing abortions did not occur until 1973.)

Bigelow appealed his conviction, and the Court ruled in his favor, noting the advertisement was accurate and the public had a right under the First Amendment to receive the information. The Court reasoned that the ad was more than just commercial in nature since it provided information concerning a public interest. The government in future cases, the Court said, would need to show a compelling state interest to prohibit commercial speech that had a legitimate interest.

A year later in *Virginia State Board of Pharmacy v. Virginia Citizens Consumer Council*, 425 U.S. 748 (1976), the Court overturned a Virginia law that prevented pharmacists from advertising the price of drugs. The stated goal of the ban was to prevent price wars. The Court said again that the information was important to the consumer and therefore protected by the First Amendment, though it noted the government could still control false and misleading advertisements. Thus, commercial speech again received partial protection from the First Amendment.

Most recently, in *Expressions Hair Design, et al., v. Schneiderman, Attorney General of New York, et al.*, 581 U.S. _____ (2017), the high Court held that a New York law that said no seller in any sales transaction could impose a surcharge on those using a credit card in lieu of cash, check or other payment was a regulation of speech. Some business owners had filed suit, alleging the law violated their First Amendment rights by regulating how they could communicate prices.

The Court of Appeals had concluded that the New York law posed no First Amendment problem because price controls regulate conduct, not speech. The Supreme Court, nevertheless, said the law was not like a typical price regulation, which simply regulates the amount a store can collect. In this case, the law was telling merchants nothing about the amount they were allowed to collect from a cash or credit card payer. Instead, the law was regulating how sellers could communicate their prices. In regulating the communication of prices rather than prices themselves, the law was regulating speech.

The Court remanded the case to the Court of Appeals for further review.

The Commercial Speech Doctrine

In 1980, the Court went even further and established a legal test to determine if and when the government could restrict commercial speech. The test is still in use today.

In *Central Hudson Gas and Electric v. Public Service Commission of New York*, 447 U.S. 557 (1980), the Court held that commercial speech was protected speech if it advertised lawful activity and was not misleading or fraudulent. The case involved a challenge by the Central Hudson Gas and Electric Company to New York Public Service Commission rules designed to promote conservation during the energy crises in 1970. In part, the rules banned advertising encouraging energy consumption. The gas company argued that it violated its First Amendment rights. The Court agreed, noting it was mere speculation such a ban would even have the desired effect to promote conservation.

In making the ruling, the Court fashioned a test known as the *Commercial Speech Doctrine* to help courts decide future commercial speech cases. Together with another later case that helped modify the test, the Court said:

1. Advertisements that are false or misleading or for unlawful goods or services are not protected by the First Amendment and can be banned, and
2. Truthful advertisements for legal goods and services may still face government regulation if
   a. the state can show a substantial interest justifying the regulation;
   b. evidence supports and advances the interest; and
   c. there is a reasonable fit between the state interest and the government regulation.

The test, sometimes also known as the *Central Hudson Test*, makes it easier to regulate commercial speech than noncommercial speech, even on the basis of content, since the government must only show a *substantial state interest* to justify regulation. As noted earlier in the text, noncommercial speech regulated on the basis of content must meet the strict scrutiny test, which means the state must show a *compelling state interest*.

The Court justifies its distinction between political speech and commercial speech largely on the basis of how people view the two. Unlike political speech, which is largely perceived as philosophical and filled with opinion, commercial speech concerns the dissemination of facts on which a consumer relies to make a purchase. Although consumers may understand that they are receiving a pitch to buy something, they also expect to learn of facts about the product within the ad. A clever advertiser may make it difficult for them to determine where the opinions leave off and the facts begin. Therefore, it's easier for the advertiser to deceive or mislead the consumer. Legal protection is thus warranted.

Moreover, the Court views commercial speech as less important than political speech in maintaining the democracy. Democracy requires robust debate and the free flow of ideas. Such speech warrants special protection. The purpose of commercial speech is largely about money, which is deemed less important than the loftier goal of self-government.

Under the Commercial Speech Doctrine, therefore, a factually inaccurate advertisement obviously could be prohibited. So could one that was misleading, such as in the case of an advertiser who leaves out important information on which the consumer might rely.

Ads for unlawful goods and services, such as heroin or prostitution (except in Nevada), could be banned to uphold the law. Laws regarding housing and employment discrimination also prohibit discriminatory advertising on the basis of race, gender, family status or sexual orientation.

Even legal speech might be prohibited if the state can show an overriding interest.

For example, protecting the welfare of children is a substantial state interest, and placing a ban on the outdoor advertising of alcoholic beverages within 500 feet of a school could be shown to directly advance that interest if evidence can be shown to prove that it reduces alcoholic consumption. Lastly, if the ban restricts only that expression necessary to achieve its goal of protecting minors without affecting other people's ability to get legal information, the Court is likely to find the law is "narrowly tailored" and a reasonable fit between the state interest and the regulation.

The Commercial Speech Doctrine has been used to regulate advertising for tobacco, gambling, prostitution in Nevada, and even outdoor billboards and lawyers' ads, as well as a whole range of other products and services.

Corporations and Noncommercial Speech

This is not to say corporations have no First Amendment rights other than those dealing with commercial speech. In *First National Bank v. Bellotti*, 435 U.S. 765 (1978), the Court said a Massachusetts law that prevented a business from speaking out in ads about ballot measures was illegal. The law had limited business advertising to matters that only affected the business. The Court countered that the free flow of information was important, even if it came from corporations instead of individuals.

In *Consolidated Edison v. Public Service Commission of New York*, 447 U.S. 530 (1980), the Court fashioned a set of guidelines regarding when a state could regulate noncommercial speech. The Court said that the government can only justify regulating noncommercial business speech if the state can show:

1. The restriction on speech satisfies a compelling state interest, or
2. The restriction regulates the time, place, and manner of the corporate speech to fulfill an important government interest while leaving open other channels of communication, or the restriction prevents a disruption of government services.

The issue of noncommercial corporate speech has since taken on more importance and generated a firestorm of controversy. In *Citizens United v. Federal Election Commission*, 558 U.S. 310 (2010), the Court ruled that the First Amendment prevented the government from interfering with the political speech of corporations, labor unions, and other organizations by restricting their campaign contributions.

Citizens United, a conservative lobbying group, made a film critical of Sen. Hillary Clinton and wanted to advertise it in possible violation of the 2002 Bipartisan Campaign Reform Act. The Court ruled that limits on corporate spending for political ads violated the First Amendment. Opponents of the ruling said that it undermined the democratic process by enabling corporations with large amounts of cash to virtually buy elections.

Media Access

Just because someone wants to advertise, however, doesn't usually mean they have a right of access to the media. Most newspapers, magazines, and TV stations are private businesses. As such, the Court has ruled repeatedly that the media are not required to carry anyone's commercial advertising.

In *Miami Herald v. Tornillo*, 418 U.S. 241 (1974), the Court struck down a Florida right-of-reply law that required newspapers to publish replies from political candidates who were attacked in editorials. The case resulted when a teacher's union leader ran for state office and was criticized in a *Miami Herald* editorial. The leader sought the right to reply but was rebuffed by the newspaper. He sued and the U.S. Supreme Court ruled unanimously that the First Amendment prohibited the government from dictating the newspaper's content. The Florida law was declared unconstitutional.

The same rule applies to broadcasters, except that Section 312(a)(7) of the Communications Act requires broadcasters to accept political advertising from candidates running for federal office. Broadcasters use public airwaves, and that gives the government some control over how they may operate. (This will be discussed further in Chapter 14.) Newspapers, magazines, and other outlets under private control are under no such obligation and can turn down ads from anyone.

Government-sponsored media, however, may be required under certain circumstances to run ads. Courts have recognized that under the 14th Amendment's equal protection clause, officials may not generally turn down advertising on public transportation systems that offer advertising space just because they don't like the content of the advertisement or the person placing the ad. They are, rather, to remain viewpoint neutral.

This does not, obviously, apply to obscene displays or other illegal communication, which may be rejected.

Neither does it mean there is always a right of access to government-sponsored media. The Supreme Court in *Lehman v. Shaker Heights*, 418

U.S. 298 (1974), held that a bus line could deny a political candidate's advertising since its policy was to only accept commercial ads.

It should be noted, however, that the Court has repeatedly said the First Amendment protects parks, sidewalks, and other public forums as places for speech.

The Far Reach of the Federal Trade Commission

Despite the evolution of the Commercial Speech Doctrine, it is the Federal Trade Commission Act that established what remains the most powerful advertising regulatory agency in the country. With few exceptions, the FTC oversees nearly all advertising in the United States.

The agency has more than 1,000 employees and a budget of more than $300 million. A five-member commission, appointed by the president with the advice and consent of the Senate, governs it. Terms last seven years. No more than three of the five commissioners can be from the same political party.

Although its power was originally limited to prevent unfair methods of business competition *in* commerce, Congress has amended the act a couple of times since. As a result, its powers have been significantly expanded.

First, in 1938, Congress adopted the *Wheeler-Lea Amendment*, which gave the agency the power to also protect *consumers* from false advertising and deceptive and unfair business practices.

Later, in 1975, Congress added to the commission's power again by passing the *Magnuson-Moss Warranty-Federal Trade Commission Improvement Act*. The law enabled the FTC, among other things, to regulate unfair business practices and ads even if they only *affected* interstate commerce.

In addition, the law established trade regulation rules that gave the FTC the power to establish regulations preventing false and deceptive advertising claims pertaining to an entire industry. Thus, the FTC no longer needs to pursue corporations in the same industry individually for making false advertising claims. The agency can go after several at once. All the agency must do is to prove that each advertiser had knowledge of the rule regarding their industry to prove an unfair or deceptive practice. The law also allows the FTC to pursue civil penalties on behalf of consumers in some situations.

The FTC investigates illegal advertising claims after it learns of them from angry citizens, competitors, other government agencies, and through its own monitoring of the media.

After receiving a complaint, however, the FTC must determine first if the ad is false or deceptive. To do this, agency <u>officials first analyze what the ad says and doesn't say</u>. They look not only to the words used, but also to the overall impression the ad gives.

<u>Next, officials look to see if any representation, omission, or practice in the ad is likely to mislead a consumer who is acting reasonably</u>. Can the consumer evaluate the ad easily?

<u>Lastly, officials will try to determine whether the alleged false or misleading claims made in the ad are material, that is, important enough to cause the consumer to make a decision to buy the product</u>. Often the claim is merely *puffery*, an exaggerated claim not to be taken literally, such as, "These shoes will make you feel like you're walking on air." A reasonable person would understand such a claim is merely a pitch. Note that this is different from saying, "These shoes will never wear out." That is a factual statement that would likely be considered false advertising since friction eventually wears out everything.

FTC Methods to Stop False Advertising

If the FTC determines an advertisement is false or misleading, the agency will attempt to stop the unfair practice. A variety of methods are at its disposal. These range from using bad publicity, to court action to halt or correct advertisements that harm consumers.

• Publicity

The first step is to notify the advertiser. If the advertiser is reluctant to remedy the problem, the agency may issue press releases noting that the agency thinks the ad is false or deceptive. Bad publicity may bring the advertiser back into compliance with the law since it undermines public confidence in the company, product, or service.

• Substantiation

Rather than to pursue costly and timely litigation, the FTC will often ask advertisers to substantiate questionable claims. This may involve the use of studies or expert testimony as well as reliable scientific evidence. If the advertiser can prove what he says in the ad is true, the case ends. Although the advertiser is under no obligation to comply with the request, it is in his best interest to make the issue go away quickly and quietly.

• Voluntary Compliance

If the advertiser is nearly finished with the ad campaign, the false claim is not too egregious, and the advertiser has a good record with the FTC, the agency may be willing to allow the advertiser to sign an *assurance of voluntary compliance*. This means the advertiser agrees not to repeat the false claim again. This saves the agency's and the advertiser's time and eliminates the legal hassle of going to court. By acting quickly to end the ad, it also protects the consumer.

• Consent Agreements

If the matter is more serious, the FTC may want the advertiser to sign a *consent agreement*. Although still an informal way to settle a false advertising claim, the agreement is placed in the public record and after 60 days, it provides penalties if the advertiser violates the agreement. The advertiser admits no guilt and only agrees that he will refrain from making the false or misleading claims in the future.

• Litigated Orders

If the advertiser refuses to sign the consent agreement, the FTC may proceed to the next level and initiate formal litigation against the advertiser in an administrative law court. The agency files a complaint against the advertiser and the parties appear before a judge. After listening to both sides, the judge makes a ruling. If the judge agrees with the FTC, he will issue a *litigated order* requiring the advertiser to comply with the FTC's demand to stop the advertising. The judge, however, may side with the advertiser.

In either case, the agency has the right to review the judge's decision and issue a formal cease and desist order anyway against the advertiser if it thinks that the judge is wrong. If, on the other hand, it agrees with the judge's ruling, it can dismiss the matter.

If the FTC ultimately rules against the advertiser, the advertiser can appeal the decision to a federal appellate court. Unless the appellate court overturns the FTC decision against the advertiser, the advertiser must comply with the order. If the advertiser violates the order, civil penalties are assessed, sometimes as much as $10,000 or more a day, until the advertiser complies.

• Corrective Advertising

If a false and misleading ad has had a long and successful run, just pulling the ad may not eliminate any damage it has already caused. As a result the FTC may force the advertiser, most often after lengthy litigation, to run ads correcting the previous false or misleading ad. Advertisers resist such action because corrective ads are an admission that they lied to or otherwise misled the consumer.

• Injunctions

In extreme cases, where the advertising campaign is not scheduled to end soon or where it poses an immediate threat to the health or safety of other individuals or businesses, the FTC may seek a restraining order in federal court. If an injunction is granted, the advertiser must immediately do whatever the court orders. Often this means stopping the ad campaign or altering the message in some way.

• Guides

Lastly, the best way to stop false and misleading advertising is to prevent it in the first place. To accomplish this, the FTC issues guides covering a variety of industries, products, services, and practices to help advertisers stay within the law. The guides are not laws, but FTC policy statements about what is permissible to say in an advertisement pertaining to a product or industry. The FTC has issued hundreds of guides to help businesses know what they can and cannot say.

Other Advertising Concerns

In addition to those regulatory tools above, the FTC has also singled out specific advertising methods and problems for comment. They are often at the forefront of false-advertising claims. Advertisers who employ these techniques should be careful that they do not overstep the law.

• Testimonials

Celebrities and consumers who claim to use a product as part of an endorsement must actually use the product. In addition, the FTC notes that those who merely promote the product must at least believe in their endorsement. Their statement should reflect their honest opinion.

Furthermore, experts who promote a product must really be experts. Claims made in the endorsements also must be verifiable. An endorser who makes a false or misleading claim may be held liable for the statement. Despite endorsements by others, commercials should note what the typical results are for someone using the product.

• Mockups

The FTC also has addressed the problem of making a product look better in an ad by using something else that resembles it. Such action can be deceptive if such mockups make the product look better than it actually is or are somehow deceptive to the central point of the advertisement. For example, hot studio lights make shooting a commercial for ice cream difficult. To avoid the problem, directors have used mashed potatoes to look like ice cream. Since the color and texture of the "ice cream" is different, the ad may be considered deceptive.

• Telemarketing

The FTC's *National Do Not Call Registry* enables consumers to block telemarketing calls. Prerecorded calls from telemarketers are banned unless the consumer has given his written permission to accept such calls. The law does permit political and charitable telemarketing calls. Many states have established similar registries banning commercial telemarketing.

• Internet Advertising

An increase in unsolicited junk mail sent over the Internet, often referred to as *spam*, prompted Congress to pass the CAN-SPAM act in 2003. Otherwise known as the *Controlling the Assault of Non-Solicited Pornography and Marketing Act*, the law bans unsolicited commercial e-mail after a recipient has notified the sender to discontinue sending such messages.

Commercial e-mails are required to contain a valid postal address, and a way to reply to the message. They also must contain information on how to opt out of receiving the messages. The FTC, the Justice Department, and the Federal Bureau of Investigation enforce the law.

• Comparison Ads

It is permissible under FTC rules for companies to compare their products with a competitors' so long as they do so objectively. The FTC notes that such advertising is of benefit to consumers so long as the basis of the comparison is clearly identified and the ads are truthful and nondeceptive.

• Bait-and-switch Advertising

Under FTC rules, it is illegal to advertise a product that the company has no intention of selling, but instead promotes in order to sell a consumer something else, usually at a higher price. The intention in such cases is to lure a customer to the store on the promise of a good deal on a certain item. When the customer gets there, he finds the product isn't available or that sales people begin pressuring him to buy something else.

Advertisers can escape a bait-and-switch claim by noting in their ads that there is a limited supply of the advertised product and the offer is good "while supplies last," or the advertiser can offer a rain check for the sold out items so the consumer can purchase them later.

Advertiser Liability and Defenses Against False-Advertising Claims

The FTC says advertising agencies have a duty to make sure their claims about a product are true. Agencies should be able to substantiate their statements. Those agencies that make false or misleading claims in ads may be held liable for their deception.

Truth is the best defense against a false-advertising claim. Another defense may be to show that the alleged false advertising statement is not material to the ad. In other words, the statement doesn't concern a matter on which the consumer would rely to make a purchasing decision.

Other Federal Agencies That Regulate Advertising

In addition to the FTC, other federal agencies also help regulate specific areas of advertising. They include:

• The Food and Drug Administration

The federal government passed the *Food, Drug, and Cosmetic Act of 1938* to protect the purity and safety of foods, drugs and cosmetics. As a result, the FDA was established to give the federal government oversight of all packaging and labeling of such items. The FDA also regulates tobacco as a drug and severely restricts advertising for tobacco products.

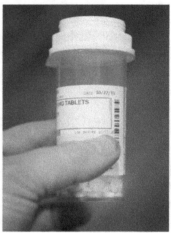

• The Federal Communications Commission

Although the FCC technically can't censor, it does have some control over advertising via its licensing regulations. When broadcast licenses come up for renewal, the agency reviews the kind and amount of advertising stations have aired. It pays particularly close attention to those commercials aired during children's shows.

FCC rules require that advertising aimed at children under age 12 not exceed 10.5 minutes during a 60-minute broadcast on weekends and 12 minutes on weekdays. Furthermore, children's programs must be separated from the commercials by a lengthy pause or other buffer to help children understand when the show stops and the advertisement starts. Lastly, shows that advertise products contained in the show—such as an ad that promotes a toy truck that appears in the show—are forbidden.

• The Securities and Exchange Commission

The Securities and Exchange Commission is responsible for enforcing federal securities laws in the United States, including those rules that govern the advertisement of stocks and other investments. The agency can bring civil actions against individuals and corporations that engage in insider trading and provide false or incomplete information about company assets and publicly-traded stocks. It also helps prosecute criminal actions against those who break securities laws.

• The Bureau of Alcohol, Tobacco, and Firearms (ATF)

The ATF is a law enforcement agency that is part of the United States' Department of Justice. It works to eliminate the illegal trafficking of firearms and explosives, acts of terrorism as well as the illegal production and sale of alcohol and tobacco products. As such, it also regulates the advertising and labeling of legal alcoholic beverages.

• The Federal Reserve Board

The Federal Reserve Board is responsible for overseeing the Federal Reserve Banks and conducting the monetary policy of the United States. Congress founded the Federal Reserve System in 1913 to provide a stable monetary and financial system. In short, it supervises and regulates the banking industry.

The Fed, as it is often called, governs consumer credit laws, including the *Truth in Lending Act*, the *Equal Credit Opportunity Act*, the *Home Mortgage Disclosure Act* and the *Truth in Savings Act*. Such laws require advertisers to disclose details about credit offers, interest rates, annual percentage rates, and other financial matters when an advertisement promotes credit financing.

Melpomene/Shutterstock.com

The Lanham Act

Thirty-two years after it passed the Federal Trade Commission Act, Congress added another level of protection for businesses known as the *Lanham Act*. Section 43(a) of the trademark law notes that any person who generates "any false designation of origin, false or misleading description of fact, or false or misleading representation of fact, which . . . in commercial advertising or promotion, misrepresents the nature, characteristics, qualities, or geographic origin of his or another person's goods, services, or commercial activities" is liable for civil damages.

Although the law is designed to protect trademarks and service marks, it also prevents an advertiser from making false claims about his product or a competitor from making false claims about another's products. Comparative advertising is legal, so long as it does not mislead the consumer.

Those who violate the act may be forced to pay actual monetary damages as well as court costs and any profits made as a result of the false or misleading claim. For particularly flagrant violations, judges can triple the damage award.

The act allows only competitors to sue one another, but as the amount of advertising has increased, so have the number of these lawsuits.

Self-regulation

The advertising industry has changed significantly since the days of the snake oil salesmen of the late 19th century. Although abuses still occur, the industry as a whole has made an effort to become more professional. Advertisers, by and large, came to realize that false, misleading and distasteful ads were undermining their ability to persuade consumers. Too, most media outlets began to develop their own advertising guidelines that determined which ads were acceptable and which were not. As a result, advertisers adopted voluntary methods of self-regulation.

By 1971, they formed the National Advertising Review Council. Known today as the Better Business Bureau's Advertising Self-Regulatory Council, the group attempts to provide good-practices advice and help advertisers resolve disputes over false or misleading claims out of court. Often, when a complaint is received, they work to help advertisers substantiate their claims. They also help advertisers examine the truth and accuracy of advertising and review whether children's advertising is age-appropriate.

CHAPTER 14

Broadcasting and the Internet

The Development of Radio

Until the late 19th century, the mass media, with the exception of the telegraph, consisted largely of newspapers, magazines, pamphlets and other written material. Then, an Italian inventor and physicist named Guglielmo Marconi changed all of that with his development of an entirely new medium—radio. The invention proved to mark the beginning of an era of unprecedented technological change in the mass media industry that continues to this day.

Unlike the telegraph, Marconi's new device enabled Morse code messages to be sent through the air and over long distances using electromagnetic radio waves instead of wires. These waves, called frequencies, carried electromagnetic impulses from a transmitter in one area to a receiver some distance away. As the power increased, the distance could be extended. So long as no one else transmitted on the same frequency, the impulses could be received easily. However, if someone else transmitted on the same wavelength at the same time, the two broadcasters would "jam" each other, and neither could be heard.

The invention, known as a "wireless," first proved useful at sea, where messages could not be received by wire. In the interest of safety, Congress passed the *Wireless Ship Act of 1910*, mandating that vessels carry the new radio devices along with trained technicians who knew how to use them.

Two years later when the *Titanic* sank after hitting an iceberg, Congress saw the need for more action. The ocean liner had sent distress signals before sinking, but radio messages from other ships and amateur radio operators on land clogged the airwaves and interfered with the Titanic's distress signals. Also, the radio operator on the ship closest to the *Titanic* was off duty and did not receive the call for help.

As a result, a new law, the *Radio Act of 1912*, required ships to have radio operators on duty at all times and authorized the secretary of commerce to issue radio licenses with assigned frequencies to prevent radio operators from jamming one another. Yet, the secretary had no authority to deny licenses or limit a station's power to send messages over a frequency, so the problem of jamming continued.

As technology improved and voice transmission became possible, commercial stations took to the airwaves in the early 1920s, making the

Paul Matthew Photography/Shutterstock.com

problem worse. Given the limited number of frequencies in the electromagnetic spectrum over which to send a message and the increasing number of stations demanding licenses, Congress was forced to act again.

Prompted by frustrated radio broadcasters, legislators passed the *Radio Act of 1927*, establishing the *Federal Radio Commission* to bring order out of the chaos. The law gave the commission the power to regulate the new industry by deciding who could and could not broadcast and when.

Perhaps most importantly, the law allowed the commission to deny licenses when there was no more room on the electromagnetic spectrum in a particular area. The commission also was given the task of trying to assist the growing industry by making sure every American could receive at least one station's broadcast. And it was charged with ensuring there were as many different radio sources as possible, thus encouraging the Miltonic theory of increasing the number of voices in the marketplace of ideas.

The plan worked. Soon, stations found they could broadcast within a certain area without interference from other nearby stations.

First Amendment Concerns

Yet such regulation also prompted a legal conundrum: The Founders had made it clear in the U.S. Constitution that government control of the Press was to be avoided. Now, little more than a hundred years later it seemed apparent that some kind of regulation was needed to make this new medium work. How could government do that without violating the Constitution? Surprisingly, the question was never really debated.

In any case, lawmakers decided they could use another part of the Constitution, the Commerce Clause, to solve the problem. Since radio signals crossed state lines, or at least could interfere with signals that did, they were technically in interstate commerce, which the federal government could regulate.

By declaring the air through which the signals passed to be public property, it was obvious the commission had the authority to regulate those frequencies on which the signals were sent. The Commerce Clause also made it clear such regulation belonged to the federal government and not the states. Furthermore, since radio operators were using public space, the commission could demand broadcasters operate in the public interest. So long as no attempt was made to regulate the content of those signals *per se*, they were not, it was argued, in violation of the other part of the Constitution—the First Amendment.

Unable to exert direct control over content, the commission was nevertheless able to influence content in other ways. In effect, the new system represented a hybrid form of mass communication. On the one hand, the First Amendment prevented direct censorship; on the other hand radio, unlike the printed press, was not a purely private endeavor. Radio depended upon the use of public airwaves, which gave the government at least some *indirect* control over what could be broadcast. As a result, over-the-air broadcast remains the most government-controlled medium to this day.

The Federal Communications Commission (FCC)

Seven years after passing the 1927 act, Congress amended the law further by passing the *Federal Communications Act*. The new law created a new agency—the *Federal Communications Commission*—and gave it control over other communication systems as well, including telephone and telegraph.

Today, the federal agency regulates all telecommunications, including radio, telephone, telegraph, television, and to a lesser extent, cable TV and direct broadcast satellite. However, unlike the telephone and telegraph, which are common carriers and must do business with everyone, radio, television and other media are under no such obligation except in certain limited situations. The industry is founded on the premise of free enterprise between station owners. So far, the Internet remains largely unregulated.

The rationale for permitting such widespread governmental regulation of radio and other over-the-air telecommunications was originally based on the concept of *spectrum scarcity*. In short, there were only so many frequencies to go around.

The U.S. Supreme Court held in *NBC v. U.S.*, 319 U.S. 190 (1943), that the FCC, because of the limited number of public airwaves over which to broadcast, had the authority to do more than regulate electromagnetic space. Because of such limitations, the Court said it was important that the agency be able to regulate the industry as a whole and dictate appropriate business practices that were in the public interest.

Technological improvements have since increased the broadcast spectrum and made such a rationale less convincing. Nevertheless, the argument is still used to justify FCC involvement.

The FCC's authority, however, is not without limits. A large portion of the radio spectrum is reserved for government use for military and emergency purposes. This area is under the control of the *National Telecommunications and Information Administration*.

Moreover, since radio and television waves cross national borders, some telecommunications regulation is governed by international treaty. *The International Telecommunications Union* in Geneva, Switzerland, assigns frequencies to prevent international interference. An increase in the number of nations transmitting by satellite has made such international cooperation even more important.

The FCC is comprised of five commissioners appointed by the president of the United States with the advice and consent of the Senate. They serve five-year terms, and only three of the members can be in the same political party. The agency adopts regulations that carry the force of law.

When the FCC proposes a rule, it publishes a *Notice of Proposed Rule-making* on the FCC website (www.fcc.gov) and in the *Federal Register*. Afterward, the agency takes comments on the proposal and then holds a hearing. If the proposed rule is adopted, it is included in the agency's regulations.

Anthonycz/Shutterstock.com

Broadcasters who violate FCC rules may receive a letter of reprimand or face a fine, called a *forfeiture*. For more serious offenses, the FCC may place conditions on the license owner's renewal or revoke the license altogether. Broadcasters who challenge the rules must file an appeal with the U.S. Court of Appeals.

Licensing

Operating a broadcast station in the United States without an FCC license is against the law, although pirate stations do exist. To combat the problem, the FCC uses direction finders to locate the illegal broadcasters and arrest them. Those who are convicted face heavy fines and the loss of their equipment.

In addition to enforcing the nation's broadcasting laws, the FCC is responsible for issuing new licenses and renewing existing broadcast licenses. Licenses are granted for eight years and can be renewed indefinitely every eight years after that.

Those applying for a new license must first either seek a channel that is not in use or petition the FCC to issue a new one. Most frequencies are already taken, and the prospect of getting a new one is remote. The spectrum is crowded. Most new licenses are awarded for existing stations that have changed hands.

It is easier to renew a license. In fact, license renewal is almost automatic unless the licensee violates some FCC rule or fails to operate the station in the public interest. Licenses are not transferrable. Assuming the station owner possesses the equipment and building, the owner is free to sell those assets, but the license is not his to sell. If he loses it or relinquishes it, it goes back to the FCC.

For many years, the FCC went through a complicated process of comparative hearings before granting a license to determine who was most qualified to serve the public interest. But today, the commission has turned to the process of auctioning licenses to the highest bidder in an effort to offset the federal deficit. The process only applies to commercial stations.

This is not to say the FCC will grant a license to anyone. Licensees must be American citizens. Foreign governments and corporations may not own stations. The rule is meant to prevent foreign governments from using the media for purposes of propaganda. Licensees also must be of good character and possess the technical skills and money necessary to run a station.

Those who wish to renew licenses also may have their application challenged by the public, though this is rare. Complaints can be filed online at www.fcc.gov/complaints. Public inspection of a station's operation is permitted. All stations must keep files containing information about station ownership as well as program content and advertising. FCC rules require compliance with a variety of day-to-day matters, including such mundane things as station break identification and more serious concerns such as children's programming.

The Effects of Deregulation

With the move toward government deregulation in the 1980s, however, several FCC rules, including some longstanding ones, were abandoned. Critics claimed the government was too paternalistic in its oversight of commercial broadcasting, deciding alone what was and what wasn't in the public interest. First Amendment concerns were raised over the FCC's interference with a station's editorial judgment, noting no federal agency has such control over print media or cable and satellite radio and television, or the Internet.

As a result, some of the original regulations that came out of the New Deal legislation of the 1930s were eliminated. The FCC instead adopted a more market-oriented philosophy that allowed station owners to determine what would be aired by looking to see what was popular with the public.

Rules eliminated included those that limited the number of commercials a station could broadcast each hour, those that prevented someone from owning a radio and television station in a top-50 market, and those that prevented one television network from owning another television network.

In addition, those rules that 1. restricted networks from owning and syndicating TV programs 2. required broadcasters to report all sides of a controversy and give reply time to people attacked in on-air editorials, 3. prevented a television station from owning a cable station—or vice versa—in the same market, and 4. prevented a cable television company from carrying the signal of a broadcast station it owns in the same market also were dropped.

These changes brought about by deregulation did not occur overnight, but gradually over three decades or so.

Broadcast Station Ownership

From the beginning, the FCC has promoted a classic libertarian philosophy—the more voices there are in the marketplace of ideas, the more likely citizens will be able to find the truth. Therefore, it has limited the number of broadcast stations one person or company can own. With the move toward deregulation, these limitations have been relaxed somewhat.

The agency has also tried to make it easier for minorities and women to own broadcast stations by making sure all areas of a community are informed about broadcast employment opportunities. Earlier, more pro-active programs designed to give preferential consideration to minorities were declared unconstitutional.

FCC rules generally prohibit one person or company from owning a major broadcast station and a daily newspaper in the same market.

Although one person or company can own an unlimited number of radio stations, the number of television stations one may own cannot exceed 39 percent of the total national viewing audience.

Other rules regarding broadcast ownership within a local market also apply. For example, one person or company can own two television stations in the same market if they don't overlap, one of the stations is not in the top four stations in the area and there are at least eight other major independently owned stations in the area.

Similarly, there are restrictions on the number of radio stations that can be owned within a particular market. Depending upon the size of the market, one generally may own anywhere from five to eight commercial stations in a local market depending upon the total number of stations in that market. Other rules limiting how many may be AM or FM stations also apply.

One person or company may also own more than one broadcast network, except that mergers between ABC, CBS, NBC, and Fox are prohibited.

The Fairness Doctrine

One of the first major rules to go in the move to deregulation was the *Fairness Doctrine*, which required broadcasters to report all sides of an important controversy. The 1949 rule was allowed to expire in 1987, during the period of deregulation. The law had required stations to air programs dealing with public controversies and to include in their overall programming differing opinions about the issues.

For years, the FCC had said the law was an important part of a station's responsibility to operate in the public interest. It was necessary because spectrum scarcity meant stations had a duty to broadcast as many different ideas on as many different issues as possible.

The Supreme Court upheld the rule in *Red Lion Broadcasting v. FCC*, 395 U.S. 367 (1969), siding with an author who demanded airtime to respond to an attack against him. Fred Cook had criticized presidential candidate Barry Goldwater during the 1964 campaign. As a result, radio evangelist Billy James Hargis attacked Cook on the air. When Cook demanded a right to reply, he was told he had to buy airtime.

The Court said the station's rights were indeed important, but not as important as the public's rights. It ordered the station to provide Cook with the time needed to respond to the attack.

But by the 1980s, broadcasters' complaints about the law had increased. They argued the law infringed on their First Amendment rights since the government was essentially dictating editorial content. Government bureaucrats were overruling the news judgments of journalists about what could be broadcast. They further argued cable and newer technologies made the FCC's spectrum scarcity argument irrelevant. Some broadcasters, meanwhile, were even avoiding controversial stories altogether out of fear they would have to provide too much airtime to competing factions on an issue. Such reluctance defeated the whole purpose of the doctrine.

The FCC finally sided with the broadcasters and abolished the rule in 1987. And a lower court echoed the decision in *Syracuse Peace Council v. FCC*, 867 F.2d 654 (D.C. Cir. 1989). In that case the Court upheld the FCC's decision to finally abolish the rule after a protest group sought airtime to counter commercials promoting the construction of a nuclear power plant.

Personal Attack Rules and Political Editorial Rules

Several years later, an appellate court also eliminated two other related rules—the *Personal Attack Rule* and the *Political Editorial Rule*. The Personal Attack Rule required broadcasters to notify those individuals or groups who had been attacked personally and give them free airtime to respond. The Political Editorial Rule similarly required broadcasters who endorsed a political candidate to give the candidate's opponent a chance to respond.

In *Radio-Television News Directors Association v. FCC*, 229 F.3d 269 (2000), the Court said the FCC could not justify the two rules and noted they interfered with the editorial judgment of journalists. Today, commercial radio and TV stations have a First Amendment right to air editorials supporting candidates. Noncommercial stations may not run editorials for candidates, although they may run editorials about public issues.

Broadcast Ascertainment Rules

By the millennium, however, the FCC had revived some of its rules. Among them were the *ascertainment rules*, FCC directives that required stations to find out from community leaders those important community issues that needed to be discussed. Although not particularly popular, programs that addressed these community issues helped stations operate in the public interest. However, given the amount of paperwork they required, most broadcasters find them burdensome.

The Equal Time Rule

Other rules were never abandoned. *Section 315* of the Communications Act, which has been part of the law since it was enacted in 1934, still requires broadcasters to give all legally qualified candidates for office an equal opportunity to respond to opponents.

Often referred to as the *Equal Time/Equal Opportunity Rule*, the provision requires broadcasters to treat all candidates equally. If one candidate gets airtime, then other candidates who seek airtime must be given the same consideration. If one candidate pays for it, the other must pay. If one candidate is given free time, the other candidate must receive free time as well.

The rule even applies when stations run old movies of actors who are running for office. Thus, if a station ran a movie of Arnold Schwarzenegger when he was running for governor, his opponent could demand equal time. And if an on-air broadcaster runs for office, the FCC has ruled his opponent must be given the same amount of airtime if he doesn't want to take a leave of absence from his job.

The FCC does allow exemptions to the Equal Opportunity Rule. For example, news programs and news interview programs, such as "Meet the Press," do not trigger the rule. Live coverage of a breaking news event of a candidate's speech will not invoke it. Candidate debates also are exempt. In *Arkansas Educational Television v. Forbes*, 523 U.S. 666 (1998), the Court held even government-owned public television stations do not need to include all candidates in a debate. Lastly, if the candidate appears in a documentary as an expert on some subject (other than himself), such a program is also exempt. His appearance is considered incidental. Such interpretation by the FCC allows for news reporters to cover events without having to include other candidates.

The rule does not apply to ballot issues like referendums and initiatives or recall elections.

The station does not have to seek out the opposing candidates to see if they want to use the station's facilities. But they must provide them with the opportunity if they ask for it within one week of the other candidate's appearance. Neither does the rule give the first candidate a right of access; it only says if the station allows one candidate to appear, it must afford the same opportunity to another candidate.

In addition, stations may not censor either candidate's message. If a candidate libels someone, the law does not hold the station responsible. The candidate, however, may still be sued.

The Equal Time Rule only applies to candidates running in the same general election. The rule changes for primary elections. In primaries, Democrats run against Democrats and Republicans run against Republicans. Thus, opposing Democrats, for example, must be given equal opportunity to appear to counter an opponent from their party, but the station does not have to give Republicans and Independents a chance to respond in the Democratic Party primary, and vice versa.

The Equal Opportunity Rule also applies to a candidate's supporters. If a supporter for one candidate appears on the air, the station must provide an equal opportunity for supporters of other candidates also. This is called the *Zapple Rule*.

In the case of state and local elections, a station may be able to avoid the Equal Opportunity Rule by not putting any candidates on the air. If no candidate is allowed on, there is no requirement to give an opposing candidate airtime.

The Candidate Access Rule

However, because of another rule in the Communications Act—*Section 312(a)(7)*—radio and television stations cannot deny *federal* candidates for office access to the airwaves. Known as the *Candidate Access Rule*, the law requires stations to provide all candidates for federal office the right to buy commercial airtime. The law applies only to commercial and cable stations. It does not apply to noncommercial stations.

Federal elections include those for the U.S. House of Representatives, the U.S. Senate, and the presidency.

Candidate Advertising

To make matters even more complicated, *Section 315(b)* requires stations to sell all candidates, including those running for local, state, and federal elections, the lowest advertising rate per minute they normally charge their best customers. It doesn't matter how much time the candidate buys—the rate stays the same. And if an advertiser is charged less for a commercial at midnight, the candidate also pays less for a commercial at that time. The *lowest unit charge provision* covers advertising within 45 days of a primary election and 60 days of a general election.

The FCC requires broadcasters to inform candidates of their rates. If a candidate's ads are preempted, the station must get the ad on at another time if it provides such makeups to other advertisers.

FCC rules also require stations to identify those who pay for commercials. This also applies to video news releases and product placement in programs. Those who sponsor political advertisements must also be identified.

Children's Programming

Despite the move toward deregulation of the broadcast industry, the FCC also still mandates that broadcasters provide quality programming for children. *The Children's Television Act of 1990* requires that broadcasters carry at least three hours of "core educational programming" each week. The programs must be designed for children aged 16 and under. They must be at least 30 minutes long, aired between 7 a.m. and 10 p.m., and be a regularly scheduled weekly program. They are not supposed to be preempted more than 10 percent of the time.

In addition, the FCC requires that stations identify children's programming on the air, note in program guides the age range the show targets, assign a staff member as a children's programming liaison, and file reports with the FCC that show the station is complying with rules regarding children's programming.

The *Child Safe Viewing Act of 2007* also directed the FCC to look for ways parents can block objectionable programming. These would be in addition to the V-chip technology mandated by earlier law that required TV sets with screens larger than 13 inches to include technology that enable parents to block programs they did not want their children to see.

Angela Waye/Shutterstock.com

FCC programming rules for children's shows apply to cable operators and direct broadcast systems as well.

As noted earlier, the FCC also keeps close watch on the advertising connected to children's shows. FCC rules require that advertising aimed at children under age 12 not exceed 10 and a half minutes during a 60-minute broadcast on weekends and 12 minutes on weekdays.

Furthermore, children's programs must be separated from the commercials by a lengthy pause or other buffer to help children understand when the show stops and the advertisement starts. In addition, shows that advertise products contained in the show—such as an ad that promotes a toy truck that appears in the program—are forbidden. These are referred to by the FCC as 'program-length commercials."

Indecency

Although obscenity is illegal, indecency is not—except in the case of over-the-air broadcasts.

Indecency—which is defined as the use of offensive language or material that in context describes in terms patently offensive to contemporary community standards sexual or excretory activities or organs—is permitted on cable and satellite television and on the Internet. Those media enjoy greater First Amendment protection.

It is, however, illegal to disseminate such material on over-the-air broadcast stations since broadcast is considered more intrusive and invasive. It can enter the home without invitation, and there is a greater chance children will be exposed to it. Thus, the FCC prohibits indecency on broadcast radio and TV.

The problem of indecency on radio and television became an issue nearly 40 years ago after a New York City radio station broadcast a recording of comedian George Carlin's "Seven Words You Can Never Say on Television." The monologue, which amounted to a verbal protest against censorship, was broadcast during the afternoon when a father and son were listening. The monologue aired without warning, and the father complained.

Subsequently, in *FCC v. Pacifica Foundation*, 438 U.S. 726 (1978), the Supreme Court held that the FCC could ban indecency from the airwaves during certain times of the day. The Court said the ban was not a violation of the First Amendment and that the ban was reasonable given that children might be in the audience. The Court said the language was not legally obscene, but noted in somewhat colorful language that the language was "merely a right thing in the wrong place—like a pig in the parlor instead of the barnyard."

The FCC has said such adult material could be broadcast during a *safe harbor* period from 10 p.m. to 6 a.m.

The problem of on-air indecency has grown in recent years. Anger erupted nationwide in 2004 when singer Janet Jackson's breast was exposed briefly during a Super Bowl halftime show broadcast by CBS. As a result, Congress increased the maximum fine the FCC could levy against stations that aired indecent content from $32,000 to $325,000. The FCC noted broadcasters had the ability to block even fleeting indecent images and words in live broadcasts and argued that its crackdown was reasonable.

At least one appellate court has expressed concern the FCC has not always applied the law equally, however, since it allowed four-letter words to be aired in the movie *Saving Private Ryan*. The FCC rationale was that the expletives were part of graphic description of a battle and created an accurate historical depiction.

Nevertheless, the broadcast industry has been put on notice on-air indecency will not be tolerated at least in some instances, and the Supreme Court, at least for the moment, has not addressed just how far the FCC can go in its quest to rid the airwaves of coarse language and pictures.

Violence on Television

Given the narrow definition of indecency, it should come as no surprise that under the FCC rules, violence is not considered indecent, despite growing complaints from the public that it is equally distasteful.

Nevertheless, after receiving a wave of complaints from parents about the increasing amount of violent programming on television, Congress included in the *Telecommunications Act of 1996* a requirement that new TV sets with screens larger than 13 inches had to include a V-chip that would enable parents to block violent shows from their children.

The law also required the industry to establish a voluntary rating system that would indicate in the corner of the TV screen if the content of a program about to be aired contained violence or sexual content. In creating the system, the television industry borrowed heavily from the motion picture industry's rating codes.

Despite the parental outcry, a Kaiser Family Foundation survey a few years later found only 15 to 16 percent of parents used the chip. Similarly, only about a quarter of the parents surveyed used the television rating system.

The News, Hoaxes, and Video News Releases

Because of the First Amendment, the FCC does not generally concern itself with news reports or attempt to second-guess the editorial judgment of journalists. Even citizen complaints about violence on evening news programs are not enough to invoke the wrath of the agency.

However, the FCC does prohibit stations from distorting the news or broadcasting false information about crimes and catastrophes if the reporter knows the information is false, is likely to harm the public, and, in fact, does cause harm.

In a related matter, the FCC also prohibits stations from airing *hoaxes*. Although not a widespread problem, at least one famous broadcast prompted the agency to address the matter. On October 30, 1938, the night before Halloween, Orson Welles directed a radio play that reported Martians were invading the earth. The play was based on H.G. Wells' novel "The War of the Worlds."

Although the broadcast was not meant to be a hoax and the director broke in several times during the broadcast to tell listeners it was a fictional radio play, the event nevertheless caused widespread panic. The FCC investigated the matter, but since it was a fictional play and not a false news broadcast, it took no action.

Video News Releases (VNRs) also have prompted FCC concern. Such public relations videos look like real news stories, although they are really subjective reports supporting a particular view on some issue. Sometimes they use actors pretending to be reporters. The FCC has warned broadcasters they must identify the sponsor of VNRs to comply with agency rules. Agency officials said listeners and viewers have a right to know who is trying to persuade them.

Other Content Rules

The FCC also has addressed other content problems. The agency requires radio deejays who are paid by promoters and record companies to play songs on the air to disclose such payola. Those who fail to disclose it violate the law.

Also, advertising and programming that promotes gambling is permitted by the FCC where gambling is legal. The permission came after the Supreme Court ruled in *Greater New Orleans Broadcasting Association v. U.S.*, 527 U.S. 173 (1999), that the federal government could not stop a broadcast station from airing a commercial for private casino gambling. However, the Court also held in *U.S. v. Edge Broadcasting*, 509 U.S. 418 (1993), that broadcasters located in states where gambling is prohibited may not advertise a nearby state's legal lottery.

Noncommercial Broadcasting

Most of the rules that affect commercial broadcasting also apply to noncommercial stations. Although the Communications Act prohibits noncommercial stations from carrying commercial advertising, they may acknowledge those viewers and listeners who contribute during fund drives. Public stations that air ads resembling commercial endorsements may be fined. Ads that contain comparative or qualitative descriptions or price information or induce people to engage in commercial activity are prohibited.

The Public Broadcasting Act established the Corporation for Public Broadcasting, which provides some congressional funding for National Public Radio (NPR) and Public Broadcasting Service (PBS) stations. The CPB also receives funding from other sources.

360b/Shutterstock.com

Unlike their commercial counterparts, public stations must provide objectivity and balance in their presentation of controversial issues. Nevertheless, the Supreme Court has allowed them to editorialize on public and political issues. The FCC uses a point system to award noncommercial stations licenses, favoring those applicants who live in the community, who do not own other nearby stations, and who have technical expertise.

Cable Television

From the beginning, over-the-air broadcast proved especially effective in urban areas where people lived close to broadcast stations. But in rural areas, where people lived farther away, receiving signals proved difficult.

To fix the problem, cable television was developed in the 1940s as a way to help those in rural communities get better television reception. First referred to as community antenna television (CATV), the technology made use of coaxial cable to deliver television broadcast signals that were impaired by long distance transmission or topography.

The new industry consisted of an elaborate antenna system that would boost signals from distant transmitters to a receiving station that would then send those signals over the wire to a subscriber's home.

In the 1960s, the system became more attractive to those in cities as well after apartment owners established rules that prevented residents from putting up antennas and then began charging residents a fee to hook up to cable. Too, viewers learned that reception from cable was clearer, and it offered more channels.

Since cable did not use the broadcast spectrum to deliver signals, and it also wasn't a common carrier like the telephone, the FCC did not get involved with the system at first. But in the 1960s, as the new industry began to grow quickly, broadcasters and program producers began to complain, noting cable operators were picking up signals from stations and airing programs for free.

To their dismay, the U.S. Supreme Court eventually held cable did nothing more than serve as an aid to reception and thus did not have to pay copyright royalties. Responding to the complaints, the FCC began to issue regulations aimed at cable systems anyway, arguing it could do so under its ancillary jurisdiction since cable was affecting on-air broadcasting. The new rules aimed at cable covered a variety of technical matters but also put limits on distant signals and franchise agreements with local governments.

The Supreme Court upheld the FCC's intervention in *U.S. v. Southwestern Cable Co.*, 392 U.S. 157 (1968), noting the Communications Act gave the agency control over wire transmissions as well. The FCC, in turn, added more rules, requiring larger cable operators to provide local public and government access channels, produce local programming, not duplicate local network programs, and not air syndicated shows to which local stations had rights. The FCC also required operators to get a certificate of compliance from the agency before entering into a franchise agreement with a local government. Such franchise agreements give a cable company the right to operate in a certain area since cable uses public rights of ways over which to run its wires. Most of the other rules affecting broadcasting were also imposed on the cable systems.

During the 1980s period of deregulation, some of the rules were abandoned. But by then the Supreme Court also made it clear that the FCC had the authority to control cable. In *Capital Cities Cable Inc. v. FCC,* 890 U.S. 691 (1984), the Court overturned an Oklahoma law that said cable systems could not advertise wine and liquor. The Court said the law violated federal must-carry rules requiring cable systems not to alter the content of nearby stations. The Court said states do not have the authority to preempt federal law.

Further curtailing state efforts to control the medium, Congress passed the *Cable Communications Policy Act of 1984* which said local governments could not charge more than 5 percent of a cable system's gross revenue for franchise fees, though local governments could require cable systems to carry education, public access, and government channels. The act, however, largely pursued a policy of deregulation.

The move was short-lived.

After receiving a flood of complaints about poor service and high rates, Congress responded by returning to more regulation. In passing the *Cable Television Consumer Protection and Competition Act of 1992*, Congress gave local governments more power to regulate rates, reduced cable rates, required cable companies to respond to consumer complaints, and prevented the cable systems from placing a station on a channel different from their on-air channel. (The *1996 Telecommunications Act* abolished the FCCs power to regulate rates.)

In addition, the FCC said stations could require cable systems in their area to carry their signal – though the cable company would not be required to compensate the station for carrying it, or the station could choose to prohibit the local cable company from transmitting its signal unless it gave its permission and received compensation. These are referred to as *must carry* and *retransmission consent* rules.

The rules are designed to protect on-air broadcasts by promoting diversity of program sources. Broadcasters had complained that if cable companies refused to carry their stations, it would undercut their businesses since nearly 85 percent of households today receive cable. Broadcasters argued that cable might drop some of their less popular programs on its system.

Unlike on-air broadcast stations, cable systems are not required to ban indecent programming during the day. In *Wilkinson v. Jones*, 480 U.S. 926 (1987), the Supreme Court held state and local governments cannot require the systems to eliminate such programming. But in *Telecommunications Consortium v. FCC*, 518 U.S. 727 (1996), the Court also added that cable systems have a First Amendment right to ban indecent material themselves on commercial leased access channels if they choose.

Direct Broadcast Satellites

Cable's main competitor is direct broadcast satellite. Instead of receiving programs by wire, subscribers to DBS rely on satellite transmission. The system relies on numerous satellites positioned more than 22,000 miles above the equator. These satellites remain in a fixed position and move with the earth as it rotates. Signals are sent up to the satellites and retransmitted down to dish antennas that are pointed at the satellite.

Newspapers, broadcasters, and wire services also use satellite transmission today.

Although DBS got off to a slow start in the 1980s, *The 1996 Telecommunications Act* enabled the FCC to promote DBS systems as a way to compete with cable. Among other things, the law allowed the FCC to overrule zoning laws that prohibited residents from placing dish antennas on their property.

Although the FCC relaxed some of its rules to help DBS succeed, it required DBS to adhere to others, including requirements to provide educational programming as well as to follow limits on advertising during children's shows. Also, if a DBS operator offers one local station to its subscribers, it must offer the other local stations as well. As with cable, television stations may choose between must-carry and retransmission consent provisions.

Low Power Television

Low-power television, which enabled stations with low power and low overhead to provide TV service to communities that had no larger local stations, were introduced in the 1980s. The FCC waived some of the regulations the larger stations had to follow in an effort to help the stations serve smaller towns and localized areas. The stations' broadcast radius only reaches up to about 10 or 15 miles. Many of these stations have had to limit their operations or switch channels to avoid interference from digital television.

Satellite Radio

A newer technology, digital radio, offers listeners a chance to receive more than 100 channels of high-quality audio by satellite for a small fee each month. The FCC reserved UHF frequencies and adopted rules for the service in the 1990s. Two services, XM and Sirius, began service in the early 2000s and by the end of the decade already had millions of listeners.

Unlike over-the-air broadcasters, which are subject to FCC regulations regarding indecency and profanity, satellite radio stations are exempt from such rules. Thus, radio personality Howard Stern, who charged the FCC was all but censoring his shock jock programs, switched to satellite radio.

FCC regulations concerning satellite radio still focus on such technical things as power levels and land antennas that pass on signals from satellites.

Low Power FM Radio

The FCC also created low-power FM radio in 2000. As with low-power television, the service is meant to reach those smaller communities without large, existing radio stations. Many also are designed to serve a limited area within a larger community, such as college campuses in a large metropolitan area.

The Internet

Finally, the FCC voted in February 2015 to regulate broadband Internet as a public service. The move was intended to make sure no Internet content is blocked and that the Internet is not divided into fast lanes of web connection for the affluent and slow lanes of web connection for everyone else. FCC officials said the goal is designed to protect net neutrality.

The new rules prevent broadband providers from deciding that some will pay more for Internet services than others. The FCC passed the rules after reclassifying high-speed Internet service as a telecommunications service rather than an information service under the Telecommunications Act. Thus, it treats the Internet more as a common carrier public utility, such as a telephone.

The move came after FCC attempts to regulate the Internet were rebuffed by at least one court. That 2010 lower court ruling said the agency had no express authority to ensure net neutrality. Neither could

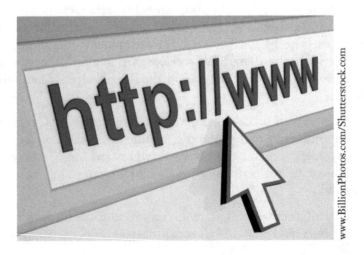

www.BillionPhotos.com/Shutterstock.com

it do so under ancillary powers granted to it by the Communications Act of 1934. This was because the FCC had classified the Internet as an information service, which the court said would place its attempts at such regulation outside the law.

The new rules, which are likely to be challenged, only attempt to keep the Internet "speed limit" the same for everyone. They do not affect what can move along that freeway since the Supreme Court had already held years earlier the Internet enjoyed wide First Amendment protection.

In *Reno v. ACLU*, 521 U.S. 844 (1997), the Court held the First Amendment protects the Internet much the same way it protects the print media. The *Reno* case challenged a provision of the Telecommunications Act of 1996 that banned indecent material from being transmitted on the Internet.

The Court overruled that provision, finding the Internet had none of the limitations that plagued broadcast. The Court said broadcast regulation is justified given spectrum scarcity, but that Internet regulation is not justified since it does not use the spectrum. Neither, said the Court, is it as invasive as broadcast. If parents don't want their children online, they need not subscribe to it.

In a more recent case, the Supreme Court said that a North Carolina law that made it a crime for a registered sex offender to access a commercial social networking website impermissibly restricted lawful speech in violation of the First Amendment. The case, *Packingham v. North Carolina*, 582 U.S. _____., 137 S.Ct. 1730 (2017), involved the innocuous posting of a statement on a personal Facebook profile about a traffic court experience.

The Court noted that while the state had a right to pass valid laws to protect children and other sexual assault victims, the law in question was not narrowly-tailored. The Court said the law barred access to a principal source for knowing current events, checking ads for employment, and speaking and listening in the modern public square, thus preventing the user from engaging in the legitimate exercise of First Amendment rights.

And in yet another Internet case, *Elonis v. United States*, 575 U.S. _____., 135 S.Ct. 2001 (2015), the Court said a man who had been convicted of making threats on Facebook by posting self-styled rap lyrics containing violent language concerning his wife, co-workers, a kindergarten class, and federal and state law enforcement officials had to understand his action as a conscious criminal act before he could be convicted. In this case, the convicted person had posted disclaimers that the lyrics were "fictitious."

APPENDIX A

The Declaration of Independence: A Transcription

IN CONGRESS, July 4, 1776.

The unanimous Declaration of the thirteen united States of America

When in the Course of human events, it becomes necessary for one people to dissolve the political bands which have connected them with another, and to assume among the powers of the earth, the separate and equal station to which the Laws of Nature and of Nature's God entitle them, a decent respect to the opinions of mankind requires that they should declare the causes which impel them to the separation.

We hold these truths to be self-evident, that all men are created equal, that they are endowed by their Creator with certain unalienable Rights, that among these are Life, Liberty and the pursuit of Happiness.— That to secure these rights, Governments are instituted among Men, deriving their just powers from the consent of the governed,—That whenever any Form of Government becomes destructive of these ends, it is the Right of the People to alter or to abolish it, and to institute new Government, laying its foundation on such principles and organizing its powers in such form, as to them shall seem most likely to effect their Safety and Happiness. Prudence, indeed, will dictate that Governments long established should not be changed for light and transient causes;

and accordingly all experience hath shewn, that mankind are more disposed to suffer, while evils are sufferable, than to right themselves by abolishing the forms to which they are accustomed. But when a long train of abuses and usurpations, pursuing invariably the same Object evinces a design to reduce them under absolute Despotism, it is their right, it is their duty, to throw off such Government, and to provide new Guards for their future security.—Such has been the patient sufferance of these Colonies; and such is now the necessity which constrains them to alter their former Systems of Government. The history of the present King of Great Britain is a history of repeated injuries and usurpations, all having in direct object the establishment of an absolute Tyranny over these States. To prove this, let Facts be submitted to a candid world.

He has refused his Assent to Laws, the most wholesome and necessary for the public good.

He has forbidden his Governors to pass Laws of immediate and pressing importance, unless suspended in their operation till his Assent should be obtained; and when so suspended, he has utterly neglected to attend to them.

He has refused to pass other Laws for the accommodation of large districts of people, unless those people would relinquish the right of Representation in the Legislature, a right inestimable to them and formidable to tyrants only.

He has called together legislative bodies at places unusual, uncomfortable, and distant from the depository of their public Records, for the sole purpose of fatiguing them into compliance with his measures.

He has dissolved Representative Houses repeatedly, for opposing with manly firmness his invasions on the rights of the people.

He has refused for a long time, after such dissolutions, to cause others to be elected; whereby the Legislative powers, incapable of Annihilation, have returned to the People at large for their exercise; the State remaining in the mean time exposed to all the dangers of invasion from without, and convulsions within.

He has endeavoured to prevent the population of these States; for that purpose obstructing the Laws for Naturalization of Foreigners; refusing to pass others to encourage their migrations hither, and raising the conditions of new Appropriations of Lands.

He has obstructed the Administration of Justice, by refusing his Assent to Laws for establishing Judiciary powers.

He has made Judges dependent on his Will alone, for the tenure of their offices, and the amount and payment of their salaries.

He has erected a multitude of New Offices, and sent hither swarms of Officers to harrass our people, and eat out their substance.

He has kept among us, in times of peace, Standing Armies without the Consent of our legislatures.

He has affected to render the Military independent of and superior to the Civil power.

He has combined with others to subject us to a jurisdiction foreign to our constitution, and unacknowledged by our laws; giving his Assent to their Acts of pretended Legislation:

> For Quartering large bodies of armed troops among us.
>
> For protecting them, by a mock Trial, from punishment for any Murders which they should commit on the Inhabitants of these States.
>
> For cutting off our Trade with all parts of the world.
>
> For imposing Taxes on us without our Consent.
>
> For depriving us in many cases, of the benefits of Trial by Jury.
>
> For transporting us beyond Seas to be tried for pretended offences
>
> For abolishing the free System of English Laws in a neighbouring Province, establishing therein an Arbitrary government, and enlarging its Boundaries so as to render it at once an example and fit instrument for introducing the same absolute rule into these Colonies.
>
> For taking away our Charters, abolishing our most valuable Laws, and altering fundamentally the Forms of our Governments.
>
> For suspending our own Legislatures, and declaring themselves invested with power to legislate for us in all cases whatsoever.

He has abdicated Government here, by declaring us out of his Protection and waging War against us.

He has plundered our seas, ravaged our Coasts, burnt our towns, and destroyed the lives of our people.

He is at this time transporting large Armies of foreign Mercenaries to compleat the works of death, desolation and tyranny, already begun with circumstances of Cruelty & perfidy scarcely paralleled in the most barbarous ages, and totally unworthy the Head of a civilized nation.

He has constrained our fellow Citizens taken Captive on the high Seas to bear Arms against their Country, to become the executioners of their friends and Brethren, or to fall themselves by their Hands.

He has excited domestic insurrections amongst us, and has endeavoured to bring on the inhabitants of our frontiers, the merciless Indian Savages, whose known rule of warfare, is an undistinguished destruction of all ages, sexes and conditions.

In every stage of these Oppressions We have Petitioned for Redress in the most humble terms: Our repeated Petitions have been answered only by repeated injury. A Prince whose character is thus marked by every act which may define a Tyrant, is unfit to be the ruler of a free people.

Nor have We been wanting in attentions to our Brittish brethren. We have warned them from time to time of attempts by their legislature to extend an unwarrantable jurisdiction over us. We have reminded them of the circumstances of our emigration and settlement here. We have appealed to their native justice and magnanimity, and we have conjured them by the ties of our common kindred to disavow these usurpations, which, would inevitably interrupt our connections and correspondence. They too have been deaf to the voice of justice and of consanguinity. We must, therefore, acquiesce in the necessity, which denounces our Separation, and hold them, as we hold the rest of mankind, Enemies in War, in Peace Friends.

We, therefore, the Representatives of the united States of America, in General Congress, Assembled, appealing to the Supreme Judge of the world for the rectitude of our intentions, do, in the Name, and by Authority of the good People of these Colonies, solemnly publish and declare, That these United Colonies are, and of Right ought to be Free and Independent States; that they are Absolved from all Allegiance to the British Crown, and that all political connection between them and the State of Great Britain, is and ought to be totally dissolved; and that as Free and Independent States, they have full Power to levy War, conclude Peace, contract Alliances, establish Commerce, and to do all other Acts and Things which Independent States may of right do. And for the support of this Declaration, with a firm reliance on the protection of divine Providence, we mutually pledge to each other our Lives, our Fortunes and our sacred Honor.

The 56 signatures on the Declaration appear in the positions indicated:

Column 1

Georgia:

Button Gwinnett
Lyman Hall
George Walton

Column 2

North Carolina:

William Hooper
Joseph Hewes
John Penn

South Carolina:

Edward Rutledge
Thomas Heyward, Jr.
Thomas Lynch, Jr.
Arthur Middleton

Column 3

Massachusetts:

John Hancock

Maryland:

Samuel Chase
William Paca
Thomas Stone
Charles Carroll of Carrollton

Virginia:

George Wythe
Richard Henry Lee
Thomas Jefferson
Benjamin Harrison
Thomas Nelson, Jr.

Francis Lightfoot Lee
Carter Braxton

Column 4
Pennsylvania:

Robert Morris
Benjamin Rush
Benjamin Franklin
John Morton
George Clymer
James Smith
George Taylor
James Wilson
George Ross

Delaware:

Caesar Rodney
George Read
Thomas McKean

Column 5
New York:

William Floyd
Philip Livingston
Francis Lewis
Lewis Morris

New Jersey:

Richard Stockton
John Witherspoon
Francis Hopkinson
John Hart
Abraham Clark

Column 6
New Hampshire:

Josiah Bartlett
William Whipple

Massachusetts:

Samuel Adams
John Adams
Robert Treat Paine
Elbridge Gerry

Rhode Island:

Stephen Hopkins
William Ellery

Connecticut:

Roger Sherman
Samuel Huntington
William Williams
Oliver Wolcott

New Hampshire:

Matthew Thornton

APPENDIX B

The Constitution of the United States: A Transcription

Note: The following text is a transcription of the Constitution as it was inscribed by Jacob Shallus on parchment (the document on display in the Rotunda at the National Archives Museum.) Items that are hyperlinked have since been amended or superseded. The authenticated text of the Constitution can be found on the website of the Government Printing Office.

We the People of the United States, in Order to form a more perfect Union, establish Justice, insure domestic Tranquility, provide for the common defence, promote the general Welfare, and secure the Blessings of Liberty to ourselves and our Posterity, do ordain and establish this Constitution for the United States of America.

Article. I.

Section 1.

All legislative Powers herein granted shall be vested in a Congress of the United States, which shall consist of a Senate and House of Representatives.

Section 2.

The House of Representatives shall be composed of Members chosen every second Year by the People of the several States, and the Electors in each State shall have the Qualifications requisite for Electors of the most numerous Branch of the State Legislature.

No Person shall be a Representative who shall not have attained to the Age of twenty five Years, and been seven Years a Citizen of the United States, and who shall not, when elected, be an Inhabitant of that State in which he shall be chosen.

Representatives and direct Taxes shall be apportioned among the several States which may be included within this Union, according to their respective Numbers, which shall be determined by adding to the whole Number of free Persons, including those bound to Service for a Term of Years, and excluding Indians not taxed, three fifths of all other Persons. The actual Enumeration shall be made within three Years after the first Meeting of the Congress of the United States, and within every subsequent Term of ten Years, in such Manner as they shall by Law direct. The Number of Representatives shall not exceed one for every thirty Thousand, but each State shall have at Least one Representative; and until such enumeration shall be made, the State of New Hampshire shall be entitled to chuse three, Massachusetts eight, Rhode-Island and Providence Plantations one, Connecticut five, New-York six, New Jersey four, Pennsylvania eight, Delaware one, Maryland six, Virginia ten, North Carolina five, South Carolina five, and Georgia three.

When vacancies happen in the Representation from any State, the Executive Authority thereof shall issue Writs of Election to fill such Vacancies.

The House of Representatives shall chuse their Speaker and other Officers; and shall have the sole Power of Impeachment.

Section 3.

The Senate of the United States shall be composed of two Senators from each State, chosen by the Legislature thereof, for six Years; and each Senator shall have one Vote.

Immediately after they shall be assembled in Consequence of the first Election, they shall be divided as equally as may be into three Classes. The Seats of the Senators of the first Class shall be vacated at the Expiration of the second Year, of the second Class at the Expiration of the fourth Year, and of the third Class at the Expiration of the sixth Year, so that one third may be chosen every second Year; and if Vacancies happen by Resignation, or otherwise, during the Recess of the Legislature of any State, the Executive thereof may make temporary

Appointments until the next Meeting of the Legislature, which shall then fill such Vacancies.

No Person shall be a Senator who shall not have attained to the Age of thirty Years, and been nine Years a Citizen of the United States, and who shall not, when elected, be an Inhabitant of that State for which he shall be chosen.

The Vice President of the United States shall be President of the Senate, but shall have no Vote, unless they be equally divided.

The Senate shall chuse their other Officers, and also a President pro tempore, in the Absence of the Vice President, or when he shall exercise the Office of President of the United States.

The Senate shall have the sole Power to try all Impeachments. When sitting for that Purpose, they shall be on Oath or Affirmation. When the President of the United States is tried, the Chief Justice shall preside: And no Person shall be convicted without the Concurrence of two thirds of the Members present.

Judgment in Cases of Impeachment shall not extend further than to removal from Office, and disqualification to hold and enjoy any Office of honor, Trust or Profit under the United States: but the Party convicted shall nevertheless be liable and subject to Indictment, Trial, Judgment and Punishment, according to Law.

Section 4.

The Times, Places and Manner of holding Elections for Senators and Representatives, shall be prescribed in each State by the Legislature thereof; but the Congress may at any time by Law make or alter such Regulations, except as to the Places of chusing Senators.

The Congress shall assemble at least once in every Year, and such Meeting shall be on the first Monday in December, unless they shall by Law appoint a different Day.

Section 5.

Each House shall be the Judge of the Elections, Returns and Qualifications of its own Members, and a Majority of each shall constitute a Quorum to do Business; but a smaller Number may adjourn from day to day, and may be authorized to compel the Attendance of absent Members, in such Manner, and under such Penalties as each House may provide.

Each House may determine the Rules of its Proceedings, punish its Members for disorderly Behaviour, and, with the Concurrence of two thirds, expel a Member.

Each House shall keep a Journal of its Proceedings, and from time to time publish the same, excepting such Parts as may in their Judgment require Secrecy; and the Yeas and Nays of the Members of either House on any question shall, at the Desire of one fifth of those Present, be entered on the Journal.

Neither House, during the Session of Congress, shall, without the Consent of the other, adjourn for more than three days, nor to any other Place than that in which the two Houses shall be sitting.

Section 6.

The Senators and Representatives shall receive a Compensation for their Services, to be ascertained by Law, and paid out of the Treasury of the United States. They shall in all Cases, except Treason, Felony and Breach of the Peace, be privileged from Arrest during their Attendance at the Session of their respective Houses, and in going to and returning from the same; and for any Speech or Debate in either House, they shall not be questioned in any other Place.

No Senator or Representative shall, during the Time for which he was elected, be appointed to any civil Office under the Authority of the United States, which shall have been created, or the Emoluments whereof shall have been encreased during such time; and no Person holding any Office under the United States, shall be a Member of either House during his Continuance in Office.

Section 7.

All Bills for raising Revenue shall originate in the House of Representatives; but the Senate may propose or concur with Amendments as on other Bills.

Every Bill which shall have passed the House of Representatives and the Senate, shall, before it become a Law, be presented to the President of the United States; If he approve he shall sign it, but if not he shall return it, with his Objections to that House in which it shall have originated, who shall enter the Objections at large on their Journal, and proceed to reconsider it. If after such Reconsideration two thirds of that House shall agree to pass the Bill, it shall be sent, together with the Objections, to the other House, by which it shall likewise be reconsidered, and if approved by two thirds of that House, it shall become a Law. But in all such Cases the Votes of both Houses shall be determined by yeas and Nays, and the Names of the Persons voting for and against the Bill shall be entered on the Journal of each House respectively. If any Bill shall not be returned by the President within ten Days (Sundays excepted) after it shall have been presented to him, the Same shall be a Law, in like Manner as if he had signed it, unless the Congress by their Adjournment prevent its Return, in which Case it shall not be a Law.

Every Order, Resolution, or Vote to which the Concurrence of the Senate and House of Representatives may be necessary (except on a question of Adjournment) shall be presented to the President of the United States; and before the Same shall take Effect, shall be approved by him, or being disapproved by him, shall be repassed by two thirds of the Senate and House of Representatives, according to the Rules and Limitations prescribed in the Case of a Bill.

Section 8.

The Congress shall have Power To lay and collect Taxes, Duties, Imposts and Excises, to pay the Debts and provide for the common Defence and general Welfare of the United States; but all Duties, Imposts and Excises shall be uniform throughout the United States;

To borrow Money on the credit of the United States;

To regulate Commerce with foreign Nations, and among the several States, and with the Indian Tribes;

To establish an uniform Rule of Naturalization, and uniform Laws on the subject of Bankruptcies throughout the United States;

To coin Money, regulate the Value thereof, and of foreign Coin, and fix the Standard of Weights and Measures;

To provide for the Punishment of counterfeiting the Securities and current Coin of the United States;

To establish Post Offices and post Roads;

To promote the Progress of Science and useful Arts, by securing for limited Times to Authors and Inventors the exclusive Right to their respective Writings and Discoveries;

To constitute Tribunals inferior to the supreme Court;

To define and punish Piracies and Felonies committed on the high Seas, and Offences against the Law of Nations;

To declare War, grant Letters of Marque and Reprisal, and make Rules concerning Captures on Land and Water;

To raise and support Armies, but no Appropriation of Money to that Use shall be for a longer Term than two Years;

To provide and maintain a Navy;

To make Rules for the Government and Regulation of the land and naval Forces;

To provide for calling forth the Militia to execute the Laws of the Union, suppress Insurrections and repel Invasions;

To provide for organizing, arming, and disciplining, the Militia, and for governing such Part of them as may be employed in the Service of the United States, reserving to the States respectively, the Appointment of the Officers, and the Authority of training the Militia according to the discipline prescribed by Congress;

To exercise exclusive Legislation in all Cases whatsoever, over such District (not exceeding ten Miles square) as may, by Cession of particular States, and the Acceptance of Congress, become the Seat of the Government of the United States, and to exercise like Authority over all Places purchased by the Consent of the Legislature of the State in which the Same shall be, for the Erection of Forts, Magazines, Arsenals, dock-Yards, and other needful Buildings;—And

To make all Laws which shall be necessary and proper for carrying into Execution the foregoing Powers, and all other Powers vested by this Constitution in the Government of the United States, or in any Department or Officer thereof.

Section 9.

The Migration or Importation of such Persons as any of the States now existing shall think proper to admit, shall not be prohibited by the Congress prior to the Year one thousand eight hundred and eight, but a Tax or duty may be imposed on such Importation, not exceeding ten dollars for each Person.

The Privilege of the Writ of Habeas Corpus shall not be suspended, unless when in Cases of Rebellion or Invasion the public Safety may require it.

No Bill of Attainder or ex post facto Law shall be passed.

No Capitation, or other direct, Tax shall be laid, <u>unless in Proportion to the Census or enumeration herein before directed to be taken</u>.

No Tax or Duty shall be laid on Articles exported from any State.

No Preference shall be given by any Regulation of Commerce or Revenue to the Ports of one State over those of another: nor shall Vessels bound to, or from, one State, be obliged to enter, clear, or pay Duties in another.

No Money shall be drawn from the Treasury, but in Consequence of Appropriations made by Law; and a regular Statement and Account of the Receipts and Expenditures of all public Money shall be published from time to time.

No Title of Nobility shall be granted by the United States: And no Person holding any Office of Profit or Trust under them, shall, without the Consent of the Congress, accept of any present, Emolument, Office, or Title, of any kind whatever, from any King, Prince, or foreign State.

Section 10.

No State shall enter into any Treaty, Alliance, or Confederation; grant Letters of Marque and Reprisal; coin Money; emit Bills of Credit; make any Thing but gold and silver Coin a Tender in Payment of Debts; pass any Bill of Attainder, ex post facto Law, or Law impairing the Obligation of Contracts, or grant any Title of Nobility.

No State shall, without the Consent of the Congress, lay any Imposts or Duties on Imports or Exports, except what may be absolutely necessary for executing it's inspection Laws: and the net Produce of all Duties and Imposts, laid by any State on Imports or Exports, shall be for the Use of the Treasury of the United States; and all such Laws shall be subject to the Revision and Controul of the Congress.

No State shall, without the Consent of Congress, lay any Duty of Tonnage, keep Troops, or Ships of War in time of Peace, enter into any Agreement or Compact with another State, or with a foreign Power, or engage in War, unless actually invaded, or in such imminent Danger as will not admit of delay.

Article. II.

Section 1.

The executive Power shall be vested in a President of the United States of America. He shall hold his Office during the Term of four Years, and, together with the Vice President, chosen for the same Term, be elected, as follows

Each State shall appoint, in such Manner as the Legislature thereof may direct, a Number of Electors, equal to the whole Number of Senators and Representatives to which the State may be entitled in the Congress: but no Senator or Representative, or Person holding an Office of Trust or Profit under the United States, shall be appointed an Elector.

The Electors shall meet in their respective States, and vote by Ballot for two Persons, of whom one at least shall not be an Inhabitant of the same State with themselves. And they shall make a List of all the Persons voted for, and of the Number of Votes for each; which List they shall sign and certify, and transmit sealed to the Seat of the Government of the United States, directed to the President of the Senate. The President of the Senate shall, in the Presence of the Senate and House of Representatives, open all the Certificates, and the Votes shall then be counted. The Person having the greatest Number of Votes shall be the President, if such Number be a Majority of the whole Number of Electors appointed; and if there be more than one who have such Majority, and have an equal Number of Votes, then the House of Representatives shall immediately chuse by Ballot one of them for President; and if no Person have a Majority, then from the five highest on the List the said House shall in like Manner chuse the President. But in chusing the President, the Votes shall be taken by States, the Representation from each State having one Vote; A quorum for this Purpose shall consist of a Member or Members from two thirds of the States, and a Majority of all the States shall be necessary to a Choice. In every Case, after the Choice of the President, the Person having the greatest Number of Votes of the Electors shall be the Vice President. But if there should remain two or more who have equal Votes, the Senate shall chuse from them by Ballot the Vice President.

The Congress may determine the Time of chusing the Electors, and the Day on which they shall give their Votes; which Day shall be the same throughout the United States.

No Person except a natural born Citizen, or a Citizen of the United States, at the time of the Adoption of this Constitution, shall be eligible to the Office of President; neither shall any Person be eligible to that Office who shall not have attained to the Age of thirty five Years, and been fourteen Years a Resident within the United States.

In Case of the Removal of the President from Office, or of his Death, Resignation, or Inability to discharge the Powers and Duties of the said Office, the Same shall devolve on the Vice President, and the Congress may by Law provide for the Case of Removal, Death, Resignation or Inability, both of the President and Vice President, declaring what Officer shall then act as President, and such Officer shall act accordingly, until the Disability be removed, or a President shall be elected.

The President shall, at stated Times, receive for his Services, a Compensation, which shall neither be encreased nor diminished during the Period for which he shall have been elected, and he shall not receive within that Period any other Emolument from the United States, or any of them.

Before he enter on the Execution of his Office, he shall take the following Oath or Affirmation:—"I do solemnly swear (or affirm) that I will faithfully execute the Office of President of the United States, and will to the best of my Ability, preserve, protect and defend the Constitution of the United States."

Section 2.

The President shall be Commander in Chief of the Army and Navy of the United States, and of the Militia of the several States, when called into the actual Service of the United States; he may require the Opinion, in writing, of the principal Officer in each of the executive Departments, upon any Subject relating to the Duties of their respective Offices, and he shall have Power to grant Reprieves and Pardons for Offences against the United States, except in Cases of Impeachment.

He shall have Power, by and with the Advice and Consent of the Senate, to make Treaties, provided two thirds of the Senators present concur; and he shall nominate, and by and with the Advice and Consent of the Senate, shall appoint Ambassadors, other public Ministers and Consuls, Judges of the supreme Court, and all other Officers of the United States, whose Appointments are not herein otherwise provided for, and which shall be established by Law: but the Congress may by Law vest the Appointment of such inferior Officers, as they think proper, in the President alone, in the Courts of Law, or in the Heads of Departments.

The President shall have Power to fill up all Vacancies that may happen during the Recess of the Senate, by granting Commissions which shall expire at the End of their next Session.

Section 3.

He shall from time to time give to the Congress Information of the State of the Union, and recommend to their Consideration such Measures as he shall judge necessary and expedient; he may, on extraordinary Occasions, convene both Houses, or either of them, and in Case of Disagreement between them, with Respect to the Time of Adjournment, he may adjourn them to such Time as he shall think proper; he shall receive Ambassadors and other public Ministers; he shall take Care that the Laws be faithfully executed, and shall Commission all the Officers of the United States.

Section 4.

The President, Vice President and all civil Officers of the United States, shall be removed from Office on Impeachment for, and Conviction of, Treason, Bribery, or other high Crimes and Misdemeanors.

Article. III.

Section 1.

The judicial Power of the United States, shall be vested in one supreme Court, and in such inferior Courts as the Congress may from time to time ordain and establish. The Judges, both of the supreme and inferior Courts, shall hold their Offices during good Behaviour, and shall, at stated Times, receive for their Services, a Compensation, which shall not be diminished during their Continuance in Office.

Section 2.

The judicial Power shall extend to all Cases, in Law and Equity, arising under this Constitution, the Laws of the United States, and Treaties made, or which shall be made, under their Authority;—to all Cases affecting Ambassadors, other public Ministers and Consuls;—to all Cases of admiralty and maritime Jurisdiction;—to Controversies to which the United States shall be a Party;—to Controversies between two or more States;—between a State and Citizens of another State,—between Citizens of different States,—between Citizens of the same State claiming Lands under Grants of different States, and between a State, or the Citizens thereof, and foreign States, Citizens or Subjects.

In all Cases affecting Ambassadors, other public Ministers and Consuls, and those in which a State shall be Party, the supreme Court shall have original Jurisdiction. In all the other Cases before mentioned, the supreme Court shall have appellate Jurisdiction, both as to Law and Fact, with such Exceptions, and under such Regulations as the Congress shall make.

The Trial of all Crimes, except in Cases of Impeachment, shall be by Jury; and such Trial shall be held in the State where the said Crimes shall have been committed; but when not committed within any State, the Trial shall be at such Place or Places as the Congress may by Law have directed.

Section 3.

Treason against the United States, shall consist only in levying War against them, or in adhering to their Enemies, giving them Aid and

Comfort. No Person shall be convicted of Treason unless on the Testimony of two Witnesses to the same overt Act, or on Confession in open Court.

The Congress shall have Power to declare the Punishment of Treason, but no Attainder of Treason shall work Corruption of Blood, or Forfeiture except during the Life of the Person attainted.

Article. IV.

Section 1.

Full Faith and Credit shall be given in each State to the public Acts, Records, and judicial Proceedings of every other State. And the Congress may by general Laws prescribe the Manner in which such Acts, Records and Proceedings shall be proved, and the Effect thereof.

Section 2.

The Citizens of each State shall be entitled to all Privileges and Immunities of Citizens in the several States.

A Person charged in any State with Treason, Felony, or other Crime, who shall flee from Justice, and be found in another State, shall on Demand of the executive Authority of the State from which he fled, be delivered up, to be removed to the State having Jurisdiction of the Crime.

No Person held to Service or Labour in one State, under the Laws thereof, escaping into another, shall, in Consequence of any Law or Regulation therein, be discharged from such Service or Labour, but shall be delivered up on Claim of the Party to whom such Service or Labour may be due.

Section 3.

New States may be admitted by the Congress into this Union; but no new State shall be formed or erected within the Jurisdiction of any other State; nor any State be formed by the Junction of two or more States, or Parts of States, without the Consent of the Legislatures of the States concerned as well as of the Congress.

The Congress shall have Power to dispose of and make all needful Rules and Regulations respecting the Territory or other Property belonging to the United States; and nothing in this Constitution shall be so construed as to Prejudice any Claims of the United States, or of any particular State.

Section 4.

The United States shall guarantee to every State in this Union a Republican Form of Government, and shall protect each of them against Invasion; and on Application of the Legislature, or of the Executive (when the Legislature cannot be convened), against domestic Violence.

Article. V.

The Congress, whenever two thirds of both Houses shall deem it necessary, shall propose Amendments to this Constitution, or, on the Application of the Legislatures of two thirds of the several States, shall call a Convention for proposing Amendments, which, in either Case, shall be valid to all Intents and Purposes, as Part of this Constitution, when ratified by the Legislatures of three fourths of the several States, or by Conventions in three fourths thereof, as the one or the other Mode of Ratification may be proposed by the Congress; Provided that no Amendment which may be made prior to the Year One thousand eight hundred and eight shall in any Manner affect the first and fourth Clauses in the Ninth Section of the first Article; and that no State, without its Consent, shall be deprived of its equal Suffrage in the Senate.

Article. VI.

All Debts contracted and Engagements entered into, before the Adoption of this Constitution, shall be as valid against the United States under this Constitution, as under the Confederation.

This Constitution, and the Laws of the United States which shall be made in Pursuance thereof; and all Treaties made, or which shall be made, under the Authority of the United States, shall be the supreme Law of the Land; and the Judges in every State shall be bound thereby, any Thing in the Constitution or Laws of any State to the Contrary notwithstanding.

The Senators and Representatives before mentioned, and the Members of the several State Legislatures, and all executive and judicial Officers, both of the United States and of the several States, shall be bound by Oath or Affirmation, to support this Constitution; but no religious Test shall ever be required as a Qualification to any Office or public Trust under the United States.

Article. VII.

The Ratification of the Conventions of nine States, shall be sufficient for the Establishment of this Constitution between the States so ratifying the Same.

The Word, "the," being interlined between the seventh and eighth Lines of the first Page, The Word "Thirty" being partly written on an Erazure in the fifteenth Line of the first Page, The Words "is tried" being interlined between the thirty second and thirty third Lines of the first Page and the Word "the" being interlined between the forty third and forty fourth Lines of the second Page.

Attest William Jackson Secretary done in Convention by the Unanimous Consent of the States present the Seventeenth Day of September in the Year of our Lord one thousand seven hundred and Eighty seven and of the Independance of the United States of America the Twelfth In witness whereof We have hereunto subscribed our Names,

G°. Washington
Presidt and deputy from Virginia

Delaware
Geo: Read
Gunning Bedford jun
John Dickinson
Richard Bassett
Jaco: Broom

Maryland
James McHenry
Dan of St Thos. Jenifer
Danl. Carroll

Virginia
John Blair
James Madison Jr.

North Carolina
Wm. Blount
Richd. Dobbs Spaight
Hu Williamson

South Carolina
J. Rutledge
Charles Cotesworth Pinckney
Charles Pinckney
Pierce Butler

Georgia
William Few
Abr Baldwin

New Hampshire
John Langdon
Nicholas Gilman

Massachusetts
Nathaniel Gorham
Rufus King

Connecticut
Wm. Saml. Johnson
Roger Sherman

New York
Alexander Hamilton

New Jersey
Wil: Livingston
David Brearley
Wm. Paterson
Jona: Dayton

Pensylvania
B Franklin
Thomas Mifflin
Robt. Morris
Geo. Clymer
Thos. FitzSimons
Jared Ingersoll
James Wilson
Gouv Morris

The U.S. Bill of Rights

The Preamble to The Bill of Rights

Congress of the United States

begun and held at the City of New-York, on

Wednesday the fourth of March, one thousand seven hundred and eighty nine.

THE Conventions of a number of the States, having at the time of their adopting the Constitution, expressed a desire, in order to prevent misconstruction or abuse of its powers, that further declaratory and restrictive clauses should be added: And as extending the ground of public confidence in the Government, will best ensure the beneficent ends of its institution.

RESOLVED by the Senate and House of Representatives of the United States of America, in Congress assembled, two thirds of both Houses concurring, that the following Articles be proposed to the Legislatures of the several States, as amendments to the Constitution of the United States, all, or any of which Articles, when ratified by three fourths of the said Legislatures, to be valid to all intents and purposes, as part of the said Constitution; viz.

ARTICLES in addition to, and Amendment of the Constitution of the United States of America, proposed by Congress, and ratified by the Legislatures of the several States, pursuant to the fifth Article of the original Constitution.

Note: The following text is a transcription of the first ten amendments to the Constitution in their original form. These amendments were ratified December 15, 1791, and form what is known as the "Bill of Rights."

Amendment I

Congress shall make no law respecting an establishment of religion, or prohibiting the free exercise thereof; or abridging the freedom of speech, or of the press; or the right of the people peaceably to assemble, and to petition the Government for a redress of grievances.

Amendment II

A well regulated Militia, being necessary to the security of a free State, the right of the people to keep and bear Arms, shall not be infringed.

Amendment III

No Soldier shall, in time of peace be quartered in any house, without the consent of the Owner, nor in time of war, but in a manner to be prescribed by law.

Amendment IV

The right of the people to be secure in their persons, houses, papers, and effects, against unreasonable searches and seizures, shall not be violated, and no Warrants shall issue, but upon probable cause, supported by Oath or affirmation, and particularly describing the place to be searched, and the persons or things to be seized.

Amendment V

No person shall be held to answer for a capital, or otherwise infamous crime, unless on a presentment or indictment of a Grand Jury, except in cases arising in the land or naval forces, or in the Militia, when in actual service in time of War or public danger; nor shall any person be subject for the same offence to be twice put in jeopardy of life or limb; nor shall be compelled in any criminal case to be a witness against himself, nor be deprived of life, liberty, or property, without due process of law; nor shall private property be taken for public use, without just compensation.

Amendment VI

In all criminal prosecutions, the accused shall enjoy the right to a speedy and public trial, by an impartial jury of the State and district wherein the crime shall have been committed, which district shall have been previously ascertained by law, and to be informed of the nature and cause of the accusation; to be confronted with the witnesses against him; to have compulsory process for obtaining witnesses in his favor, and to have the Assistance of Counsel for his defence.

Amendment VII

In Suits at common law, where the value in controversy shall exceed twenty dollars, the right of trial by jury shall be preserved, and no fact tried by a jury, shall be otherwise re-examined in any Court of the United States, than according to the rules of the common law.

Amendment VIII

Excessive bail shall not be required, nor excessive fines imposed, nor cruel and unusual punishments inflicted.

Amendment IX

The enumeration in the Constitution, of certain rights, shall not be construed to deny or disparage others retained by the people.

Amendment X

The powers not delegated to the United States by the Constitution, nor prohibited by it to the States, are reserved to the States respectively, or to the people.

[Amendments XI – XXVII]
Amendment XI

Passed by Congress March 4, 1794. Ratified February 7, 1795.

Note: Article III, section 2, of the Constitution was modified by amendment 11.

The Judicial power of the United States shall not be construed to extend to any suit in law or equity, commenced or prosecuted against one of the United States by Citizens of another State, or by Citizens or Subjects of any Foreign State.

Amendment XII

Passed by Congress December 9, 1803. Ratified June 15, 1804.

Note: A portion of Article II, section 1 of the Constitution was superseded by the 12th amendment.

The Electors shall meet in their respective states and vote by ballot for President and Vice-President, one of whom, at least, shall not be an inhabitant of the same state with themselves; they shall name in their ballots the person voted for as President, and in distinct ballots the person voted for as Vice-President, and they shall make distinct lists of all persons voted for as President, and of all persons voted for as Vice-President, and of the number of votes for each, which lists they shall sign and certify, and transmit sealed to the seat of the government of the United States, directed to the President of the Senate;—the President of the Senate shall, in the presence of the Senate and House of Representatives, open all the certificates and the votes shall then be counted;—The person having the greatest number of votes for President, shall be the President, if such number be a majority of the whole number of Electors appointed; and if no person have such majority, then from the persons having the highest numbers not exceeding three on the list of those voted for as President, the House of Representatives shall choose immediately, by ballot, the President. But in choosing the President, the votes shall be taken by states, the representation from each state having one vote; a quorum for this purpose shall consist of a member or members from two-thirds of the states, and a majority of all the states shall be necessary to a choice. [And if the House of Representatives shall not choose a President whenever the right of choice shall devolve upon them, before the fourth day of March next following, then the Vice-President shall act as President, as in case of the death or other constitutional disability of the President.—]* The person having the greatest number of votes as Vice-President, shall be the Vice-President, if such number be a majority of the whole number of Electors appointed, and if no person have a majority, then from the two highest numbers on the list, the Senate shall choose the Vice-President; a quorum for the purpose shall consist of two-thirds of the whole number of Senators, and a majority of the whole number shall be necessary to a choice. But no person constitutionally ineligible to the office of President shall be eligible to that of Vice-President of the United States.

---

*Superseded by section 3 of the 20th amendment.

Amendment XIII

Passed by Congress January 31, 1865. Ratified December 6, 1865.

Note: A portion of Article IV, section 2, of the Constitution was super-seded by the 13th amendment.

Section 1.

Neither slavery nor involuntary servitude, except as a punishment for crime whereof the party shall have been duly convicted, shall exist within the United States, or any place subject to their jurisdiction.

Section 2.

Congress shall have power to enforce this article by appropriate legislation.

Amendment XIV

Passed by Congress June 13, 1866. Ratified July 9, 1868.

Note: Article I, section 2, of the Constitution was modified by section 2 of the 14th Amendment.

Section 1.

All persons born or naturalized in the United States, and subject to the jurisdiction thereof, are citizens of the United States and of the State wherein they reside. No State shall make or enforce any law which shall abridge the privileges or immunities of citizens of the United States; nor shall any State deprive any person of life, liberty, or property, without due process of law; nor deny to any person within its jurisdiction the equal protection of the laws.

Section 2.

Representatives shall be apportioned among the several States according to their respective numbers, counting the whole number of persons in each State, excluding Indians not taxed. But when the right to vote at any election for the choice of electors for President and Vice-President of the United States, Representatives in Congress, the Executive and Judicial officers of a State, or the members of the Legislature thereof, is denied to any of the male inhabitants of such State, being twenty-one years of age,* and citizens of the United States, or in any way abridged, except for participation in rebellion, or other crime, the basis of representation therein shall be reduced in the proportion which the number of such male citizens shall bear to the whole number of male citizens twenty-one years of age in such State.

Section 3.

No person shall be a Senator or Representative in Congress, or elector of President and Vice-President, or hold any office, civil or military, under the United States, or under any State, who, having previously taken an oath, as a member of Congress, or as an officer of the United States, or as a member of any State legislature, or as an executive or judicial officer of any State, to support the Constitution of the United States, shall have engaged in insurrection or rebellion against the same, or given aid or comfort to the enemies thereof. But Congress may by a vote of two-thirds of each House, remove such disability.

Section 4.

The validity of the public debt of the United States, authorized by law, including debts incurred for payment of pensions and bounties for services in suppressing insurrection or rebellion, shall not be questioned. But neither the United States nor any State shall assume or pay any debt or obligation incurred in aid of insurrection or rebellion against the United States, or any claim for the loss or emancipation of any slave; but all such debts, obligations and claims shall be held illegal and void.

Section 5.

The Congress shall have the power to enforce, by appropriate legislation, the provisions of this article.

Amendment XV

Passed by Congress February 26, 1869. Ratified February 3, 1870.

---

*Changed by section 1 of the 26th amendment.

Section 1.

The right of citizens of the United States to vote shall not be denied or abridged by the United States or by any State on account of race, color, or previous condition of servitude—

Section 2.

The Congress shall have the power to enforce this article by appropriate legislation.

Amendment XVI

Passed by Congress July 2, 1909. Ratified February 3, 1913.

Note: Article I, section 9, of the Constitution was modified by amendment 16.

The Congress shall have power to lay and collect taxes on incomes, from whatever source derived, without apportionment among the several States, and without regard to any census or enumeration.

Amendment XVII

Passed by Congress May 13, 1912. Ratified April 8, 1913.

Note: Article I, section 3, of the Constitution was modified by the 17th amendment.

The Senate of the United States shall be composed of two Senators from each State, elected by the people thereof, for six years; and each Senator shall have one vote. The electors in each State shall have the qualifications requisite for electors of the most numerous branch of the State legislatures.

When vacancies happen in the representation of any State in the Senate, the executive authority of such State shall issue writs of election to fill such vacancies: *Provided*, That the legislature of any State may empower the executive thereof to make temporary appointments until the people fill the vacancies by election as the legislature may direct.

This amendment shall not be so construed as to affect the election or term of any Senator chosen before it becomes valid as part of the Constitution.

Amendment XVIII

Passed by Congress December 18, 1917. Ratified January 16, 1919. Repealed by amendment 21.

Section 1.

After one year from the ratification of this article the manufacture, sale, or transportation of intoxicating liquors within, the importation thereof into, or the exportation thereof from the United States and all territory subject to the jurisdiction thereof for beverage purposes is hereby prohibited.

Section 2.

The Congress and the several States shall have concurrent power to enforce this article by appropriate legislation.

Section 3.

This article shall be inoperative unless it shall have been ratified as an amendment to the Constitution by the legislatures of the several States, as provided in the Constitution, within seven years from the date of the submission hereof to the States by the Congress.

Amendment XIX

Passed by Congress June 4, 1919. Ratified August 18, 1920.

The right of citizens of the United States to vote shall not be denied or abridged by the United States or by any State on account of sex.

Congress shall have power to enforce this article by appropriate legislation.

Amendment XX

Passed by Congress March 2, 1932. Ratified January 23, 1933.

Note: Article I, section 4, of the Constitution was modified by section 2 of this amendment. In addition, a portion of the 12th amendment was superseded by section 3.

Section 1.

The terms of the President and the Vice President shall end at noon on the 20th day of January, and the terms of Senators and Representatives at noon on the 3d day of January, of the years in which such terms would have ended if this article had not been ratified; and the terms of their successors shall then begin.

Section 2.

The Congress shall assemble at least once in every year, and such meeting shall begin at noon on the 3d day of January, unless they shall by law appoint a different day.

Section 3.

If, at the time fixed for the beginning of the term of the President, the President elect shall have died, the Vice President elect shall become President. If a President shall not have been chosen before the time fixed for the beginning of his term, or if the President elect shall have failed to qualify, then the Vice President elect shall act as President until a President shall have qualified; and the Congress may by law provide for the case wherein neither a President elect nor a Vice President elect shall have qualified, declaring who shall then act as President, or the manner in which one who is to act shall be selected, and such person shall act accordingly until a President or Vice President shall have qualified.

Section 4.

The Congress may by law provide for the case of the death of any of the persons from whom the House of Representatives may choose a President whenever the right of choice shall have devolved upon them, and for the case of the death of any of the persons from whom the Senate may choose a Vice President whenever the right of choice shall have devolved upon them.

Section 5.

Sections 1 and 2 shall take effect on the 15th day of October following the ratification of this article.

Section 6.

This article shall be inoperative unless it shall have been ratified as an amendment to the Constitution by the legislatures of three-fourths of the several States within seven years from the date of its submission.

Amendment XXI

Passed by Congress February 20, 1933. Ratified December 5, 1933.

Section 1.

The eighteenth article of amendment to the Constitution of the United States is hereby repealed.

Section 2.

The transportation or importation into any State, Territory, or possession of the United States for delivery or use therein of intoxicating liquors, in violation of the laws thereof, is hereby prohibited.

Section 3.

This article shall be inoperative unless it shall have been ratified as an amendment to the Constitution by conventions in the several States, as provided in the Constitution, within seven years from the date of the submission hereof to the States by the Congress.

Amendment XXII

Passed by Congress March 21, 1947. Ratified February 27, 1951.

Section 1.

No person shall be elected to the office of the President more than twice, and no person who has held the office of President, or acted as President, for more than two years of a term to which some other person was elected President shall be elected to the office of the President more than once. But this Article shall not apply to any person holding the office of President when this Article was proposed by the Congress, and shall not prevent any person who may be holding the office of President, or acting as President, during the term within which this Article becomes operative from holding the office of President or acting as President during the remainder of such term.

Section 2.

This article shall be inoperative unless it shall have been ratified as an amendment to the Constitution by the legislatures of three-fourths of the several States within seven years from the date of its submission to the States by the Congress.

Amendment XXIII

Passed by Congress June 16, 1960. Ratified March 29, 1961.

Section 1.

The District constituting the seat of Government of the United States shall appoint in such manner as the Congress may direct:

A number of electors of President and Vice President equal to the whole number of Senators and Representatives in Congress to which the District would be entitled if it were a State, but in no event more than the least populous State; they shall be in addition to those appointed by the States, but they shall be considered, for the purposes of the election of President and Vice President, to be electors appointed by a State; and they shall meet in the District and perform such duties as provided by the twelfth article of amendment.

Section 2.

The Congress shall have power to enforce this article by appropriate legislation.

Amendment XXIV

Passed by Congress August 27, 1962. Ratified January 23, 1964.

Section 1.

The right of citizens of the United States to vote in any primary or other election for President or Vice President, for electors for President or Vice President, or for Senator or Representative in Congress, shall not be denied or abridged by the United States or any State by reason of failure to pay any poll tax or other tax.

Section 2.

The Congress shall have power to enforce this article by appropriate legislation.

Amendment XXV

Passed by Congress July 6, 1965. Ratified February 10, 1967.

Note: Article II, section 1, of the Constitution was affected by the 25th amendment.

Section 1.

In case of the removal of the President from office or of his death or resignation, the Vice President shall become President.

Section 2.

Whenever there is a vacancy in the office of the Vice President, the President shall nominate a Vice President who shall take office upon confirmation by a majority vote of both Houses of Congress.

Section 3.

Whenever the President transmits to the President pro tempore of the Senate and the Speaker of the House of Representatives his written declaration that he is unable to discharge the powers and duties of his office, and until he transmits to them a written declaration to the contrary, such powers and duties shall be discharged by the Vice President as Acting President.

Section 4.

Whenever the Vice President and a majority of either the principal officers of the executive departments or of such other body as Congress may by law provide, transmit to the President pro tempore of the Senate and the Speaker of the House of Representatives their written declaration that the President is unable to discharge the powers and duties of his office, the Vice President shall immediately assume the powers and duties of the office as Acting President.

Thereafter, when the President transmits to the President pro tempore of the Senate and the Speaker of the House of Representatives his written declaration that no inability exists, he shall resume the powers and duties of his office unless the Vice President and a majority of either the principal officers of the executive department or of such other body as Congress may by law provide, transmit within four days to the President pro tempore of the Senate and the Speaker of the House of Representatives their written declaration that the President is unable to discharge the powers and duties of his office. Thereupon Congress shall decide the issue, assembling within forty-eight hours for that purpose if not in session. If the Congress, within twenty-one days after receipt of the latter written declaration, or, if Congress is not in session, within twenty-one days after Congress is required to assemble, determines by two-thirds vote of both Houses that the President is unable to discharge the powers and duties of his office, the Vice President shall continue to discharge the same as Acting President; otherwise, the President shall resume the powers and duties of his office.

Amendment XXVI

Passed by Congress March 23, 1971. Ratified July 1, 1971.

Note: Amendment 14, section 2, of the Constitution was modified by section 1 of the 26th amendment.

Section 1.

The right of citizens of the United States, who are eighteen years of age or older, to vote shall not be denied or abridged by the United States or by any State on account of age.

Section 2.

The Congress shall have power to enforce this article by appropriate legislation.

Amendment XXVII

Originally proposed Sept. 25, 1789. Ratified May 7, 1992.

No law, varying the compensation for the services of the Senators and Representatives, shall take effect, until an election of Representatives shall have intervened.

BIBLIOGRAPHY

A&M Records, Inc. v. Napster, Inc., 239 F3d 1004, (2001).

Action for Children's Television v. F.C.C., 58 F.3d 654, (D.C. Cir. 1995).

Advertising Self-Regulatory Council. (2012). ASRC website. Retrieved from www.asrcreviews.org

Administrative sanctions, 47 U.S.C. § 312(a)(7).

Alexander v. Haley, 460 F.Supp. 40, (1978).

Alexander v. U.S. 509 U.S. 544. (1993).

Ali v. Playgirl, 447 F. Supp. 723, (S.D.N.Y. 1978).

Alien Registration Act of 1940, Pub. L. No. 76-670, 54 Stat. 670 (1940).

Alliance for Community Media v. F.C.C., 56 F.3d 105, (1995).

Alpha Therapeutic Corp. v. Nippon HosoKyokai (HNK), 199 F.3d 1078, (1999).

American Civil Liberties Union of Illinois v. Alvarez, 133 S. Ct. 651, (7th Cir. 2012).

American Law Institute. (1957). *Restatement of the law second: Torts.* Philadelphia: The Institute.

American Law Institute. (1995). *Restatement of the law, unfair competition: As adopted and promulgated by the American Law Institute at Washington, D.C., May 11, 1993.* St Paul, MN: The Institute.

American Amusement Machine Ass'n v. Kendrick. 534 U.S. 994. (2001).

Annenberg Public Policy Center. (2017). *Americans Are Poorly Informed About Basic Constitutional Provisions.* Retrieved from https://www. annenbergpublicpolicycenter.org/americans-are-poorly

Announcement of payment for broadcast, 47 U.S.C. § 317.

Anticybersquatting Consumer Protection Act, Pub. L. No. 106-113, 113 Stat. 1501 (1999).

A.P. v. U.S. District Court, 705 F. 2d 1143, (1983).

Applications for Court Orders, 50 U.S.C.§§ 1804(a)(7)(B)–1823(a)(B).

Application for license, 47 U.S.C. § 309(j).

Application for registration; verification, 15 U.S.C. § 1051 et seq.

Arkansas Educational Television v. Forbes. 523 U.S. 666. (1998).

Armstrong v. H&C Communications, 575 So.2d 280, (1991).

Ashcroft v. Free Speech Coalition. 535 U.S. 234. (2002).

Associated Press v. All Headline News Corp., 608 F. Supp. 2d 454, (2009).

Associated Press v. Walker. 388 U.S. 130. (1967).

Austin v. U.S. 509 U.S. 602. (1993).

Baker v. Selden. 101 U.S. 99. (1879).

Baltimore Sun v. Ehrlich, 437 F.3d 410, (4th Cir. 2006).

Barber v. Time, 159 S.W. 2d 291, (Mo. 1942).

Barron, J. (1967). Access to the press—a new first amendment right. *Harvard Law Review*, 80, 1641.

Bartnicki v. Vopper. 532 U.S. 514. (2001).

Basic Books v. Kinko's Graphics Corp., 758 F. Supp. 1522, (1991).

Belmas, G., & Overbeck, W. (2015). *Major principles of media law*. Boston, MA: Cengage Learning.

Berne convention for the protection of literary and artistic works. (1886).

Berne Convention Implementation Act, Pub. L. No. 100-568, 102 Stat. 2853 (1988).

Bethel School District v. Frasier. 478 U.S. 675. (1986).

Bigelow v. Virginia. 421 U.S. 809. (1975).

Biography.com editors. (n.d). Charles-Louis de Secondat. *Biography.com*. Retrieved from http://www.biography.com/people/charles-louis-de-secondat-21292453#fame-as-political-thinker

Black, H.C., & Garner, B.A. (2014). *Black's law dictionary* (10th ed.). St. Paul, MN: Thomson Reuters.

Blackstone, W. (1979). *Commentaries on the laws of England: A facsimile of the first edition of 1765*. Chicago, IL: University of Chicago Press.

Boisson v. Banian, Ltd., 273 F.3d 262, 268, (2d Cir. 2001).

Board of Governors of the Federal Reserve System. (2015).

Booth v. Curtis Publishing Co., 11 N.Y.2d 907, (1962).

Bowers v. Hardwick. 478 U.S. 186. (1986).

Branch v. F.C.C., 824 F.2d 37, (D.C. Cir. 1987).

Brandenburg v. Ohio. 395 U.S. 444. (1969).

Branzburg v. Hayes. 408 U.S. 665. (1972).

Bristol-Myers Co., 102 F.T.C. 21, 366 (1983).

Broadcast of telephone conversation. 47 C.F.R. § 73. 1206. (1970).

Broadcasting obscene language, 18 U.S.C. § 1464.

Brooke, J. (1998). FCC supports TV news. *New York Times*. Retrieved from http://www.nytimes.com/1998/05/03/us/rejecting-petitions-fcc-supports-tv-news-as-free-speech.html

Broughton v. McClatchy Newspapers, Inc., 588 S.E.2d, (N.C. App. 2003).

Brown v. Entertainment Merchants Association, 564 U.S. 786 (2011).

Bureau of Alcohol, Tobacco, Firearms, and Explosives .(n.d.) Retrieved from ATF website https://www.atf.gov/

Burnham, W. (2006). *Introduction to the law and legal system of the United States* (4th ed.). St. Paul, MN: Thomson/West.

Burstyn v. Wilson. 343 U.S. 495. (1952).

Butler v. Michigan. 352 U.S. 380. (1957).

Butterworth v. Smith. 494 U.S. 624. (1990).

Cable channels for commercial use, 47 U.S.C. §532(h).

Cable Communications Policy Act, Pub. L. No. 98-549, 98 Stat. 2779 (1984).

Cable Television Consumer Protection and Competition Act, 106 Stat. 1460 (1992).

Campbell v. Acuff-Rose Music Co. 510 U.S. 569. (1994).

Cantrell v. Forest City Publishing Co. 419 U.S. 245. (1974).

Capital Cities Cable, Inc. v. F.C.C. 890 U.S. 691. (1984).

Carreau, M. (2003, July 9). Another shuttle, another breach. *Houston Chronicle*.

Carson v. Here's Johnny Portable Toilets Inc., 698 F.2d 831, (1983).

Catsouras v. Department of California Highway Patrol, 181 Cal. App. 4th 856 (2010).

C.B.S. v. F.C.C. 453 U.S. 367. (1981).

C.B.S. Corp. v. F.C.C., 663 F.3d 122, (2011).

Censorship, 47 U.S.C. § 326.

Central Hudson Gas and Electric v. Public Service Commission of New York. 447 U.S. 557. (1980).

Chandler v. Florida. 449 U.S. 560. (1981).

Channel 10, Inc. v. Gunnarson, 337 F. Supp. 634, (D. Minn. 1972).

Chaplinsky v. New Hampshire. 315 U.S. 568. (1942).

Cher v. Forum International, 692 F.2d 634, (1982).

Child Pornography Prevention Act, Pub. L. No. 104-208, 110 Stat. 3009 (1996).

Child Safe Viewing Act, Pub. L. No. 110-452 (2007).

Children's Internet Protection Act, Pub. L. No. 106–554 (2003).

Children's Television Act, 104 Stat. 996 (1990).

Circumvention of copyright protection systems, 17 U.S.C. § 1201.

Citicasters v. Finkbeiner, No. 07-CV-00117 (N.D. Ohio 2007).

Citizens United v. Federal Elections Commission. 558 U.S. 310. (2010).

City of Eric v. Pap's A.M. 529 U.S. 277. (2000).

City of Los Angeles v. Alameda Books, Inc. 535 U.S. 425, 438. (2002).

Clark, G. (1962). *Famous libel and slander cases of history*. New York, NY: Collier.

Coblenz, W., & Pakula, A.J. (1976). *All the president's men*. USA: Warner Bros.

Cohen v. California. 403 U.S. 15. (1971).

Cohen v. Cowles Media Co. 501 U.S. 663. (1991).

Common Law. (n.d.). In *Wikipedia*. Retrieved January 15, 2015, from https://en.wikipedia.org/wiki/Common_law

Communications Act, Pub.L. 73–416, 48 Stat. 1064, §§ 312(a)(7), 315, 315(b), 326 (1934).

Communications Decency Act, Pub. L. 104-104, 110 Stat. 133 (1996).

Complaints Against Various Television Licensees Regarding Their Broadcast on November 11, 2004, of the ABC Television Network's Presentation of the Film "Saving Private Ryan," Memorandum Opinion and Order, File No. EB-04-IH-0589 (Feb. 28, 2005).

Computer Matching and Privacy Protection Act of 1988, Pub. L. No. 100-503 (1988).

Comstock Act, 17 Stat. 598 (1873).

Consolidated Edison v. Public Service Commission of New York. 447 U.S. 530. (1980).

Controlling the Assault of Non-Solicited Pornography and Marketing Act (CAN-SPAM), Pub.L. No. 108-187, 117 Stat. 2699 (2003).

Copyright Act, 1 Stat. 124 (1790).

Copyright registration in general, 17 U.S.C. §§ 408(a), 408(b).

Copyright Revision Act, Pub. L. 94-553, 90 Stat. 2541 (1976).

Cosmopolitan Broadcasting Corp., 59 F.C.C. 2d 558 (1976).

Costlow v. Cusimano, 311 N.Y.S. 2d 92, (1970).

Cox Broadcasting v. Cohn. 420 U.S. 469. (1975).

Coyote Publishing, Inc. v. Miller, 5l98 F.3d 592, (9th Cir. 2010).

Crime Awareness and Campus Security Act of 1990, Pub. L. No. 101-542, 20 U.S.C. § 1092(f) (1990).

Criminal infringement of a copyright, 18 U.S.C. § 2319A.

Criminal offenses, 17 U.S.C. § 506.

Crown v. John Peter Zenger. (1735).

Curtis Publishing Co. v. Butts. 388 U.S. 130. (1967).

DeBenedictis, D.J. (1994, Oct.). The national verdict. *American Bar Association Journal*, 80(10), 52–54.

Definitions, 17 U.S.C. § 101.

Definitions for chapter, 18 U.S.C. §2256(8), (2)(A).

Dendrite v. Doe, 775 A.2d 756, (N.J. Super. Ct. 2001).

Dept. of the Air Force v. Rose. 425 U.S. 352, 361. (1976).

Deposit of copies or phonorecords for Library of Congress, 17 U.S.C. § 407.

Desnick v. American Broadcasting Co., 44 F.3d 1345, (1995).

Dietemann v. Time, Inc., 449 F.2d 245, (9th Cir. 1971).

Digital Millennium Copyright Act, Pub.L. No. 105-304, 112 Stat. 2860 (1998).

Digital Performance Right in Sound Recordings Act, Pub. L. No. 104-39, 109 Stat. 336 (1995).

Documents of Freedom editors. (n.d.). *The role of government*. Retrieved from Bill of Rights Institute https://www.docsoffreedom.org/readings/the-role-of-government

Doe v. McFarlane, 207 S.W. 3d 52, (Mo. Ct. App. 2006).

Doe v. New York City, 15 F. 3d 264, (2d Cir. 1994).

Driver's Privacy Protection Act, Pub. L. No. 114-38, 18 U.S.C. 2721–2725 (1994).

Dr. Seuss Enterprises v. Penguin Books, 109 F.3d 1394, (1997).

Duration of copyright: Works created on or after January 1, 1978, 17 U.S.C. § 302(c).

Durations, affidavits and fees, 15 U.S.C. § 1058.

Electronic Freedom of Information Act Amendments, Pub.L. No. 104-231, 110 Stat. 3048 (1996).

Elonis v. United States. 575 U.S. _____. 135 S.Ct. 2001 (2015).

eMarketer editors. (2014). Total U.S ad spending to see largest increase since 2004.

eMarketer Daily Newsletter. Retrieved from http://www.emarketer.com/Article-/Total-US...Spending.../1010982

Enforcement of 18 U.S.C. 1464, 47 C.F.R. §73.3999.

Equal Credit Opportunity Act, Pub. L. No. 90-321, 88 Stat. 1521 (1974).

Estes v. Texas. 381 U.S. 532. (1965).

ETW Corp. v. Jireh Publishing, Inc., 332 F. 3d 915, (2003).

Ex parte Jackson. 96 U.S. 727. (1878).

Exclusive rights in copyrighted works, 17 U.S.C. §§ 106A, 106(4).

Expressions Hair Design v. Schneiderman, 581 U.S. _____ (2017).

Family Educational Rights and Privacy Act, 20 U.S.C. § 1232g (1974).

Family Entertainment and Copyright Act, Pub.L. No. 109-9, 119 Stat. 218 (2005).

Fairness in Music Licensing Act, Pub.L. No. 105-298, 112 Stat. 2827 (1998).

Farmers Educational and Cooperative Union of America v. W.D.A.Y. 360 U.S. 525. (1959).

F.C.C. v. Fox Television Stations, Inc., 132 S. Ct. 2307, (2012).

F.C.C. v. League of Women Voters. 468 U.S. 364. (1984).

F.C.C. v. Midwest Video. 440 U.S. 689. (1979).

F.C.C v. Pacifica Found. 438 U.S. 726. (1978).

F.C.C. v. Pacifica Foundation. 438 U.S. 726. (1978).

Federal Advisory Committee Act, Pub. L. No. 92-463 (1972).

Federal Communications Act, 48 Stat. 1064 (1934).

Federal Communications Commission. (2015). *Updates and releases.* Retrieved from https://www.fcc.gov/encyclopedia/fcc-updates-and-releases

Federal Open Meetings Law, 5 U.S.C. § 552b.

Federal Trade Commission. (n.d.). Retrieved from https://www.ftc.gov/

Federal Trade Commission Act, 15 U.S.C. §§ 41-58 as amended. (1914).

Federal Trade Commission Improvement Act of 1980, Pub. L. No. 96-252, 94 Stat. 374 (1980).

Federal Trademark Dilution Act, Pub. L. No. 104-98, 109 Stat. 985 (1995).

Federal trademark law, 15 U.S.C. 1125 § 43(a)(1)(A), (B).

Feist Publications v. Rural Telephone Service Co. 499 U.S. 340. (1997).

First National Bank v. Bellotti. 435 U.S. 765. (1978).

Florida Publishing Co. v. Fletcher, 340 So.2d 914, (1976).

Florida Star v. B.J.F. 491 U.S. 524. (1989).

Fly Fish, Inc. v. City of Cocoa Beach, 337 F.3d 1301, (11th Cir. 2003).

Food, Drug and Cosmetic Act, Pub.L. No. 75-717, 52 Stat. 1040 (1938).

Forfeitures, 47 U.S.C. §503(b)(1)(D).

Forsham v. Harris. 445 U.S. 169, 183, 184. (1980).

Foster v. City of El Paso, 396 S.W.3d 244,(Tex. Ct. App. 2013).

Fox Television v. F.C.C., 489 F.3d 444 (2007).

Franks, J.B. (1977). The Commercial Speech Doctrine and the First Amendment. *Tulsa Law Review*, 12(4), 699–730.

Freedman v. Maryland. 380 U.S. 51. (1965).

Freedom House. (n.d). Retrieved from https://freedomhouse.org/

Freedom of Information Act, Pub. L. 89-487, 80 Stat. 250 (1967).

Friend, C. (n.d.). Social Contract Theory. In *Encyclopedia of philosophy*. Retrieved from www.iep.utm.edu/soc-cont/

F.R.C. v. Nelson Brothers. 289 U.S. 266. (1933).

Frisby v. Schultz. 487 U.S. 474. (1988).

F.T.C. v. Colgate-Palmolive Co. 380 U.S. 374. (1965).

F.T.C. v. National Urological Group, 645 F.Supp.2d 1167, (U.S. Dist. Ct. 2008).

F.T.C. v. Sperry Hutchinson Co. 405 U.S. 233. (1972).

F.T.C. v. Winsted Hosiery Co. 258 U.S. 483. (1922).

Gallela v. Onassis, 487 F.2d 986, (2nd Cir. 1973).

Gannett v. DePasquale. 443 U.S. 368. (1979).

Geer, J.G., Schiller, W.J., Segal, J.A., & Glencross, D.K. (2012). *Gateways to democracy: An introduction to American government*. Boston, MA: Cengage.

Gentile v. Nevada State Bar, 111 S. Ct. 2770, (1991).

Gertz v. Robert Welch, Inc. 418 U.S. 323. (1974).

Gill v. Hearst Corp., 40 E.2d 224, (1953).

Ginsberg v. New York. 390 U.S. 629. (1968).

Ginzburg v. U.S. 383 U.S. 463. (1966).

Gitlow v. New York. 268 U.S. 652. (1925).

Glik v. Cunniffe, 655 F.3d 78, (1st Cir. 2011).

Globe Newspaper Co. v. Superior Court. 457 U.S. 596. (1982).

Government in the Sunshine Act, Pub. L. No. 94-409, 90 Stat. 1241 (1976).

Greater New Orleans Broadcasting Association v. U.S. 527 U.S. 173 (1999).

Griswold v. Connecticut, 381 U.S. 479. (1965).

Grosjean v. American Press. 297 U.S. 233. (1936).

Guides against Bait Advertising, Bait Advertisement, 16 C.F.R. § 238.1 (2008).

Guides against Bait Advertising, Bait Advertising Defined, 16 C.F.R. § 238.0 (2008).

Guides against Bait Advertising, Discouragement of Purchase of Advertised Merchandise, 16 C.F.R. § 238.3 (2008).

Haelan Laboratories v. Topps Chewing Gum, 202 F2d 866, (1953).

Hamling v. United States. 418 U.S. 87. (1974).

Hanebutt, M. (2013). *The journalist's primer: A no-nonsense guide to getting and reporting the news*. Dubuque, IA: Kendall Hunt Publishing.

Harper & Row Publishers v. The National Enterprises. 471 U.S. 539. (1986).

Hartford Courant v. Pellegrino, 371 F. 3d 49, (2004).

Hazelwood v. Kuhlmeier. 484 U.S. 260. (1988).

Health Insurance Portability and Accountability Act, Pub.L. 104–191, 110 Stat. 1936 (1996).

Heffernan v. City of Patterson. 578 U.S. _____., 136 S.Ct. 1412 (2016).

Higher Education Act Amendments of 1998, Pub. L. No. 105-244, (1998).

Hoffman v. Capital Cities/ABC Inc., 255 F3d 1180, (2001).

Home Mortgage Disclosure Act, Pub. L. No. 94-200, 89 Stat. 1124 (1975).

Honest Leadership and Open Government Act, Pub.L. 110–81, 121 Stat. 735 (2007).

Houchins v. KQED. 438 U.S. 1. (1978).

Howell v. New York Post Co., 612 N.E. 2d 699, (1993).

Hustler Magazine v. Falwell. 485 U.S. 46 (1988).

Hutchinson v. Proxmire. 443 U.S. 11. (1979).

Idaho v. Salsbury, 924 P. 2d 208, (1996).

Importation or transportation of obscene matters, 18 U.S. Code § 1462 (1940).

Infringement of copyright, 17 U.S.C. § 501(b).

Integrity of copyright management information, 17 U.S.C. § 1202.

International News Service v. Associated Press. 248 U.S. 215. (1918).

International Telecommunications Union. (n.d). Retrieved from ITU website www.itu.int

Irvin v. Dowd. 366 U.S. 717. (1961).

Jacobellis v. Ohio. 378 U.S. 184, 197. (1964).

Jenkins v. Georgia. 418 U.S. 153. (1974).

Jones v. Corbis Corp., 815 F. Supp. 2d 1108, (C.D. Cal. 2011).

Jones v. Herald Post Co., 18 S.W. 2d 972, (1929).

Joyce, J. (1992). Ulysses. New York, NY: Modern Library.

Junk Fax Prevention Act, Pub. L. No. 109-21, 119 Stat. 359 (2005).

Kaiser Family Foundation. (2015). New v-chip and TV ratings study release. Retrieved from http://kff.org/other/report/new-v-chip-and-tv-ratings-study/

Katz v. U.S. 389 U.S. 347. (1967).

Keeton v. Hustler. 465 U.S. 770. (1984).

Kissinger v. New York City Transit Auth., 274 F. Supp. 438, (1967).

Kissinger v. Reporters Committee for Freedom of the Press. 445 U.S. 136. (1980).

Knight Foundation. (2017). *Future of the First Amendment survey.*Retrieved from http://www.knightfoundation.org/future-first-amendment-survey/

Kopelson, A., & Davis, A. (1993). *The fugitive.* USA: Warner Bros.

Korematsu v. United States. 323 U.S. 214. (1944).

Kyllo v. U.S. 533 U.S. 27. (2001).

Lanham Act, Pub. L. No. 79-489, 60 Stat. 427 (1946).

Lawrence v. Texas. 539 U.S. 558. (2003).

Lawyers Co-operative Publishing Company, Bancroft-Whitney Company, & West Group. (1962). *American jurisprudence: A modern comprehensive text statement of American law, State and Federal* (2nd ed.). St. Paul, MN: West Group.

Lehman v. Shaker Heights. 418 U.S. 298. (1974).

Leverton v. Curtis Publishing Co., 192 F. 2d 974, (1951).

License for radio communication or transmission of energy, 47 U.S.C. § 301.

License ownership restrictions, 47 U.S.C. § 310(b).

Lieb v. Topstone Industries, Inc., 788 F.2d 151, 153, (3d Cir. 1986).

Limitations on exclusive rights: Effect of transfer of particular copy or phonorecord, 17 U.S.C. § 109(b)(1)(A).

Limitations on exclusive rights: Ephemeral recordings, 17 U.S.C. § 112(a).

Limitations on exclusive rights: Secondary transmissions of distant television programming by satellite, 17 U.S.C. § 119.

Limitations on liability relating to material online, 17 U.S.C. § 512(c).

Lipman v. Commonwealth, 475 F.2d 565, (1973).

Lovell v. City of Griffin. 303 U.S. 444. (1938).

Lowi, T., Ginsberg, B., & Shepsle, K.A. (2002). *American government: Power and Purpose* (7th ed.). New York, NY: W.W. Norton & Co.

Machleder v. Diaz, 538 F. Supp. 1364, (S.D.N.Y. 1982).

Madison, J. (1900). *The writings of James Madison: Comprising his public papers and his private correspondence including numerous letters and documents now for the first time printed.* In G. Hunt (Ed.). New York, NY: G.P. Putnam's Sons.

Magnuson-Moss Warranty Act, Pub. L. No. 93-637 (1975).

Mandatory restitution, 18 U.S.C. §2259.

Marbury v. Madison. 5 U.S. 137. (1803).

Marketos v. American Employers Insurance Co., 460 N.W. 2d 272, (1990).

Marsh v. County of San Diego, 680 F. 3d 1148, (9th Cir. 2012).

Matal v. Tam. 582 U.S. ____., 137 S.Ct. 1744 (2017).

Matthews v. Wozencraft, 15 F.3d 432, (1994).

May Seed and Nursery, 2 F.C.C. 559 (1936).

McCray et al., 41 Media L. Rep. 1313 (2013).

McCulloch v. Maryland.17 U.S. 316. (1819).

Medical Laboratory Management Consultants v. American Broadcasting Co., Inc., 306 F.3d 806, (9th Cir. 2002).

Meiklejohn, A. (1948). *Free speech and its relationship to self-government.* New York, NY: Harper and Brothers.

Melvin v. Reid, 112 C.A. 285, (1931).

Memoirs v. Massachusetts. 383 U.S. 413. (1966).

Miami Herald v. Tornillo. 418 U.S. 241. (1974).

Midler v. Ford Motor Co., 849 F.2d 460, (9th Cir. 1988).

Milkovich v. Lorain Journal Co. 497 U.S. 1. (1990).

Miller v. California. 413 U.S. 15. (1973).

Morse v. Frederick. 551 U.S. 393. (2007).

Moseley v. Victoria's Secret Catalogue, Inc. 537 U.S. 418. (2003).

Multiple ownership, 47 C.F.R. §§ 73.3555(a), (b), (e).

Mu'Min v. Virginia. 501 U.S. 1269. (1991).

Murphy v. Florida. 421 U.S. 784. (1975).

Mutual Film Corp. v. Industrial Commission of Ohio. 236 U.S. 230. (1915).

National Endowment for the Arts, 20 U.S.C. § 954.

National Paralegal College.(2007). *History of equal protection and the levels of review.* Retrieved from http://nationalparalegal.edu/conLaw-CrimProc_Public/EqualProtection/HistoryOfEqualProtection.asp

National Telecommunications and Information Administration.(n.d.). Retrieved from NTIA website http://www.ntia.doc.gov/

N.B.C v. U.S. 319 U.S. 190. (1943).

N.E.A. v. Finley. 524 U.S. 569. (1998).

Near v. Minnesota. 283 U.S. 697. (1931).

Nebraska Press Association v. Stewart. 427 U.S. 539, 559. (1976).

Newseuminstitute. (2017). *2017 State of the First Amendment Survey Report*. Retrieved from http://www.newseuminstitute.org/first -amendment-center/state-of-the-first-amendment/

New York v. Ferber. 458 U.S. 747. (1982).

New York Times. (2015). Net neutrality. Retrieved from http://topics. nytimes.com/top/reference/timestopics/subjects/n/net_neutrality/ index.html

New York Times v. Sullivan. 376 U.S. 254. (1964).

New York Times v. Tasini. 533 U.S. 483. (2001).

New York Times v. U.S. 403 U.S. 713. (1971).

New York Times Co. v. Gonzales, 459 F. 3d 160, (2d Cir. 2006).

Nixon v. Warner Communications. 434 U.S. 591. (1978).

Oklahoma Publishing Co. v. District Court. 430 U.S. 308. (1977).

Ollman v. Evans, 750 F.2d 970 (U.S. App. D.C. Cir. 1985).

Olmstead v. U.S. 277 U.S. 438. (1928).

One Book Entitled Ulysses v. U.S., 72 F.2d 705, (1934).

Organization for a Better Austin v. Keefe. 402 U.S. 415. (1971).

Osborne v. Ohio. 495 U.S. 103. (1990).

Ownership of copyright, 17 U.S.C. § 201(b).

Packingham v. North Carolina. 582 U.S. ____., 137 S.Ct. 1730 (2017).

Pandering Advertisement Act, Pub. L. 91–375, 84 Stat. 748 (1970).

Parkinson, S. (Ed.). (1995). The Areopagitica. *Discourse* 14. http://www. stlawrenceinstitute.org/vol14mit.html.

Paroline v. U.S. 572 U.S. ____ (2014).

Patterson, P., & Wilkins, L. (2014). *Media ethics: Issues and cases* (8th ed.). New York, NY: McGraw-Hill.

Peavy v. WFAA-TV, 221 F.3d 158, (2000).

Pell v. Procunier. 417 U.S. 817. (1974).

Pember, D., & Calvert, C. (2015). *Mass media law* (19th ed.). New York, NY: Mcgraw Hill.

Pinkus v. United States. 436 U.S. 293. (1978).

Planned Parenthood of S.E. Pennsylvania v. Casy. 505 U.S. 833. (1992).

Pope v. Illinois. 481 U.S. 497. (1987).

Presley v. Georgia. 558 U.S. 209. (2010).

Preemption with respect to other laws, 17 U.S.C. § 301.

Press-Enterprise Co. v. Superior Court. 464 U.S. 501. (1984).

Preston v. Martin Bregman Productions, Inc., 765 F. Supp. 116, (S.D.N.Y. 1991).

Printers' Ink Editors. (n.d.). *Printers' Ink.*

Privacy Act of 1974.Pub.L. No. 93–579, 88 Stat. 1896 (1974).

Privacy Protection Act, Pub. L. No. 96-440, 94 Stat. 1879 (1980).

Production and transportation of obscene matters for sale or distribution, 18 U.S.C. § 1465.

Prometheus Radio Project v. F.C.C., 373 F.3d 372, (3d Cir. 2004).

Prosser, W.L. (1960). Privacy. *California Law Review*, 48(3), 383–423.

Protection of Children Against Sexual Exploitation Act, Pub. L. No. 95-225, 92 Stat. 7 (1977).

Pruneyard Shopping Center v. Robins. 447 U.S. 74. (1980).

Public Access to Court Electronic Records. (n.d.). *Pacer case locator.* Retrieved from www.pacer.gov

Public Broadcasting Act, Pub. L. No. 90-129, 81 Stat. 365 (1967).

Public Citizen v. Dept. of Justice. 491 U.S. 440. (1989).

Public information; agency rules, opinions, orders, records, and proceedings.5 U.S.C. § 552 (f)(1).

Pure Power Fitness Camp v. Warrior Fitness Boot Camp, 813 F. Supp. 2d 489, (S.D.N.Y. 2011).

Racketeer Influenced and Corrupt Organization Act, Pub. L. No. 91-452, 84 Stat. 922–923 (1970).

Radio Act, 27 Stat. 302 (1912).

Radio Act, 44 Stat. 1162 (1927).

Radio-Television News Directors Association. (n.d). *Archives.*Retrieved from www.rtnda.org

Radio-Television News Directors Association v. F.C.C., 229 F.3d 269, (2000).

R.A.V. v. St. Paul. 505 U.S. 377. (1992).

Reagen, R.T. (2010). *Sealing court records and proceedings: A pocket guide.* Retrieved from FJC website at www.fjc.gov

Red Lion Broadcasting v. F.C.C. 395 U.S. 367. (1969).

Reed v. Town of Gilbert. 576 U.S. _____. 135 S.Ct. 2218 (2015).

Regina v. Hicklin, L.R. 3 Q.B. 360, (1868).

Registration and civil infringement actions, 17 U.S.C. § 411(a).

Registration as prerequisite to certain remedies for infringement, 17 U.S.C. § 412.

Registration on principal register as evidence of exclusive right to use mark; defenses, 15 U.S.C. § 1115(a), (b).

Regulation of services, facilities, and equipment, 47 U.S.C. § 544(d)(2).

Rehnquist, W.H. (1987). *The Supreme Court: How it was, how it is.* New York, NY: Morrow.

Rehnquist, W. H. (2000). *All the laws but one: Civil liberties in wartime.* New York, NY: Vintage Books.

Remedies for infringement: Costs and attorney's fees, 17 U.S.C. § 505.

Remedies for infringement: Damages and profits, 17 U.S.C. §§ 504(c) (1), 504(c)(2).

Remedies for infringement: Injunctions, 17 U.S.C. § 502.

Remedies; infringement; innocent infringement by printers and publishers, 15 U.S.C. § 1114(1).

Renewal of registration, 15 U.S.C. § 1059.

Reno v. A.C.L.U. 521 U.S. 844. (1997).

Reno v. A.C.L.U., 117 S.Ct. 2329, (1997).

Reno v. Condon. 528 U.S. 141. (2000).

Renton v. Playtime Theatres, Inc. 475 U.S. 41. (1986).

Report on editorializing by broadcast licensees, 13 F.C.C. 1246 (1949).

Reporters Committee for Freedom of the Press.(n.d.). How to use the federal FOI Act.

Retrieved from www.rcfp.org/foiact/index.html

Reporters Committee for Freedom of the Press. (n.d.). News. Retrieved from www.rcfp.org/newsitems/index.php?!=6907

Reporters Committee for Freedom of the Press. (n.d.). The reporter's privilege. Retrieved from www.rcfp.org/privilege

Reporter's Committee for Freedom of the Press (2011). *First Amendment handbook.* Arlington, VA: RCFP.

Requirements for license, 47 U.S.C. § 308(b).

Revell v. Hoffman, 309 F.3d 1228 (10th Cir. 2002).

Richards, R.D., & Calvert, C. (2003). Nadine Strossen and freedom of expression. *George Mason University Civil Rights Journal,* 13, 185.

Richmond Newspapers v. Virginia. 448 U.S. 555. (1980).

Riley v. California, 134 S.Ct. 2473, (2014).

Robinson v. American Broadcasting Co., 441 F.2d 1396, (6th Cir. 1971).

Roche, J.P. (1964). *Shadow and substance.* New York, NY: Macmillan.

Roe v. Wade. 410 U.S. 113. (1973).

Rogers v. Grimaldi, 875 F. 2d 994, (2nd. Cir. 1989).

Romaine v. Kallinger, 537 A.2d 284, (1988).

Roth v. U.S. 354 U.S. 476. (1957).

Rousseau, J.J. (1762). *The Social Contract.* (G.D.H. Cole, Trans.). Retrieved from http://www.constitution.org/jjr/socon.htm

Rowan v. Post Office. 397 U.S. 728. (1970).

Sable Communications of California, Inc. v. F.C.C. 492 U.S. 115, 126. (1989).

Satellite Home Viewer Improvement Act, Pub. L. No. 106, 113 Stat. 1501 (1999).

Saxbe v. Washington Post. 417 U.S. 843. (1974).

Schad v. Mt. Ephraim. 452 U.S. 61. (1981).

Schenck v. U.S. 249 U.S. 47. (1919).

Schifano v. Greene Country Greyhound Park, Inc., 624 So. 2d, (Ala. 1993).

Schneider v. State of New Jersey. 308 U.S. 147. (1939).

Scope of exclusive rights in nondramatic musical works: Compulsory license for making and distributing phonorecords, 15 U.S.C. § 115(b)(4).

Scope of exclusive rights in sound recordings, 17 U.S.C. § 114(b).

Securities and Exchange Commission. (n.d.). Retrieved from SEC website http://www.sec.gov/

Sedition Act of 1798, Ch. 74, 1 Stat. 596 (1798).

Sexual exploitation of children, 18 U.S.C. § 2251(a).

Sheppard v. Maxwell. 384 U.S. 333. (1966).

Shields, Christopher. (2015). Aristotle. In E.N. Zalta (Ed.), *Stanford encyclopedia of Philosophy* (Fall 2015 ed.). Retrieved from http://plato. stanford.edu/archives/fall2015/entries/aristotle/

Shoen v. Shoen, 5 F.3d 1289, (1993).

Shulman v. Group W. Productions, 18 C.4th 200, (1998).

Sidis v. F-R Publishing Co., 113 F.2d 806, (1940).

Silkwood v. Kerr McGee, 563 F.2d 433, (1977).

Simon & Schuster v. New York State Crime Victims Board. 502 U.S. 105. (1991).

Skilling v. U.S., 130 S. Ct. 2896, (2010).

Smith v. California. 361 U.S. 147. (1959).

Smith v. Daily Mail. 443 U.S. 97. (1979).

Smith v. U.S. 431 U.S. 291. (1977).

Snepp v. U.S. 444 U.S. 507. (1980).

Snyder v. Phelps. 562 U.S. 443.131 S.Ct. 1207. (2011).

Society of Professional Journalists. (n.d.). *Code of ethics.* Retrieved from SPJ website at www.spj.org/ethicscode.asp

Sony Corp. of America v. Universal City Studios. 464 U.S. 417. (1984).

Sponsorship Identification Rules and Embedded Advertising, 23 F.C.C.R. 10682 (2008)

Stanley v. Georgia. 394 U.S. 557. (1969).

Star Athletica v. Varsity Brands, 580 U.S. _____., 136 S.Ct. 1823 (2017).

Statista. (2017). *U.S Advertising Industry—statistics and facts.*[Date file]. Retrieved from http://www.statista.com/topics/979/advertising-in-the-us/

Statute of Anne, 8 Anne, C. 19 (1710).

Stickels v. General Rental Co., Inc., 750 F. Supp. 729, (1990).

Subject matter of copyright: In general, 17 U.S.C. § 102(a)(7).

Subject matter of copyright: National origin, 17 U.S.C. § 104A.

Subject matter of copyright: United States Government works, 17 U.S.C. § 105.

Supplemental register, 15 U.S.C. § 1091.

Support of political candidates prohibited, 47 U.S.C. § 399.

Sussman v. ABC, 186 F.3d 1200, (1999).

Syracuse Peace Council v. F.C.C., 867 F.2d 654, (D.C. Cir. 1989).

Telecommunications Act, Pub. L. No. 104-104, 110 Stat. 56 (1996).

Telecommunications Consortium v. F.C.C. 518 U.S. 727. (1996).

Texas v. Johnson. 491 U.S. 397. (1989).

Time, Inc. v. Firestone. 424 U.S. 448. (1976).

Time, Inc. v. Hill. 385 U.S. 374. (1967).

Times Mirror Co. v. Superior Court of San Diego County, 198 C.A. 3d 1420, (1988).

Tinker v. Des Moines Independent Community School District. 393 U.S. 503. (1969).

Tinker v. Des Moines School District. 393 U.S. 503. (1969).

Tocqueville, A. (1954). *Democracy in America.* New York, NY: Vintage Books.

Trademarks registrable on principal register; concurrent registration, 15 U.S.C. § 1052.

Trager, R., Russomanno, J., Ross, S.D., & Reynolds, A. (2014). *The law of journalism and mass communication* (4th ed.). Los Angeles, CA: CQ Press.

Triangle Publications v. Knight-Ridder, 626 F.2d 1171, (1980).

Trinity Methodist Church, South v. F.R.C., 62 F.2d 650, (1932).

Truth in Lending Act, Pub. L. No. 90-321, 82 Stat. 146 (1968).

Truth in Savings Act, Pub. L. No. 102-242, 105 Stat. 2236 (1991).

Turner Broadcasting System, Inc. v. F.C.C., 114 S.Ct. 2445, (1994).

Turner Broadcasting System, Inc. v. F.C.C., 117 S.Ct. 1174, (1997).

Turner Broadcasting System, Inc. v. F.C.C. 520 U.S. 180. (1997).

Unauthorized fixation and trafficking in sound recordings and music videos, 17 U.S.C. § 1101.

United States. (1990). *Federal rules of civil procedure.* Washington, D.C.: U.S. G.P.O.

United States. (1990). *Federal rules of criminal procedure.* Washington, D.C.: U.S. G.P.O.

United States.(1900). *Federal rules of evidence.* Washington: U.S. G.P.O.

U.S. Const. art.I, § 8.

U.S. v. Alvarez. 567 U.S. 709 (2012).

U.S. v. American Library Association. 539 U.S. 194. (2003).

U.S. v. Blagojevich, 612 F.3d 558, (7th Cir. 2010).

U.S. v. Bryan. 339 U.S. 323, 331. (1950).

U.S. v. Carolene Products. 304 U.S. 144. (1938).

U.S. v. Cleveland, 128 F. 3d 267, (1997).

U.S. v. Dickinson, 465 F. 2d 496, (1972).

U.S. v. Edge Broadcasting. 509 U.S. 418. (1993).

U.S. v. Hotaling, 634 F.3d 725, (2d.Cir. 2011).

U.S. v. Jones, 132 S. Ct 945, (2012).

U.S. v. Kokinda. 497 U.S. 720. (1990).

U.S. v. Midwest Video Corp. 406 U.S. 649. (1972).

U.S. v. Monzel, 641 F.3d 528, (D.C. Cir.2011).

U.S. v. National Treasury Employees Union. 513 U.S. 454. (1995).

U.S. v. Nixon. 418 U.S. 683. (1974).

U.S. v. O'Brien. 391 U.S. 367. (1968).

U.S. v. Playboy Entertainment Group. 529 U.S. 803. (2000).

U.S. v. Smith, 992 F. Supp. 743, (D.N.J. 1998).

U.S. v. Southwestern Cable Co. 392 U.S. 157. (1968).

U.S. v. Williams. 553 U.S. 285. (2008).

U.S. Judicial Conference. (n.d.). *Handbook for jurors.* Washington, D.C.: Administrative Office of the U.S. Courts.

USA Patriot Act, Pub. L. No. 107-56, 115 Stat. 272 (2001).

Use of Endorsements and Testimonials in Advertising, Consumer Endorsements, 16 C.F.R. § 255.2 (2008).

Use of Endorsements and Testimonials in Advertising, Expert Endorsements, 16 C.F.R. § 255.3 (2008).

Use of Endorsements and Testimonials in Advertising, General Considerations, 16 C.F.R. § 255.1 (2008).

Use of Endorsements and Testimonials in Advertising, Purpose and Definitions, 16 C.F.R. § 255.0 (2008).

Uzgalis, W. (2012). John Locke. In E. N. Zalta (Ed.), *Stanford encyclopedia of philosophy* (Fall 2012 ed.). Retrieved from http//plato.standord.edu/archives/fall 2012/entries/locke/

Valentine v. Chrestensen. 316 U.S. 52. (1942).

Vance v. Universal Amusement. 445 U.S. 308. (1980).

Vernor v. Autodesk, 621 F.3d 1102, (2010).

Violation of Great Lakes Agreement, 47 U.S.C § 507.

Violent television programming and its impact on children, 22 F.C.C.R. 7929 (2007).

Virgil v. Time Inc., 527 F. 2d 1122, (1975).

Virginia v. Black. 538 U.S. 343. (2003).

Virginia v. Hicks. 539 U.S. 113, 119. (2003).

Virginia State Board of Pharmacy v. Virginia Citizens Consumer Council. 425 U.S. 748. (1976).

Volkomer, W.E. (2011). *American government* (13th ed.). Boston, MA: Longman.

Wal-Mart Stores v. Samara Brothers. 529 U.S. 205. (2000).

Walker v. Texas Division, Sons of Confederate Veterans. 576 U.S. ____., 135 S.Ct. 2239 (2015).

Warren, S., & and Brandeis, L. (1890). The Right to Privacy. *Harvard Law Review*, 4(5), 193–220.

Weathers v. American Family Mutual Insurance Co., 17 M.L.R. 1534, (1990).

Wendt v. Host International, 125 F.3d 806, (1997).

West Publishing Company. (1936). *Corpus Juris Secundum*. St. Paul, MN: West Publishing Co.

West Virginia State Board of Education v. Barnette. 319 U.S. 624. (1943).

Wheaton v. Peters. 33 U.S. 590. (1834).

Wheeler v. Goulart, 18 M.L.R. 2296, (1990).

Wheeler-Lea Act, Pub. L. No. 75447, 52 Stat. 111, 114 (1938).

White v. Samsung, 971 F.2d 1395, (1992).

Whitney v. California. 274 U.S. 357. (1927).

Wikileaks. (n.d.). Retrieved from https://wikileaks.org/index.en.html

Wilkinson v. Jones. 480 U.S. 926. (1987).

Willis, J. (1910). Common Law. In *Catholic encyclopedia*. Retrieved from http://www.newadvent.org/cathen/09068a.htm

Wilson v. Layne. 526 U.S. 603. (1999).

Wireless Ship Act, 36 Stat. 629 (1910).

Wisconsin v. Mitchell. 508 U.S. 476. (1993).

Wooley v. Maynard. 430 U.S. 705. (1977).

Young People's Association for the Propagation of the Gospel, 6 F.C.C. 178 (1936).

Young v. American Mini-Theatres. 427 U.S. 50. (1976).

Zacchini v. Scripps-Howard Broadcasting. 433 U.S. 562. (1977).

Zelenka v. Wisconsin, 266 N.W. 2d 279, (1978).

Zurcher v. Stanford Daily. 436 U.S. 547. (1978).

ABOUT THE AUTHOR

Mark Hanebutt is professor of journalism in the department of mass communication at the University of Central Oklahoma where he teaches courses in news reporting and media law. In addition, he is a member of the Oklahoma Bar Association and is of counsel to Magill & Magill, P.L.L.C., Attorneys and Counselors at Law, in Oklahoma City, where he mediates and consults on media law issues and cases. A former reporter, editor, and syndicated writer with *The Orlando Sentinel*, he is also the author of *The Journalist's Primer: A No-Nonsense Guide to Getting and Reporting the News* (Kendall Hunt 2013). He holds a Bachelor of Arts degree in journalism, a Master of Arts degree in English and a Juris Doctor degree in law and has received fellowships from the American Press Institute and the Gannett Foundation.

INDEX

S

CPSIA information can be obtained
at www.ICGtesting.com
Printed in the USA
FFHW01n0142110818
47701950-51361FF